Webster's English Usage Guide

Webster's English Usage Guide

Created in Cooperation with the Editors of

MERRIAM-WEBSTER

A Division of Merriam-Webster, Incorporated
Springfield, Massachusetts

This 2006 edition published by
Federal Street Press,
A Division of Merriam-Webster, Incorporated
P.O. Box 281
Springfield, MA 01102

Federal Street Press books are available for bulk purchase for sales promotion and premium use.
For details write the manager of special sales,
Federal Street Press, P.O. Box 281, Springfield, MA 01102

ISBN 13 978-1-59695-010-8
ISBN 10 1-59695-010-2

Printed in the United States of America

06 07 08 09 10 5 4 3 2 1

Contents

Preface

This book presents over 1,500 brief discussions of common problems in English usage. Its main strengths are its recognition of the historical background to questions of usage and the fact that it is based on a thorough examination of present-day usage. Merriam-Webster's extensive citation files of 15 million examples of English words used in context have been a valuable resource in developing this book.

While English, like some other languages, has long had its commentators who seek to proscribe certain usages and prescribe others, standard usage tends to evolve quite independently of such critics. This book sets out in concise form the standard uses to which common English words, phrases, and grammatical constructions are actually put, especially in writing.

Articles. Each article is introduced by one or more boldface words indicating the subject for discussion.

data

glance, glimpse

reason is because

In cases where it seemed helpful to do so, homographs are distinguished by italic labels indicating part of speech.

account, *noun*

account, *verb*

Otherwise such distinctions are made as part of the accompanying discussion.

An article that treats more than one aspect of its subject may be divided into sections, each section introduced by a boldface numeral. The topic of the section is occasionally indicated by an introductory word or phrase in italics.

allow 1. *Allow, permit.* Usage commentators have long sought to distinguish between *allow* and *permit.* . . .
2. *Allow of.* The intransitive *allow,* used with *of,* occurs primarily. . . .
3. *Allow* in the sense "admit, concede". . . .

Verbal Illustrations. This book includes thousands of verbal illustrations offering examples primarily of standard, but also occasionally of nonstandard, usages. Standard usages are shown within angle brackets, with the particular word or words at issue in italics.

When the verb *date* is used to point to a date of origin, it may be used with *from, back to,* or *to* <these vases *date from* the early Ming period> <the poem *dates back to* 1843> <the dispute *dates to* Japan's annexation of the islands>.

When two different but equally acceptable alternatives

are exemplified, the second appears in square brackets immediately after the first.

> *Farther and further* . . . continue to be used interchangeably when distance in space or time . . . is involved <traveled *further* [*farther*] today than yesterday> <taking the principle one step *farther* [*further*]>.

Nonstandard usages, as well as some that are standard but are associated with casual speech rather than with writing, are shown in quotation marks, usually inside parentheses.

> The conjunction *being* survives in various dialects (as in "*Being* you are family, I can tell you").
>
> *Off* in the sense of "from" (as in "we bought the tools *off* Joe" or "we recorded the show *off* the TV") . . . is found most often in speech and speechlike writing.

Cross-References. Directional cross-references to articles where relevant discussion may be found are shown in small capital letters. They may appear within or at the end of an article or section, or they may receive a separate entry.

> **gamut . . .** Some caution against confusing it with *run* the gauntlet (see GAUNTLET, GANTLET).
> . . .

> **different from, different than** Both of these phrases are standard. . . . See also THAN.

> **either . . . or** See EITHER 3, 5.

Cross-references to articles appearing in the Glossary, which begins on page 348, are identified as such.

> Because of the strength of NOTIONAL AGREEMENT (see Glossary), however, a plural verb is not uncommon. . . .

Pronunciation. The symbols used in most of the articles on pronunciation are explained in the table on page xi.

The text of this work was prepared by Michael Shally-Jensen. Jocelyn White Franklin helped compile the Glossary. Mark A. Stevens, E. Ward Gilman, and Frederick C. Mish reviewed the entire manuscript. Georgette B. Boucher assisted substantially in the keyboarding of the manuscript. Cross-referencing was done by Maria A. Sansalone and Adrienne M. Scholz, and proofreading was performed by Donna L. Rickerby and Adrienne M. Scholz under the direction of Madeline L. Novak.

Pronunciation Symbols

Slant lines (\ . . . \) used in pairs indicate the beginning and end of a pronunciation respelling. The symbol ˈ indicates primary (strongest) stress on the syllable that follows; the symbol ˌ indicates secondary (medium) stress. Parentheses surrounding an element indicate that it is optional.

ə	banana, collide
ˈə, ˌə	humdrum, abut
ər	further, merger, bird
a	mat, snap
ā	day, fade, aorta
ä	cart, cot, father
au̇	now, loud
ch	chin, nature \ˈnā-chər\
ē	beat, nosebleed
e	bet, red, peck
i	tip, banish
ī	side, buy
ō	bone, know, beau
ȯ	saw, all, caught
ȯi	coin, destroy
ü	rule, youth
u̇	pull, wood, book, fury \ˈfyu̇r-ē\
y	yard, mute \ˈmyüt\

A

a, an In both speech and writing, *a* is used before a word beginning with a consonant <*a* door> <*a* symphony>. Before a word beginning with a vowel, *an* is usual <*an* icicle> <*an* operation>, but when the vowel is pronounced with an initial consonant sound, *a* is used <*a* one-time deal> <*a* union>. Before nouns beginning with *h*, *a* is used if the *h* is pronounced <*a* human> <*a* headache>; in a few cases where the first syllable is unaccented, either *a* or *an* can be used <*a(n)* historic event> <*a(n)* Hispanic applicant> <*a(n)* habitual liar>. *An* is used if the *h* is not pronounced <twice *an* hour>.

abhorrence *Abhorrence*, when followed by a preposition, takes of <an *abhorrence of* winter>. *To, for,* and *against* can also be found following *abhorrence* in older literature.

able to In sentences where *able* is followed by *to* and the infinitive, the infinitive is nearly always in the active voice <you used to be *able to* smoke in movie theaters>, whether the subject is human or nonhuman. The passive infinitive (as in "a simple test *able to* be performed at home") is generally thought to sound awkward and may usually be avoided easily <a test that can be performed at home>.

abound When something abounds—that is, is copiously supplied—it usually abounds *in* or *with* <the

house *abounded in* warmth and sunlight> <he *abounded with* good spirits>.

about See AT ABOUT.

above The use of *above* as both a noun <none of the *above*> and an adjective <please refer to the *above* table> has long been established as standard, even though some critics disapprove of it.

absent The use of *absent* as a preposition <*absent* any backing from the government, the project was forced to shut down> has been criticized, but it is currently in good use and is standard.

absolutely The use of *absolutely* as an intensifier may sometimes be judged overdramatic (as in "she was *absolutely* devastated when she wasn't invited"). In more measured uses, criticism of the word is not justified <no drug can be proved *absolutely* harmless>.

absolve When *absolve* is followed by a preposition, it is usually either *from* <*absolved from* their obligations> or *of* <cannot be *absolved of* blame>. Only rarely is *for* used <were *absolved for* the crimes they allegedly committed>.

abstain When *abstain* is followed by a preposition, it is normally *from* <decided to *abstain from* meat>. In reference to voting, *abstain* usually takes no preposition <20 delegates *abstained*>.

abstract When the verb *abstract* takes a preposition, it is generally *from* <*abstracted* the essential data *from* the report> but occasionally *by* <*abstracted by* a researcher>.

abut *On* is the preposition most frequently used with *abut* <land *abuts on* the road>. *Upon* and *into* are also occasionally used. The transitive *abut* is sometimes followed by a prepositional phrase <the horizontal piece *abuts* the vertical one at the base>.

accede *Accede* is normally followed by *to* <*acceding to* their demands>.

accept, except The verb *except* (meaning "omit") is sometimes mistakenly written in place of *accept* (meaning "receive willingly" or "agree to"). Be careful not to confuse the words because of their similarity in sound.

access When followed by a preposition, the noun access usually takes *to* <*access to* information>.

accidently, accidentally Though the spelling *accidently* has been used by some reputable writers, it is usually regarded as a misspelling.

accommodate When a preposition follows intransitive *accommodate,* it is usually *to* <she *accommodated* quickly *to* the changed circumstances>. *To* is also used with transitive *accommodate,* after a reflexive pronoun <he *accommodated* himself *to* these demands>; less frequently, *with* is used <*accommodate* you *with* a bowl of soup>. When the transitive *accommodate* is in the passive, it may take various other prepositions <we were *accommodated at* the station for the night>.

accompany *Accompanied by* is the usual form; *by* is always used with persons <children should be *accompanied by* an adult> and is usual with things as well <explosions *accompanied by* random gunfire>. *Accompanied with* is limited to things <has *accompanied* her drawings *with* some verse> and was used more in the past than it is now.

account, *noun* See ON ACCOUNT OF.

account, *verb* When *account* is used as an intransitive verb, it is normally followed by the preposition *for* <fails to *account for* the results>.

accountable One is accountable *to* someone who is due an explanation *for* something done or not done <elected officials are *accountable to* the people *for* their actions>.

accrue *Accrue* as an intransitive verb takes various prepositions, including *to* <*accrues to* her account>, *on* <interest *accrues on* a daily basis>, *with* <the wisdom that *accrues with* age>, *for* <whatever benefits *accrue for* their efforts>, *through* <market exposure *accruing through* the use of new business channels>, and *from* <have *accrued from* the current system>. It can be used without prepositions as well <no serious effects have *accrued*>. *Accrue* is also used as an transitive verb <*accruing* a mass of support>.

acknowledgment, acknowledgement *Acknowledgment* and *acknowledgement* are both acceptable spellings, but the first is much more prevalent in the U.S.

a couple of See COUPLE, *noun* 2.

acquaint *Acquaint* is most often followed by the preposition *with* <is *acquainted with* them>.

acquiesce *Acquiesce* is frequently followed by in <*acquiesced in* the decision>, less frequently by *to* <would *acquiesce to* those demands>.

acquit *Acquit* is often used in the construction *acquit* (a person) *of* (something charged). Far less frequently, *for* is used instead of *of* <should be *acquitted for* the crime>.

act, action Both *act* and *action* can be used to denote something done. When *act* is modified, it tends to be followed by *of* and a noun <an *act of* arson> <*acts of* kindness>. *Action* tends to be preceded by its modifier <a protest *action*> <unilateral *actions*>. *Action* is also used attributively <environmental *action* groups> <*action* photographs>, while *act* is not. In addition, both words appear in standard idioms <caught in the *act*> <a piece of the *action*>.

activate, actuate These two words are usually distinguished when applied to persons and things. *Activate* is more often used of things thought of as mechanical in their operation <*activate* the heat-exchange system>; when applied to people, it almost always indicates some external spur to action <he

lacked the charisma to *activate* voters>. *Actuate,* which has a long history of literary use, generally indicates internal motivation <people who are *actuated* by the hope of personal gain>.

actual, actually Both *actual* and *actually* are sometimes used in ways that do not add much meaning to a sentence (as in "made more in *actual* wages than in tips," or "I had been *actually* involved"). But they can sometimes improve the rhythm of a sentence or help to set off the more important words <whatever the *actual* human and physical cost> <but *actually* there is a pattern that underlies these facts>. In general, you should check to see whether they are actually necessary for meaning or style in your writing.

actuate See ACTIVATE, ACTUATE.

ad Although *ad* is considered by some to be an inappropriate shortening of *advertisement,* it is used widely in general and informal writing <found the *ad* too expensive to run>.

A.D., B.C. Do these abbreviations go before or after the year? Can they be used after the word *century?* *B.C.* almost always follows the year <sometime before 2000 *B.C.*> <from the fourth century *B.C.*>. *A.D.*, on the other hand, is usually, but not always, placed *before* the year <*A.D.* 22> <flourished 125–190 *A.D.*>. Both are standard when used after *century* <the third century *A.D.*>. Both are usually either capitalized or set in small capitals, and both generally use periods.

adapt, adopt These words may be distinguished as follows: *Adopt* suggests taking something over as it is <the committee voted to *adopt* a new set of rules>. *Adapt* suggests changing something to meet new needs <*adapt* a short story for television>.

adequate 1. *Adequate* is most often used without a complement <an *adequate* sum>. When a complement is used, *adequate* is often followed by *to* and either a noun <a supply *adequate to* the demand> or an infinitive <more than *adequate to* cover the cost>. It is also frequently followed by *for* <seemed *adequate for* our needs>.

2. *Adequate* is considered by many to be an absolute adjective that doesn't lend itself to use with qualifiers like *more* or *less. More,* however, is sometimes used, usually with the meaning "more nearly" <were hoping for *more adequate* funding>.

adjacent *Adjacent* is often followed by *to* <the region *adjacent to* the Highlands>. The word can describe objects that touch each other <*adjacent* warm and cold masses of air> or do not touch <the *adjacent* islands of Nantucket and Martha's Vineyard>.

admission, admittance Both *admittance* and *admission* mean "permitted entrance." *Admittance* is usually applied to mere physical entrance to a locality or a building <members must show their cards upon *admittance*>, whereas *admission* applies to entrance or formal acceptance (as into a club) that carries with it rights, privileges, standing, or membership <two recommendations are required for *admission* to the club>. *Admission* is much more common for a fee to gain entrance <*admission* $5.00> <worth the price of *admission*>.

adopt See ADAPT, ADOPT.

adult The pronunciation with stress on the second syllable, \ə-'dəlt\, is the most common one in the U.S., although the alternative pronunciation, \'ad-ˌəlt\, is also widely used (and is usual in Great Britain).

adverse, averse These words are similar in meaning, but *adverse* is the more generally useful word. It is commonly used to modify a following noun <*adverse* circumstances> <an *adverse* reaction>, whereas *averse* is not. *Adverse to* is used as a predicate adjective to describe things <testimony that was *adverse to* their cases>. For describing people, *averse to* is more common today and is especially frequent in negative constructions <is not *averse to* receiving praise>. See also AVERSE TO, AVERSE FROM.

advice, advise These two words are occasionally confused. Be careful not to mix up the noun *advice* <she offered good *advice*> with the verb *advise* <I must *advise* you>.

adviser, advisor Although both of these spellings are currently acceptable, *adviser* is the more frequently used.

advocate Though the verb *advocate* usually takes no preposition <*advocates* affirmative action>, it may be followed by a prepositional phrase introduced by *for, in, on,* or *by* <*advocates* affirmative action *for* economically disadvantaged groups>. The noun *advocate* usually takes *of* to introduce what is being advocated <an *advocate of* affirmative action>, although *for* is also sometimes used <is an *advocate for* the rights of minorities>.

affect, effect These words are commonly confused, but they are not synonyms. The verb *affect* means "to influence or act upon" <how the cutbacks will *affect* the company>, while the noun *effect* means "result" <the *effects* will be devastating>. Thus if you *affect* something, the result is an *effect. Effect* is also a verb meaning "to bring about" <a mandate to *effect* some serious changes>, and *affect* is a much rarer noun used by psychologists in describing emotional states.

affiliate As a verb (in participial form) *affiliate* is commonly used with the preposition *with* <he is *affiliated with* the University>. The noun *affiliate* is commonly followed by *of* <it is an *affiliate of* Encyclopaedia Britannica> or preceded by an attributive adjective <it is an Encyclopaedia Britannica *affiliate*>.

affinity *Affinity* is most often used with the prepositions *for* and *with* <have a real *affinity for* each other> <a language having some *affinity with* Norwegian>. Somewhat less often, it is used with *to* or *between*

<people with an *affinity to* darkness> <certain *affinities between* autism and genius>.

afflict See INFLICT, AFFLICT.

affluent The pronunciation in which the first syllable is accented is more standard than the one that puts the stress on the second syllable.

aforementioned This word is used in legal contexts but is generally avoided in ordinary writing, except when a humorous effect is intended <said the *aforementioned* spouse with a snarl>.

afraid *Afraid* can be followed by a *that* clause <is *afraid* that the request may be denied> or by an infinitive <is *afraid* to cross the street>. The usually preposition after *afraid* is *of,* which can be followed by a noun <*afraid of* machines> or a gerund <*afraid of* making waves>. *Afraid* is followed by *for* when the object is not the source of the threat but rather what is threatened <*afraid for* his job>.

African-American *African-American* (noun) is on its way to becoming the preferred term for an American of African descent, but *black* (sometimes capitalized) is still just about as frequent. *African-American* is used both in the singular and the plural, but *black* (which means "African-American") is almost always used in the plural <southern *blacks*>. As an adjective, *African-American* is applied to both people <an *African-American* author> and things <*African-Ameri-*

can music>, as is *black* <*black* voters> <*black* churches>. *Black,* however, seems to be used slightly more often of things than of people.

after *After* meaning "afterwards" can be found in the works of standard authors <we arrived shortly *after*> <returned 20 years *after*>, but it is not found in the most formal writing today.

afterward, afterwards *Afterward* is the more common form in the U.S., though both are quite common; *afterwards* is the form generally used in British English.

agenda Although it originated as the plural of the Latin *agendum, agenda* is standard in English as a singular noun <a political *agenda*>, with *agendas* as its plural <the *agendas* of the last three faculty meetings>.

aggravate, aggravation, aggravating *Aggravate* is used chiefly in two meanings, "to make worse" <*aggravated* her shoulder injury> <their financial position was *aggravated* by the market downturn> and to "irritate, annoy" <the President was *aggravated* by French intransigence>. The first sense is more common than the second in published prose. This is not true, however, of *aggravation,* which usually means "irritation" <an *aggravation* for him>, or *aggravating,* which almost always expresses annoyance <an *aggravating* situation>.

agree *To, on,* and *with* are the prepositions most frequently used with *agree* <the company *agreed to* mediation> <they *agreed on* a payment schedule> <she *agrees with* the experts>.

a half a(n) See HALF 2.

ahold See GET HOLD OF, GET AHOLD OF.

aim Some critics regard *aim to* as an outworn Americanism, but it is still widely used in both British and American English <a design *aimed to* give pleasure> <this provision *aims to* ensure stability>. *Aim at* is also very common <a story *aimed at* helping youths> <will *aim at* savings for homeowners>. *Aim for* may also be used <the thing to *aim for* in these negotiations>.

ain't Although widely disapproved, avoided in formal writing, and most common in the habitual speech of the less educated, *ain't* in the senses "am not, are not, is not" and "have not, has not" is flourishing in American English. It is used in both speech and writing to catch attention and emphasize. It is used especially in journalistic prose as part of a consistently informal style <things just *ain't* what they used to be>. This informal *ain't* is commonly distinguished from habitual *ain't* by its tendency to occur in fixed constructions and phrases <say it *ain't* so> <if it *ain't* broke, don't fix it>. In fiction *ain't* is used for purposes of characterization; in familiar correspondence it tends to be a mark of an easygoing friendship.

à la This imported (French) preposition is printed more often in English with its accent than without. Used in English since the end of the 16th century, it need not be italicized as a foreign term <chomping on a large cigar *à la* Groucho Marx>.

albeit Although some writers consider *albeit* old-fashioned, it is still very much in use <was treated as a partner, *albeit* a junior one>.

alien When *alien* is used with a preposition, the choice is most often *to* <a quality *alien to* the rest of his personality>.

all of The usage question here is whether *all* should be followed by *of* in expressions such as "all (of) the percussion instruments." While *all of* is required before personal pronouns <*all of* them>, *all* and *all of* are about equally common in most other cases <*all* the lawyers got together> <*all of* these rocks are striated>. See also BOTH 2.

allow **1.** *Allow, permit.* Usage commentators have long sought to distinguish between *allow* and *permit,* claiming that *permit* is for the giving of express consent or authorization <yes, you are *permitted* to go> and *allow* is for those instances in which no objection is attempted <employees are *allowed* 10 sick days>. Good writers, however, do as seems best to them: some observe the distinction, others do not.

2. *Allow of.* The intransitive *allow,* used with *of,* occurs primarily with impersonal subjects <problems that do not *allow of* easy solutions>.

3. *Allow* in the sense "admit, concede" <he *allows* that he might be wrong> is considered by some a regionalism, but it has a long tradition of mainstream use. Two senses of *allow* that *are* chiefly regional are those of "say" (as in "she *allowed* she saw you yesterday") and "suppose, think" (as in "we *allowed* you wasn't coming"). However, when these two senses combine to imply that someone both holds an opinion and expresses it <she *allows* that the subject is a timely one>, the usage is standard—particularly when followed by *that. Allow* with *as how* <the manager *allowed as how* he disliked making decisions> is sometimes used in journalism and other general writing, but is usually avoided in the most formal contexts. See also AS HOW.

all ready, already The distinction between *all ready* and *already* is one that some still get wrong. *All ready* as a fixed phrase <we are *all ready* to leave> means simply "ready" (*all* serves as an intensive). *Already* is an adverb; it is used in sentences like "They had *already* finished by the time we got there."

all right See ALRIGHT, ALL RIGHT.

all that Although this phrase is regarded by some as substandard in writing, it is commonly found in fiction, reportage, and occasionally more serious writing

<her upstate mansion was not *all that* impressive>. It is used for understatement, sometimes with ironic intent.

all the Commonly used as a simple intensifier of a comparative adverb <the crime was *all the* more heinous considering the victim's age>, *all the* is also used in many different regions of the country in spoken sentences like "That's *all the* higher I can jump." The conventional *as* . . . *as* construction <that's *as* high *as* I can jump> prevails in print.

all-time Though objected to by some as redundant or overused, *all-time* is often a useful intensifier <he holds the *all-time* record for runs batted in> <temperatures reached an *all-time* high>.

all together, altogether Occasionally the phrase *all together,* meaning "in a group" <taken *all together,* these developments indicate a positive trend>, is confused with the adverb *altogether,* meaning "completely" <she was *altogether* uninterested in the details>. You will want to take care in your choice of spelling.

allude **1.** Some insist that *allude* can mean only "to make indirect reference" and that use of the word to mean "refer" is a mistake. But in practice the word is frequently used in a way that makes it impossible to identify one meaning or the other <they did not *allude* to the subject at all> <the person whose work he was

alluding to was there>. *Allude* is also commonly used in the sense "to mention in passing" <the book *alludes* to her husband several times>. In short, the "indirect" sense often shades into the "direct" sense; you should not feel compelled to adhere to any strict distinction.

2. *Alude, elude.* Very occasionally these words are confused. Allude means "to refer" (see 1 above), elude "to evade" <*eluded* police>.

ally *Ally* is used with *to, with,* and *against* <*allied to* this concern was their fear of creating instability> <their efforts are *allied with* those of the Red Cross> <both provinces were *allied against* the central government>.

aloof The usual preposition with *aloof* is *from* <remains *aloof from* the family's financial affairs>. Occasionally *to* is used <*aloof to* the criticisms>. Other prepositions may be used to indicate somewhat different relationships <is *aloof with* strangers> <holds himself *aloof in* such matters>.

alot, a lot *A lot* is often written as one word, but two words is the accepted norm <*a lot* of junk in the attic>. See also LOTS, A LOT.

aloud See OUT LOUD.

already See ALL READY.

alright, all right *All right* is the commonly preferred form <it is *all right* to think that> <everyone is *all right*>. *Alright* is often found in journalistic and business publications <that's *alright* by his fans> and in transcribed speech <he said "*Alright* darling, I was wrong">.

also **1.** Some critics dislike *also* used like *and* <found some old nails, *also* bits of pottery>. This use is common in wills but is not found very often elsewhere. *And also* is sometimes recommended as a replacement.

2. One of those traditional rules is that you should never begin a sentence with *also,* except when the sentence is inverted <*Also* discovered were three kittens>. Writers of high repute, however, have long used *also* as an opener <*Also,* he was in love>. You can ignore the old rule.

alternate, *verb* One person or one thing may alternate *with* another or others <able to *alternate* blue blocks *with* red ones>; one person or thing may alternate *between* two things <his views *alternate between* rigid orthodoxy and freewheeling independence>.

alternate, alternative, *adjectives* Traditionalists recommend using *alternate* to mean "occurring or succeeding by turns" <a day of *alternate* sunshine and rain>, and *alternative* to mean "offering or expressing a choice" <we had a set of *alternative* plans in case of rain>. The distinction is not always maintained in practice, however. In fact, *alternative* is becoming more and more a noun <the only *alternative* to intervention>, and the adjective is in the process of being replaced by *alternate* <they found an *alternate* source of merchandise> <they liked the *alternate* plans better>. The adjective *alternate* in its sense "by turns" is also undergoing change, giving way to the verb *alternate* and its participle *alternating* <strove to *alternate* men and women participants> <we'll see *alternating* sunshine and rain>. The antiestablishment use of the 1960s—"alternative journalism," "alternative schools," and the like—is expressed by both adjectives, with *alternative* somewhat more common.

alternative, *noun* Though some critics insist that alternatives come only in pairs, the evidence from usage indicates this is not true <we were given three *alternatives*>.

although, though These conjunctions have been essentially interchangeable for centuries, though people keep wondering whether one or the other is preferable. The difference is merely a matter of personal choice, but *though* is used more frequently than *although,* perhaps because it is shorter.

altogether See ALL TOGETHER, ALTOGETHER.

alumnus, alumna *Alumna* is the singular form of *alumnae, alumnus* the singular form of *alumni. Alumna* is used for female graduates and *alumnus* for males. *Alumni* is the form usually used for a mixed bag of graduates of both sexes. The clipped form *alum* is also used in less formal contexts.

amalgam *Amalgam* (in its nontechnical sense) takes *of* when it needs a preposition <an *amalgam of* fetishism, spiritism, and transcendentalism>.

amateur In recent years the adjective *amateur* has been used more frequently than the noun. Whereas in the past you might have been an *amateur of, in,* or *at* photography, for example, nowadays you are much more likely to be an *amateur photographer.*

ambiguous See AMBIVALENT, AMBIGUOUS; EQUIVOCAL, AMBIGUOUS.

ambition Both the prepositions *for* and *of* are used with *ambition* <an *ambition for* fame> <she harbors the *ambition of* becoming a broadcaster>. However, the infinitive follows even more commonly <her *ambition* to become a psychiatrist>.

ambivalent, ambiguous *Ambivalent* is used as a descriptive word for a state in which one experiences simultaneous contradictory feelings or in which one wavers between two polar opposites. *Ambiguous,* too, may connote duality, but it most often tends to stress uncertainty and is usually applied to external things <eyes of an *ambiguous* color> whereas *ambivalent* tends to stress duality and is usually applied to internal things <an *ambivalent* attitude toward his father>. *Ambivalent* may be followed by the prepositions *toward* and *about* <*ambivalent toward* her> <*ambiva-*

lent about taking the job>. See also EQUIVOCAL, AMBIGUOUS.

amenable *Amenable* is regularly followed by *to* <*amenable to* the idea>.

amend, emend *Amend,* the more common of these two words, means "to alter (in writing)" but is usually used figuratively <*amended* his ways>. *Emend* is much less often used and is usually applied to the correction of text <was *emended* in this edition>.

America, American People have long questioned the propriety or accuracy of using *America* to mean the United States only and *American* to mean an inhabitant or citizen of the United States. Despite the perceived difficulty with these uses, however, both are fully established. Other inhabitants of the Americas generally prefer using different terms for themselves.

American Indian See NATIVE AMERICAN.

amid, amidst **1.** Different writers have different preferences regarding use of these words. Some feel that neither should be used, while others feel that one or the other is somehow preferable. Actual usage indicates that both are standard; you can use whichever sounds better to you.

2. *Amid, amidst, among.* There exists a curious belief that *amid* and *amidst* should go with singular nouns and *among* with plural nouns. This distinction is not found in actual usage: *amid* and *amidst* are followed by both singular and plural nouns <*amid* a flood of gossip> <*amidst* charges of ethics violations>, and *among,* though commonly used with a plural noun, cannot always serve as a substitute for *amid* or *amidst.*

among **1.** For information about choosing between *among* and *between,* see BETWEEN, AMONG.

2. Some would restrict *among* to use with plural nouns <*among* the players>. While this use is common, an almost equally common use of *among* is with collective nouns <*among* a certain class of people> <*among* the evidence is a note>. Collective nouns are notionally plural, which is why they fit with *among* (see NOTIONAL AGREEMENT in Glossary).

3. *Among, amongst.* Our evidence shows amongst to be a bit less common in American than in British use.

amongst See AMONG 3.

amount **1.** *Amount, number. Amount* is most frequently used with singular mass nouns <a certain *amount* of trust> <the *amount* of money involved>; it is also used with plural nouns considered as an aggregate <requires a fixed *amount* of calories>. *Number* is regularly used with plural count nouns to indicate an indefinite number of individuals or items <a *number* of journalists> <a *number* of objections>.

2. The phrase *in the amount of* is sometimes considered wordy. One recommendation is to replace it with *for* or *of.* But the phrase is useful with large amounts of money <a trade balance favorable *in the amount of* $103,518,000>.

3. The verb *amount* is regularly followed by *to* <it *amounted to* a little more than $200>.

amuse The verb *amuse* (and its past participle *amused,* used as an adjective) is commonly followed by *at, by,* and *with; at* is somewhat less common than the others <we were *amused at* this observation> <he was *amused by* the childrens play> < busy *amusing* themselves *with* video games>. *Amuse* can also be followed by the infinitive <I was *amused* to find an article about it>.

an See A, AN.

analogous When it is followed by a prepositional phrase (as a complement), *analogous* almost always takes *to* <a situation *analogous to* that of Russia's following the collapse of Communism>.

analogy This noun is used with the prepositions *between* <an *analogy between* the Internet and the telephone system>, *among* <*analogies among* the classes of data>, *with* <on *analogy with* a library>, *of* <presents the *analogy of* a family>, and *to* <makes an *analogy to* rock climbing>.

anchorperson See PERSON 2.

and **1.** It is all right to begin a sentence with *and,* though the practice is apparently still cautioned against by some schoolteachers.

2. For other usage problems involving *and,* see AND SO; AND WHICH, AND WHO; GOOD AND; TRY AND; ETC.; and in Glossary: AGREEMENT: SUBJECT-VERB; COMPOUND SUBJECT; PARALLELISM: FAULTY PARALLELISM.

and etc. See ETC.

and/or *And/or* has established itself as an acceptable term, but it should be used only between two alternatives, where the meaning will obviously be "A or B or both" <the student's test scores *and/or* general preparedness will help us determine eligibility>. If used in longer series, *and/or* is likely to be either vague or unnecessary.

and so *And so,* though disparaged by some, is in perfectly good use <*and so* they moved on>.

and which, and who The issue here, which involves faulty parallelism, is better exemplified than described: In the phrase "a lady very learned in stones, ferns, plants, and vermin, and who had written a book about petals" (Anthony Trollope, *Barchester Towers*), *and* joins a clause ("who had written a book . . . ") with an adjective phrase ("very learned in stones . . . ") that is not parallel to it. The usual correction would be to insert *who was* after *lady* and, optionally, omit the *who* after *and* <a lady who was very learned in stones . . . and had written a book>.

angle *Angle* in the sense "the viewpoint from which something is considered" is criticized in various handbooks, but is nevertheless standard; it is used frequently in reviews <the story describes the event from two different *angles*>.

Anglo *Anglo* is an ethnic term of relatively recent vintage (mid-1930s in the U.S., significantly earlier in Canada) used to distinguish those of English ethnic or English-speaking background from others. There are at present two chief uses. The first distinguishes a Canadian of English ethnic and language background from one whose background is French. The second generally distinguishes an American of English-speaking background from one of Spanish-speaking background. *Anglo* has occasionally been considered a derogatory term, but it seems not to be considered so by most people.

angry The chief prepositions used with *angry* are *with, at,* and *about. With* is the most frequently used when the object is a person <she was *angry with* me>, though *with* is also sometimes used with inanimate or abstract objects <*angry with* the decision>. *At* is used with objects that are persons, actions, or things <*angry at* her boss> <*angry at* the world>. *About* is likewise used of persons or actions or things <*angry about* her partner> <*angry about* it>.

annoy The prepositions that commonly go with *annoy* are *with* <I was *annoyed with* her>, *at* <she is *annoyed at* the gossip>, and *by* <he was *annoyed by* their lack of understanding>. Other constructions are also possible <it *annoyed* them to have to listen to it> <she was *annoyed* to see him there> <it's *annoying that* they're so careless>.

ante-, anti- *Ante-* means "earlier, before," and *anti-* "opposite, opposed, against." See a good dictionary for fuller definition.

anticipate Some criticize the use of *anticipate* to mean "expect" <we *anticipate* an early conclusion to the talks> <I *anticipate* that they will follow suit>. The criticism is ill-founded, however; use of the word in this sense is fully established.

antipathy *To* is the preposition most commonly used with *antipathy* <an *antipathy to* outdoor work>, though *for* and *toward* are also in regular use <an *antipathy for* the theater> <an *antipathy toward* intellectuals>. The use of *between,* while not common, is still current <the *antipathy between* Ms. Gross and Mr. Salinger> <an *antipathy between* development and conservation>.

anxious There are two issues here: whether *anxious* can be used to mean "eager" <she was *anxious* for another meeting>, and whether *anxious* can be followed by an infinitive <*anxious* to see the movie> <*anxious* to ease employees' fears>. Both uses are in fact standard and the latter use, especially when *anxious* means "worried," is in fact the most common. Other common uses of *anxious* (in the "worried" sense) are as an attributive adjective <an *anxious* demand> or a predicate adjective without any following prepositional phrase <left him feeling *anxious*>.

any 1. The pronoun *any* can be either singular <*is any* of these solutions the one for us?> or plural <*are any* of these solutions right for us?>.

2. Some maintain that *any* with a singular noun must be referred to by a singular pronoun <*any* participant who spots the difference can test *his or her* knowledge further>. But it is not at all uncommon to find singular *any* referred to by a plural pronoun <*any* driver here can have *their* privileges revoked>. See THEY, THEIR, THEM; AGREEMENT (in Glossary).

3. *Of any, than any* (illogical comparison). Constructions like "has written a better account *than any* before him" and "the finest *of any* I have seen" are sometimes objected to as illogical comparisons. (*Any* is said to logically *include* that which is being spoken of, making *any other* or *all* the better choice.) But such constructions have been around for centuries, even though in recent years they seem to be on the wane. You can revise *any* to *any other* or *all* if you want to, but you need not feel you must do so on logical grounds.

anybody, anyone 1. These indefinite pronouns take a singular verb <*is anybody* home?>, and either a singular or a plural pronoun <*anyone* requiring this service should contact *his or her* [*their*] physician>. The use of the plural pronoun—

they, their, them—has traditionally been disapproved by grammarians, but the use has long been established and is winning greater acceptance. See THEY, THEIR, THEM; and in Glossary: AGREEMENT: INDEFINITE PRONOUNS; NOTIONAL AGREEMENT.

2. *Anybody else's.* See ELSE.

anymore, any more **1.** Both *anymore* and *any more* are found in current written use <she scarcely knows him *anymore* [*any more*]>; the one-word styling is more common.

2. *Anymore* is regularly used in negative contexts <we don't go there *anymore*>. It is also widely used in positive contexts <all I do *anymore* is go to funerals>; this use continually surprises those unfamiliar with it, but it is widespread in most dialect areas except New England.

anyone See ANYBODY, ANYONE.

any other See ANY 3.

anyplace This adverb seems to be American in origin, having emerged in 1916 and later established itself as standard in American English <we could play *anyplace* but in the living room>. See also EVERYPLACE, SOMEPLACE.

anytime This adverb is generally spelled as one word (unless you mean to write "at any time"). It seems to be largely an Americanism <they were not leaving *anytime* soon>.

anyways None of the senses of *anyways* are standard contemporary English; they are limited to various American and English regional dialects.

anywheres *Anywheres* is a generally disparaged Americanism that seldom appears in print outside of dialogue in fiction. It is best avoided in other contexts.

apathy When *apathy* is used with a preposition, it is most frequently *toward* (or *towards*) <*apathy toward* her sister>. *About, to,* and *regarding* are also in use <*apathy about* the matter> <*apathy to* his cousin> <*apathy regarding* the election>.

apparently, evidently *Evidently* generally suggests that there is some overt reason for drawing an inference <*evidently* our team had won the game, because we could hear the cheering>. *Apparently* is used as a disclaimer, as if the author were telling us, "This is what it seems to be, but I wont vouch for it" <*apparently* his previous company let him go, but they wouldn't say so directly>. *Apparently* is used much more frequently than *evidently.*

append *Append* usually takes *to* <should *append* it *to* the file>.

appendix Both *appendixes* and *appendices* are standard and acceptable plurals for *appendix.*

apportion The verb *apportion* may take the prepositions *among, to,* and *between* when a prepositional phrase is required (as a complement) <to be *appor-*

tioned among the states> <*apportioned* duties *to* her subordinates> <*apportioned* responsibility *between* the higher and lower courts>.

apprehensive *Of* is the most frequently used preposition with *apprehensive* <*apprehensive of* so high a cost>, but *about* is also quite common <*apprehensive about* her situation> and *regarding* is sometimes chosen <*apprehensive regarding* his lack of stamina>.

appraise, apprise These words are sometimes confused, especially in speech. *Apprise,* which means "give notice to," usually occurs in the construction *apprise one of* <*apprised him of* her views>. *Appraise,* which means "evaluate," is used with inanimate or abstract objects <*appraised* the house> <*appraised* the situation> and sometimes people <*appraised* him>.

approve *Approve,* when used as an intransitive verb with the meaning "to take a favorable view," takes *of* <he generally *approves of* the effort>. When used as a transitive verb—usually in the sense "to sanction officially"—it can take *by* to indicate the agent of approval <the plan was *approved by* the board>. Some object to using the "favorable view" sense in such transitive constructions as "School officials could not *approve* such behavior on the part of students." This use, however, is standard.

approximately A common recommendation is that the adverb *approximately* should be replaced by the shorter *about* or *nearly* or *almost* when it can be.

However, in business and technical writing and in general prose of a serious cast, the word is standard. It is most commonly applied to numerical quantities <*approximately* 2 percent of the total> but also is used of other things <a boundary running *approximately* north and south>. In casual or informal contexts, you probably will have no need for it.

apropos, apropos of *Apropos of* has been functioning as a compound preposition in English since the middle of the 18th century <a story *apropos of* your interest in meeting him>. Early in the 20th century *apropos* began to be used without *of* as a preposition having the same meaning <I should mention, *apropos* our earlier discussion, that there is one condition>. Both are now standard.

apt See LIABLE, APT, LIKELY.

arguably Some feel that this word is overused and that *perhaps* or *probably* are preferable substitutes. But while *arguably* may be close in meaning to these other two words, it carries its own connotation. It functions as a hedge against too absolute a statement <*arguably* a plan that will satisfy everyone>, or as the qualifier of a superlative <*arguably* the fittest person for the job>. There seems to be no compelling reason to avoid using it.

around **1.** *Around, about.* The use of *around* in senses it share with *about,* especially the sense "approximately" or "near," has long been objected to

<*around* 30 percent> <*around* 4 oclock>. But this use of *around* is standard in American English. You can use it without apologizing.

2. *Around, round. Around* is more common in American English and *round* more common in British English. Both words are, however, in use on both sides of the Atlantic.

array The verb *array* is used with many prepositions. When used in the sense of "dress," it usually takes *in* <*arrayed in* finery>. If the sense is close to "equip," *in* or *with* may be used <towns in the war zone were *arrayed in* arms> <the boat was *arrayed with* sheet and sail>. When the meaning is "to get or place in order," many prepositions are possible <marchers *arrayed on* the parade grounds> <an orchestra *arrayed in front of* the stage> <Secret Service members *arrayed before* the podium> <lights *arrayed in* a Christmas-tree shape>. When there is a notion of drawing up forces, *against* is usual <officials *arrayed against* their opponents>.

arrive The question of what prepositions to use with *arrive* has been a matter of comment since 1770. Our evidence shows the following: When the place of arrival is the object, *in* and *at* are used <*arrived in* New York> <*arrive at* the courtroom>; *on* or *upon* may be used in some instances <will *arrive on* stage> <*arrived upon* the scene>. When things—material or immaterial—arrive, we find *in, at,* or *on* <word *arrived in* the classroom> <the letter *arrived at* her

desk> <the dinghy *arrived on* the beach>. If the object is the point of departure, *from* is the most common <*arrived from* Seattle>. When the object is the means of arrival, we find *by, on,* and occasionally *in* <*arriving by* limousine> <*arrive on* horseback> <*arrived in* a skiff>. In figurative use, the object is almost always the point of arrival and the preposition is at <*arrived at* his conclusion>.

as **1.** The use of *as* to mean "because" or "since" <I needed an answer on the spot, *as* my plane was about to depart> is sometimes said to be ambiguous. However, the surrounding context usually makes the meaning clear, and *as* used in this way is a standard and acceptable alternative to *because* and *since,* though less frequently used than either. See also SINCE.

2. The relative pronoun *as* may be preceded by *such* or *same* <*such* a racket *as* had never been heard before> <faced with much the *same* set of problems *as* confronted Europe in 1914>. The relative pronoun *as* without a preceding *such* or *same* (as in "took decisions *as* ought not to have been taken") is a dialectal form surviving from an older use.

3. The use of *as* as a conjunction where *that,* or sometimes *if* or *whether,* could be substituted (as in "I don't know *as* it matters") is primarily a speech form and is not found in ordinary written prose.

4. When *as* is used as a preposition in the same sense as *like* <he is not *as* other men>, it is standard. But care must be taken not to choose *as* simply to avoid *like* lest ambiguity with other senses of prepositional *as* result <the judge said they acted *as* buffoons>. See also LIKE.

as . . . as **1.** *As . . . as, so . . . as.* *As . . . as* is used in positive statements <*as* good *as* it will ever be>, while either *as . . . as* or *so . . . as* may be used in negative statements <were not *as* accommodating *as* we had expected> <not *so* lucky *as* he used to be>.

2. If a pronoun follows an *as . . . as* comparison, is it to be in the nominative case <she is *as* tall as I> or the objective case <she is *as* tall as me>? Some object to the former as pretentious (though correct), while others object to the latter as ungrammatical (though common). The trend seems to be toward using the nominative case in rather formal contexts and the objective case in most others.

as bad or worse than See AS GOOD OR BETTER THAN.

as best In expressions like "We must carry on *as best* we can," *as best* is a perfectly respectable English idiom. *As best as,* as in "*As best as* I can recall," is disapproved by some critics and is mostly restricted to speech.

as far as, so far as The use of the phrase *as far as* (or *so far as*) without a following verb (such as *goes* or *is concerned* <there has been little improvement *as far as* eliminating street crime in the area> has been much objected to. Our evidence shows that this use is firmly established in speech but is not much used in writing.

as good as Complaints are sometimes heard about the use of *as good as* for *practically* <the plan is *as good as* dead> <she *as good as* told him to print the story>. But you can safely ignore the complaints, as this use is standard.

as good or better than This phrase—as in "Her work is *as good or better than* his"—and others of similar construction (e.g., *as good if not better than, as bad or worse than, as much or more than, as great or greater than*), have been the subject of corrective efforts since the 18th century. The usual suggestion is to supply the missing *as* ("*as* good *as* or better than"), but in a written sentence *or better than* should be set off with commas. Our evidence shows that *as good or better than* (like the others) is an old, well-established English idiom; it need not be routinely revised out unless you are striving for a more formal style.

as great or greater than See AS GOOD OR BETTER THAN.

as how *As how* has been aspersed as simply incorrect and as substandard for *that.* It is neither, however; it is simply dialectal. The expression, particularly in the combination *allow as how,* has current use in journalism, and especially political journalism <the group's spokesperson *allows as how* the decision could affect their most recent plans>. The combinations *being as how* and *seeing as how* are speech forms that do not often appear in print. See also ALLOW 3; BEING, BEING AS, BEING AS HOW, BEING THAT; SEEING AS, SEEING AS HOW, SEEING THAT.

Asian, Oriental *Asian* is now the preferred word, noun or adjective, especially for ethnic purposes <a number of *Asian* students>; *Oriental* is held to be mildly offensive.

aside from *Aside from* can mean either "besides" <*aside from* professional archaeologists, several amateurs have made discoveries> or "except for" <*aside from* this one accomplished piece, her contribution is negligible>. Because it can sometimes happen that you intend "besides" but your reader understands "except for," you must be sure to make your context clear.

as if, as though **1.** At one time the propriety of *as though* used for *as if* was considered dubious. Nowadays most observers find the two to be interchangeable <it's *as though* [*as if*] no one cared>.

2. In sentences like "She felt *as if* someone were [was] watching her," some critics insist on the subjunctive *were,* whereas others accept the indicative *was.* The evidence from usage shows both subjunctive and indicative in frequent respectable use. You may use whichever form you are most comfortable with.

3. See also LIKE 1.

ask *Ask* may be followed by an infinitive <was *asked* to return> or a clause <I *ask* that you not use it> <she *asked* how you were doing>.

When prepositions are used with *ask,* one convention is as follows: "Ask *of* a person *for* what is wanted, *after* one's health." *Of* may also be used with inanimate objects <*asks* too much *of* the program> and *for* with persons <*ask for* Ms. Smith>. *About* is often used when information is sought <*asking about* our plans>. When *ask* means "invite," it may be used with the adverb *out* or the preposition *to* <*asked* her *out* on a date> <was *asked to* the prom>.

as long as, so long as *As long as* and *so long as* are simply variants, being pretty much interchangeable in the sense "provided that" <*as long as* [*so long as*] you get it done in time> and in the more literal sense "for the period of time that" <*so long as* [*as long as*] I am in charge here>. *As long as* (but not *so long as*) is also used to mean "since" <*as long as* you're going out, could you return this video?>

as much or more than See AS GOOD OR BETTER THAN.

as of Although the use of *as of* has been disparaged, the phrase is in reputable American use, especially in business contexts <the figures are current *as of* June 30>. *As of* is also used with words relating to time other than dates. Combinations such *as of now, as of the moment, as of late* are primarily speech forms that are not often used in writing for publication.

as per *As per* is in use—perhaps overuse—in business correspondence and other types of more or less straightforward prose <*as per* the agreement> <*as per* our catalog description>. If you want to avoid it, you may try substituting *in accordance with* or using other constructions beginning with *as* <*as* described in our catalog>, or you may simply use *per* <*per* your memo>.

aspire *To* is the preposition most frequently used with *aspire* <*aspires to* a singing career>; *to* followed by the infinitive is also common <*aspired to* be the nation's best billiards player>. *Toward* (and *towards*) are also both found <*aspiring toward* full-scale arms-reduction talks>.

as regards See REGARD.

assent When the verb *assent* takes a preposition, it is *to* <*assented to* their demands>.

assimilate When the verb *assimilate* takes a preposition, it is most often *to* <*assimilate to* the conditions> and next most often *into* <*assimilated into* the platoon>. *By* indicates the agent <*assimilated by* her new country>.

assist **1.** The most common construction using *assist* appears in phrases like "*assist* patrons *in* using the library" (i.e., *assist* + object + *in* + gerund). Standard but somewhat less common are phrases like "*assisting* his parents *to* build a house" (*assist* + object + *to* + infinitive). Other constructions are found more rarely.

2. When *assist* clearly means "help," *in* or *with* are the usual prepositions <*assist in* finding the pet's owner> <*assisted with* clearing the table>. When *assist* means "be present," it regularly takes *at* <several ministers *assisted at* the signing>.

assume, presume These words are not synonymous, but they share the sense "suppose, expect, believe." *Presume* tends to convey more certainty than *assume* <he is *presumed* to be armed and dangerous> <she *assumed* that her friends would be there>. *Assume* has more meanings than *presume* and is the more common word.

assure **1.** For information about choosing among synonyms of *assure,* see ENSURE, INSURE, ASSURE.

2. *Assure* can take an ordinary noun object <to *assure* success> <we *assure* the quality of our workmanship>. The direct object may also be a clause <wanting to *assure* that their savings are safe>. But most often *assure,* much like *promise,* takes two objects—a direct and an indirect <thus *assuring* us another victory>. Usually the direct object is a clause, with or without *that* <*assured* them *that* they have nothing to worry about> <we were *assured* this wouldn't happen>. Sometimes the clause is replaced by a phrase with *of* <to assure them *of* a seat at the negotiating table>.

as though See AS IF, AS THOUGH.

as to **1.** *As to,* contrary to the opinion of some, is not legalese. Rather, it is a common compound preposition in wide use at every level of formality. It is used as an introducer <*As to* his suggestion about retiring, . . .> and to link a noun, an adjective, or a verb with the following matter <offered no opinion *as to* the likelihood of a settlement> <she was less sanguine *as to* the couple's long-term prospects> <slow to decide *as to* the best route to take>. You can use any of these constructions when they sound right to you.

2. Various commentators have complained about using *as to* in front of such conjunctions as *how, why,* and especially *whether* <questions were raised *as to how* to treat it> <no one can be certain *as to why* they left> <a disagreement *as to whether* she is capable of it>. There is, however, no solid basis to these complaints; use of *as to* in such constructions is standard.

astonished *Astonished* can be used with either *at* or *by,* though *at* is perhaps the more common <we were *astonished at* the force of the hurricane>. *By* is frequently followed by a gerund <he *astonished* the judging panel *by* withdrawing the piece>.

as well as *As well as,* besides being used in the literal, comparative way <she performed it *as well as* anyone could>, is used as a preposition and conjunction. As a preposition, it is usually followed by a gerund <*as well as* serving as chief counsel, Jim is the group's treasurer>. The most common use of the phrase, however, is as a conjunction. It joins nouns and noun phrases <two department stores *as well as*

a pharmacy>. It joins prepositional phrases <the room opens into the dining room *as well as* onto the deck>. It joins verbs <she drove *as well as* navigated> and verbal phrases <the firm was floundering financially *as well as* running into legal difficulties>. It joins adjectives <she seemed relaxed *as well as* confident>.

Sometimes *as well as* joins two words or phrases that are the subject of the same verb. Usually the first subject is plural, the verb is plural, and no commas are used <recent legislative actions *as well as* tighter enforcement make it unlikely>. Where the first subject is singular and the second plural, usage is somewhat mixed: the plural verb tends to be chosen when no commas are used <the harbor *as well as* the many inlets are quickly filling with sand>, and the singular is chosen when commas are used <the harbor, *as well as* the many inlets, is quickly filling with sand>. When both subjects are singular, commas and a singular verb are preferred <this statement, *as well as* the earlier one, is tantamount to libel>.

at See WHERE . . . AT.

at about Although various commentators have complained that *at about* is redundant <we left the arena *at about* two oclock> and have recommended eliminating one or the other of the two terms, our files show that *at about* is thoroughly reputable and firmly established.

at present, at the present time Though a few critics have discouraged the use of these phrases as merely wordy ways of saying *now,* it is difficult to see why. Both phrases can be useful in subtly emphasizing a contrast with time past or time future in a way that the less noticeable *now* cannot <his work is *at present* not widely supported within the scientific community>. You should feel free to use either phrase when it sounds right.

attain When used intransitively, *attain* is normally followed by *to* <he could only *attain to* a low-level job in the ministry>.

attempt **1.** The noun *attempt* frequently takes the preposition at <her first *attempt at* bareback riding>. *On* is the usual preposition when *attempt* means "an attempt to kill" <an *attempt on* the prime minister's life>; *against* and *upon* are also used <the failed *attempt against* Hitler> <*attempts upon* the crown>. And the infinitive is quite common <an *attempt* to escape>.

2. The idea that *try* should be substituted for *attempt* is occasionally put forward, but may be disregarded. Many good writers find *attempt* to be perfectly satisfactory <it is futile to *attempt* to eradicate a speech form by denouncing it in books on writing>.

at the present time See AT PRESENT, AT THE PRESENT TIME.

at this point in time See POINT IN TIME.

attitude *Attitude* is generally followed by the prepositions *toward, towards,* and *to. Toward* is the most frequent in American English <the assistants *attitude toward* the boss>. *Towards* is found chiefly in British English, and *to* is more common in British than American English <a critical *attitude to* her work>. *About* has some use, usually spoken, in American English <developed an *attitude about* it>.

augment *Augment,* often in the form of its past participle *augmented,* is used frequently with the preposition *by* <these resources were *augmented by* funds of her own>, and less frequently with *with* <ended up *augmenting* the divider *with* concrete barriers>.

auger, augur These two words are sometimes confused because of their similar spelling. *Auger* refers to tools for boring holes; *augur* (as in the phrase *augur well*) deals with foretelling future events from omens.

authority When *authority* refers to a person, it is most often followed by *on* <an *authority on* airplane disasters>, but a couple of other prepositions are possible <an *authority upon* virtually all subjects> <an *authority in* the field of high-density physics>. When *authority* refers to a cited source, *for* is usual <his *authority for* this observation is an 18th-century grammarian>. When it refers to a power or convincing force, *over* often follows *authority* <the state has no *authority over* federal wetlands> and *by* and *on* often precede it <*by* the *authority* invested in me> <*on* the *authority* of agency head Dixon>. *Authority* is also used with the infinitive <has *authority* to institute a manhunt if necessary>.

average According to some, *average* should not be used to mean "customary, ordinary, usual." But even though an occasional writer puts this sense in quotation marks <the "*average*" New Yorker> to indicate that the use is dubious, the issue is dead since this meaning has been completely standard for many years <the *average* Beltway politician> <the *average* dictionary user>.

averse to, averse from *Averse* to is the more common phrase in both British and American English <not *averse to* making money>, though *averse from* is still used in Britain.

aversion Of the prepositions that go with *aversion*, *to* is the most common <an *aversion to* being questioned>. *From* is the next most common <his *aversion from* sex>. The use of *for* goes back many years, but seems to be less common now than either *to* or *from* <a pronounced *aversion for* reading>.

awake, awaken *Awake* is a verb that, like WAKE (see entry), derives from a blend of two older verbs, one transitive (or causative) and the other intransitive. Because of this, it employs a mixture of regular and irregular principal parts. The past tense is either *awoke* or *awaked* <we *awoke* [*awaked*] from our reverie>, while the past participle is either *awoken* or *awaked* <they had *awoken* [*awaked*] to their own misery>.

The separate verb *awaken,* on the other hand, which has essentially the same meaning as *awake,* is perfectly regular, with *awakened* as its past <the experience *awakened* memories> and past participle <the company has *awakened* from its self-induced torpor>.

awesome The use of *awesome* as a generalized term of approval has been part of the standard hyperbole of sports broadcasting and writing for several years <an *awesome* fastball>. It has also been popular in speech, often attracting the intensifier *totally* <"the waves are *totally awesome,*" he reported>. In more formal contexts this "extraordinary" sense is probably best avoided.

The word also continues to carry its primary meaning of "inspiring awe" <an *awesome* show of force> <the *awesome* responsibility of becoming the child's permanent guardian>.

awful, awfully Any use of *awful* and *awfully* that doesn't convey the original sense of being "filled with awe" has traditionally been criticized. However, *awful* has long been acceptable in the meanings "extremely objectionable" <what an *awful* color> and "exceedingly great" <an *awful* lot of money> in speech and casual writing. Use of the adverbs *awful* and *awfully* as intensifiers <I'm *awful* tired> <he's *awfully* rich> is likewise common in informal prose. You probably will not want these where a formal tone is called for.

awhile, a while *Awhile,* like several other adverbs of time and place, is often used as the object of a preposition <after *awhile* I felt better> <for *awhile* she was silent>, though many consider this an error. If you want to play it safe, however, you should stick to the spelling *a while* <they had parted *a while* earlier>.

B

background Some have criticized the use of *background* in the senses "the sum of a person's experience or training" <the two boys' *backgrounds* are very different> and "the circumstances preceding a phenomenon or event" <gave us some *background* on the candidate's decision>. But the criticisms can be safely ignored; the use of *background* in these senses is standard.

back of, in back of Both *back of* and *in back of* are standard in American English <set up a dog kennel *in back of* [*back of*] the garage>.

bad, badly **1.** The standard use of the adverb *bad* is equivalent in meaning to *badly;* it often occurs with *off* <just how *bad off* were they?>. In speech and in some informal writing, *bad* is interchangeable with *badly* after *do, want,* and *need* <we didn't *do too bad,* considering the circumstances> <he says he *wants* justice *bad* enough to bring the case to trial>.

2. See FEEL BAD, FEEL BADLY.

bail, bale Watch your spelling here. *Bail* means "security given" <managed to post *bail*>, while *bale* means "a bundle of goods" <*bales* of hay>.

balance The extension of the meaning of this word to the remainder or rest of something other than money is a standard Americanism <the *balance* of the book's chapters>.

balding Though once criticized as nonexistent, *balding* has established itself as standard <a *balding* gentleman of middle years>.

bale See BAIL, BALE.

bare, bear Confusion or misspelling of these two words sometimes occurs. *Bare* as a verb means "to uncover" <*bared* his soul> and as an adjective "uncovered" <*bare*-headed>. The verb *bear* has a variety of meanings, among them "to carry" <*bears* the stamp of approval>, "to endure" <couldn't *bear* to watch>, "to press" <*bear* down hard>, and "to give birth to or produce" (see BORN, BORNE).

bargain The verb *bargain* takes *with* with a person or group of persons <the rules forbid *bargaining with* anyone>. *With* may also be used with something considered as a helpful tool <not much capital to *bargain with*>. You bargain *for* something <no one had *bargained for* these results>, and *about, over,* or *on* something or some subject <the right to *bargain about* [*over, on*] pensions>.

based *Based,* when used to mean "established, founded" and followed by a preposition, is most often used with on <*based on* the facts>. Less often, *based* is used with *upon* <*based upon* the sources>; and least often, it is used with *in* <*based in* a thorough modernism>. When used to mean "stationed or located at a base," *based* is most often followed by the prepositions *at* or *in* <a fleet *based at* Guantanamo> <she was *based in* California>.

based on, based upon When *based on* (or *based upon*) begins a sentence, it often ends up becoming a dangling modifier: "*Based on* this analysis, Porkco Inc. is running little risk." However, such sentences are usually perfectly understandable. When a *based on* phrase clearly modifies an element later in the sentence <*Based on* this analysis, the risk to Porkco Inc. is minimal>, it is not dangling and is fully acceptable.

basically Some object to what they consider the unnecessary use of *basically* as a sentence adverb: "*Basically,* they want to raze the neighborhood and build a highway." But *basically,* as used here, is one of those little space-makers carried over from speech to speechlike prose; it does not seem to be a serious fault in the kind of journalistic writing in which it usually appears. It should not be overdone, however.

basis **1.** *Basis* figures in two somewhat long-winded phrases that are often criticized—namely, *on the basis of* and *on a . . . basis.*

The first of these phrases is often considered a candidate for replacement by *on, by, after,* or *because of.* In the clause "not *on the basis of* the merits of that view but rather . . . ," for example, you could replace "on the basis of the merits of that view" with "on its own merits." Other cases are not so clear-cut, however; and sometimes the phrase is necessary <this cannot be proved *on the basis of* the postulates stated>. Conclusion: though mechanical substitution of another preposition or phrase will not necessarily make your text more readable, *on the basis of* can often be replaced by something shorter. Consider how the phrase fits the whole context of your piece and how it fits the rhythm and sense of the sentence.

The more challenging phrase is *on a . . . basis.* This phrase functions as an adverb <service *on a* pay-per-view *basis*>, and is found quite often in less-than-elegant writing. Its awkwardness seems to be its chief virtue, though, for it allows a writer to write what might otherwise not be easily expressible. Care and judgment are required in revising it out of your text; it may be better left alone than hastily revised.

2. When used with a preposition, *basis* usually takes *of* or *for* <the *basis of* the objection> <simple designs which became the *basis for* more elaborate ones>.

be *Be* continues to be used in its subjunctive function <any young man, *be* he rich or poor, . . .>, especially in a few fixed phrases <*be* that as it may> <so *be* it>. More frequently, however, *is* or *are* is used instead <if this *is* Tuesday, I must be in Moscow> <though they *are* down, they are not defeated>. *Be* is also used in various English dialects, such as Black English and

Irish English, to indicate habitual or continued action (as in "he *be* the one" and "sure the afternoon *be* a warm one"), but these usages are not yet part of ordinary standard English.

bear See BARE, BEAR; BORN, BORNE.

beat, beaten *Beaten* is by far the more common form of the past participle <he was *beaten* to a pulp>. *Beat* appears more often in older writing, but is still found in respectable circles <she had *beat* the odds>. *Beat* is common in sports writing after *get* <when they got *beat* in the finals>, and it is usual in the phrase *can't be beat* (where *beaten* is not used).

because **1.** The notion that *because* can be used only to introduce an adverbial clause and not a noun clause seems to be connected with opposition to the phrase *reason is because* (see REASON IS BECAUSE). Such sentences as "It is *because* he has never performed the stunt before a large crowd that he is so uneasy" (noun clause) and "*Because* he has never performed the stunt before a large crowd, he is uneasy" (adverbial clause) are, however, both entirely standard.

2. Some have criticized the practice of making a clause beginning with *because* or *just because* the subject of a sentence, as in "*Just because* I forgot to call doesn't mean I don't love you." This construction is more typical of speech than of highly serious writing. It is not wrong, but you probably will not want to use it in anything of a formal nature.

3. The rule that you can never begin a sentence with *because* is a myth. *Because* is frequently used to begin sentences, particularly in magazine and newspaper writing <*Because* no one returned her call, she took them to be less than enthusiastic about meeting with her>.

4. It is commonly observed that there can be ambiguity when *because* follows a negative verb in a sentence: "He didn't leave *because* he was afraid." The question here is, did he leave or did he stay? The usual advice is to solve the ambiguity with a comma: "He didn't leave, *because* he was afraid" means he stayed; "He didn't leave *because* he was afraid" means he left, but not because he was afraid. But sentences like this are better rewritten; professional writers seem to revise them, and you should too.

5. See AS 1; SINCE.

beg the question This phrase originated in a 16th-century translation of Aristotle, where the verb literally meant "beg" but was really closer in meaning to "assume." Thus the phrase was not clear to many readers and developed a second sense "to evade, sidestep." Both these uses are standard. More recently the phrase has been used in contexts in which *beg* is literal <the title "Improve Your Grammar" *begs the question:* Why?> This use seems to be on the way to establishing itself as standard.

behalf Some commentators have insisted on distinguishing between *in behalf of* (meaning "for the benefit of") and *on behalf of* (meaning "as the agent for"). But evidence from actual usage shows that there has never been a clear-cut distinction in meaning based on the choice of preposition. Both *in* and *on* are used interchangeably in American English in both the "benefit" sense and the "agent" sense, while modern British usage tends to favor *on* in all instances.

behest Sometimes criticized as old-fashioned or formal, *behest* is indeed an old word but it is still in current use in a variety of contexts. It suggests a stronger urging than *request* does <will investigate the matter at the *behest* of the Senate panel>.

behoove, behove *Behoove* is the usual spelling in the U.S. and *behove* the usual spelling in the U.K.

being, being as, being as how, being that The conjunction *being* survives in various dialects (as in "*Being as* you are family, I can tell you"). If any of these phrases are in your dialect and you use them in writing, it is likely to be noticed by those who do not have them in their dialect.

belabor, labor These two verbs are interchangeable in expressions such as "*belabor/labor* a point."

beside, besides *Beside* is used as a preposition <the table *beside* the couch>, and it also appears in two standard idioms: *beside oneself,* and *beside the point. Besides* is both an adverb <she was an experienced professional and a loving mother *besides*> and a preposition meaning "except, other than, together with" <she had nothing to worry about, *besides* the wedding>.

bestow In modern use, *upon* and *on* are the prepositions that usually go with *bestow* <*bestowed* good fortune *upon* them>.

be sure and See TRY AND.

bet The verb *bet* has two forms of the past tense and past participle: *bet* and *betted.* In the U.S., *bet* is usual <had not yet *bet* on the race>. In the U.K. both are used, but *bet* is more common.

better **1.** For the use of *better* in constructions like "a *better* kind of company," where no explicit comparison is made, see ABSOLUTE COMPARATIVE (in Glossary).

2. The use of *better* for *had better* is an acceptable idiom <you *better* not complain>, but it is not found in very formal surroundings.

3. The idiom *better than* used to mean "more than" (as in "*better than* two thirds were lawyers") is primarily a spoken idiom and is not generally found in formal writing.

between, among The notion that *between* can be used only of two items and that *among* must be used for more than two is persistent but unfounded. *Between* is especially appropriate to denote a one-to-one relationship, regardless of the number of items. It can be used when the number is unspecified <eco-

nomic cooperation *between* nations>, when more than two are mentioned <this is *between* you and me and the lamppost>, and even when only one item is noted but repetition is implied <paused *between* every sentence). *Among* is more appropriate when the emphasis is not strictly on individual relationships <discontent *among* the stockholders>. Automatically using *among* when more than two items are mentioned can result in awkwardness and may strain natural idiom.

between you and I Critical opinion holds that *between you and I* (or *between he and Jane*) should be *between you and me* (or *between him and Jane* or *between Jane and him*). The problem here is that *between* takes a compound object, which resists the government of the preposition. A few commentators think *between you and I* should be accepted as good English (it dates back as far as Shakespeare), but most resist it. You need not eliminate it from your speech, but you will probably want to avoid it in writing.

biannual, biennial These two words are usually differentiated, *biannual* meaning "occurring twice a year" and *biennial* usually meaning "occurring once in two years." See also BIMONTHLY, BIWEEKLY.

bid The verb *bid* has irregular inflected forms. When it means "to make a bid" it usually has the unchanged *bid* as both past tense and past participle <he *bid* on the piano> <we had *bid* for the job>. In other senses the most common past is *bade*, though *bid* is sometimes also found <she *bade* [*bid*] him farewell>. As past participle in those senses, *bid* and *bidden* are the most usual <we have *bid* adieu to the problem> <was *bidden* to speak>.

biennial See BIANNUAL, BIENNIAL.

bimonthly, biweekly Many people are puzzled about these two words, which are often ambiguous because the meaning of *bi-* in this context can be either "coming or occurring every two" (i.e., every other month, every other week) or "coming or occurring two times" (i.e., twice a month, twice a week). This ambiguity has existed for well over a century and seems unlikely to go away soon. The chief difficulty is that many users of these words, assuming that their readers know exactly what they mean, do not bother to make their context clear. So if you use *bimonthly* or *biweekly,* you should leave some clues to your meaning. See also BIANNUAL, BIENNIAL.

bite *Bitten* is the usual past participle <the shark has already *bitten* two bathers>. *Bit,* however, continues to be used in spoken dialect and now and then in various fixed phrases with *bite* <many such mining operations long ago *bit* the dust>.

biweekly See BIMONTHLY, BIWEEKLY.

black See AFRICAN-AMERICAN.

blame, *noun* The noun *blame* may be followed by the prepositions *for* or *on* <took all the *blame for* allowing it> <placed *blame* on the managers>.

blame on, blame for The real difference between "blame someone for" and "blame something on" is the direct object. In the first, the direct object is the cause of the problem <they *blamed* Kathy *for* the error> <the technicians were *blamed for* the outage>; in the second, the direct object is the problem <they *blamed* the error *on* Kathy> <the outage was *blamed on* the technicians>. The evidence shows *blame on* and *blame for* to be about equally frequent.

blend *Blend* is followed by *with* or *into* <*blending* these ideas *with* similar ones of his partner> <the structure *blends into* its surroundings>. Sometimes the phrase *blend in* is followed by *with* <we *blended* right *in with* the crowd>. In cookery, *blend* is regularly followed by *in* <*blend in* three eggs>.

bloc, block The spelling *bloc* is usual for the sense of a political combination <a *bloc* of voters>.

blow The usual inflected forms of *blow* are irregular: *blew* and *blown* <the wind *blew*> <our cover was *blown*>. *Blowed* is a speech form limited to some regional dialects.

boast **1.** Though questioned by some, the transitive sense of *boast,* "to possess and call attention to," has been in use since the late 17th century and is standard <the city *boasts* one of the largest convention centers in the nation>.

2. When *boast* is used as an intransitive with a preposition, *of* and *about* are usual <they would some-

times *boast of* their links to the underground> <she *boasts* too much *about* her experience and training>.

boost Occasionally someone complains about use of the noun *boost* to mean "increase, raise, rise." It is nevertheless standard <a *boost* in the prime lending rate> <a real *boost* to morale>.

border When *border* is used to mean "to approach the nature of a specific thing" and is followed by a preposition, *on* is the usual choice <a statement *bordering on* the ridiculous>. When the literal sense of *border* is used in the passive, the preposition most often used is *by; with* is less frequent <grounds *bordered by* [*with*] potted flowers>.

born, borne These two words, both past participles of the verb *bear,* are sometimes misused. *Born* should be used only in the passive of the literal or figurative act of birth <was *born* in 1989> or as an adjective <a *born* loser>. The active past participle for giving birth is *borne* <had *borne* three children>. *Borne* is used for all other senses <a pain that could hardly be *borne*> <not *borne* out by the facts>. See also BARE, BEAR.

borrow The usual preposition linking *borrow* to the person or source is *from* <she *borrowed* it *from* Sarah>. *Of* is used sometimes to link *borrow* with the object borrowed <he *borrowed* freely *of* Shakespeare's words in composing these lines>. *Against* and *on* tend to be used in more specialized contexts <*borrowed against* revenues> <he *borrows on* the philosophy of

Pragmatism>. The prepositions *off* and *off of* are limited to speech.

both **1.** *Both . . . and.* To achieve parallelism in your prose, it is best to place the same construction after both *both* and *and* <rights to *both* the cottage *and* the lakefront> <bowing *both* out of respect for her elders *and* out of fear in the presence of her mother-in-law>. In speech, this convention is not always adhered to.

2. *Both of. Both of* is just like ALL OF (see entry). The *of* after *both* can be omitted before a plural noun (although it need not be) <*both (of)* these rates are likely to increase>, but it must be kept before a pronoun in the objective case <we visited *both of* them>.

3. *The both. The both* is a fairly common spoken idiom (as in "To bed, *the both* of you!"), usually avoided in writing.

brand *Brand,* in the sense "a characteristic or distinctive kind" <a lively *brand* of theater>, is occasionally criticized. It is nevertheless standard.

bridegroom See GROOM.

break The past tense of *break* is *broke* <I *broke* the latch> and the standard past participle is *broken* <was *broken* in two>. *Broke* as a past participle was once standard but is now dialectal, except in the usage of those who train horses; they distinguish *broke* (desirable) from *broken* (undesirable).

bring, take The oft-stated and simple rule that *bring* implies movement toward the speaker and *take* implies movement away is reasonable as far as it goes, but it does not go far enough to account for actual use. The fact is that often direction or point of view is of little or no relevance to the reader (or hearer) <students must *bring* [*take*] report cards home to their parents> <"Be sure to *take* [*bring*] the umbrella," she told him>. In such instances, *bring* and *take* become virtually interchangeable. You should follow your natural inclination and not worry about what critics might prefer.

bring up See RAISE, REAR.

Brit, Briton, Britisher *Brit* is a relatively modern word (about a century old) that is a shortening of *Briton, Britisher,* or *British.* It is used to designate a native of England, and its use has been accelerating rapidly since the 1970s. Despite some British touchiness about it, *Brit* seems to be on its way to becoming a neutral, informal term on both sides of the Atlantic. *Briton* and *Britisher* also remain in reputable use.

broke **1.** Although *broke* in the sense "without funds, penniless" is maligned by some as slangy, it has been in good use for some three centuries.

2. See BREAK.

bulk of *The bulk of* is used with plural count nouns that may be thought of as a mass <*the bulk of* the voters> <*the bulk* of the books>. It is equally often used with mass nouns <*the bulk of* the evidence> <*the bulk of* the work>.

bunch *Bunch* is sometimes criticized as colloquial. Our evidence shows that it has long been in good use both as a generalized collective <a *bunch* of boys> <*bunches* of tourists> and as a word for a group of people <a literate *bunch*> <a tough-looking *bunch*>. It is also standard when used with mass nouns <a *bunch* of money> <a *bunch* of nonsense>. You can avoid it in formal contexts if you want, but there is no reason to do so other than your own preference.

burgeon It was decided in the 1960s that the use of *burgeon* to mean "bloom" or "flourish" <a *burgeoning* industry> was an error. It was not an error, having been in established use for well over a century. It is entirely standard.

burn Both the past tense and past participle of *burn* are spelled two different ways—*burned* and *burnt.* In American English *burned* is the more common form of the past tense <we were *burned* by the market> <the fire *burned* furiously>, while both *burnt* and *burned* are used as adjectives <a *burnt* almond flavor>. Intransitive *burned* and transitive *burnt* are preferred in British English.

bust The verb *bust,* though disparaged by some, has been gaining in respectability for a half century, and in some contexts is the right word to use <*busting* loose> <was *busted* for dealing drugs> <had to *bust* our butts

to get it done>. None of these suggest use in highly formal situations.

but **1.** Commentators agree that, contrary to what many people believe, it is okay to begin a sentence with *but.* The only caution they offer is that *but* is best not followed with a comma (as in "*But,* you won't know until you try it"), as this will weaken its force, unless the comma is one of a pair setting off a parenthetical clause <*But,* however you add it up, the fact remains . . .>.

2. *But* has functioned as both a conjunction and a preposition since Old English, and still does. As a conjunction, it is sometimes followed by a pronoun in the nominative case, particularly when it forms part of the subject <no one *but* I saw through the ruse>. When followed by a pronoun in the objective case that stands in a position normally calling for the objective, *but* can be interpreted either as a preposition or a conjunction <they questioned everyone *but* him>. Sometimes *but* is clearly a preposition and must be followed by the objective case of the pronoun <It seemed obvious to everyone in the group *but* her>. In such instances the style tends to be more conversational than when *but* is followed by a nominative pronoun. You may use *but* either way, depending on your audience and your preference.

3. *But for,* though used infrequently, functions as a compound preposition in exactly the same way that *except for* does <there *but for* the grace of God go I>.

4. When *but* (as an adverb) means "only," constructions such as "had he *but* informed the family of his wishes" are standard in written prose. An older, negative form (as in "We weren't *but* two months into the project when . . .") is now found chiefly in speech.

5. *But that,* as in "There is no question *but that* the game has changed" or "I don't doubt *but that* Congress will succeed," is a standard idiom, though in many contexts either word by itself will serve. *But what* (as in "I don't know *but what* you could find it there") is also a standard idiom, but one more likely to be found in speech and in the most informal kinds of writing.

buy **1.** *Noun. Buy* in the sense "bargain" has been in standard use since at least 1879 <many good *buys* at the flea market>.

2. *Verb.* The sense of the verb meaning "accept, believe" is no longer considered slang <few *buy* the idea that such increases are necessary>.

by means of Some assert that this "wordy" preposition should be replaced by *by, in,* or *with.* But *by means of* is often used precisely to avoid a simpler preposition when the simpler one might be ambiguous <learning about the past *by means of* artifacts discovered by archaeologists>. "Short and simple" may often be better, but longer is sometimes clearer.

C

callous, callus These two words are sometimes confused because of similar sound and spelling. *Callous* is generally limited to the sense "feeling no emotion or sympathy" <a *callous* person>. *Callus* is used to refer to a hard area on the skin.

can, may *Can* and *may* are frequently interchangeable in senses denoting possibility <do you think he *may* still be alive?> <those things *can* happen>. Because the possibility of one's doing something may depend on another's acquiescence, *can* and *may* have also become interchangeable in the sense denoting permission <you *can* [*may*] go now if you like>. The use of *can* to ask or grant permission has been common since the 19th century and is well established, though some language commentators feel that *may* is more appropriate in formal contexts. *May* is relatively rare in negative constructions; *cannot* and *can't* are more common in such constructions <the groom *cannot* see the bride until the ceremony begins>.

cannot, can not Both spellings are in use, but *cannot* is more frequent, especially in edited prose.

cannot but, cannot help, cannot help but These phrases all mean the same thing— "to be unable to do otherwise than"—and they are all standard <I *cannot but* recall that I too was once in that position> <I *can-*

not help thinking that their efforts are somehow misdirected> <one *cannot help but* admire his zeal>.

can't seem The expression *can't seem* <I *can't seem* to get any sleep lately> is an idiom that is mostly used in speech. It is an example of what linguists call "raising," the process by which a negative element like *can't* (or some other element) gets moved from a subordinate clause to the main clause. Another well-known example of raising is "I don't think it'll rain today" for "I think it won't rain today." Negative elements often tend to be raised in conjunction with *seem.* Thus, related expressions like *cannot seem, don't seem, did not seem,* etc., are all standard idioms and are not uncommon in print.

canvas, canvass *Canvas,* meaning "strong cloth" or "oil painting," is occasionally spelled *canvass,* but *canvas* remains more common. Similarly, *canvass,* meaning "to solicit votes or opinions," is sometimes spelled *canvas,* but the latter is only a secondary spelling variant.

capability *Capability* is commonly followed by *of* or *for* when it is used with a preposition <they are taught to trust in the *capabilities of* their superiors> <our *capability for* mutual destruction>. It is also commonly followed by *to* and an infinitive <the *capability to* produce mass quantities>.

capable When followed by a preposition, *capable* nearly always appears with *of* <*capable of* eliminating pests>. Use of *capable of* in passive constructions is also found <a substance *capable of* being altered by changes in temperature>, although some language arbiters would insist on converting these to active constructions.

capacity *Capacity*, when it refers to ability, potential, facility, or power, may be followed by *to* and the infinitive <a *capacity to* love>. It may also be followed by *for* and a noun <his *capacity for* mischief>, or *for* and a gerund phrase <a *capacity for* stirring controversy>. When *capacity* is used to designate volume, the preposition *of* follows it <a seating *capacity of* 500>. When denoting a position or role, *capacity* is used more often in the construction *in his* (*her, our*, etc.) *capacity as* than in the construction *in the* (*his, her*, etc.) *capacity of* <in her [the] *capacity* as [of] editor>.

capful See -FUL.

capital, capitol There are a number of things that the spelling *capital* is used for—letters, money, cities—but *capitol* always refers to a building (and is capitalized when denoting the federal Capitol).

care **1.** The verb *care* is often followed by *for* and *about* <the animal was being *cared for* by shelter volunteers> <I don't *care about* that>. *To* and the infinitive may also follow *care* <do you *care to* comment?>.

2. The noun *care* is commonly followed by *for* or *of* <specialized *care for* the aged> <in the *care of* his doctor>.

careen, career The verbs *careen* and *career* look a lot alike, sound a lot alike, and in fact are used a lot alike to refer to movement that is headlong, reckless, or uncontrolled. *Career* is used almost entirely in this sense; *careen* has other meanings as well. Consult a good dictionary for clarification.

careful, careless 1. *Careful,* when used with a complement, is most often followed by the preposition *of* and a noun or a pronoun, or by *to* and an infinitive <be *careful of* your father-in-law> <had been *careful to* remove their belongings>. When *careful* is used to mean "exercising prudence," however, it may be followed by *about* or *with* <they are *careful about* such things> <be *careful with* the baby>.

2. *Careless* is most often used with *of* or *about* when it takes a complement <*careless of* time> <*careless about* dress>.

3. Both *careful* and *careless* are also used with *in* followed by a noun or gerund <*careful in* choosing a partner> <*careless in* style>.

catsup See CATSUP, KETCHUP, CATCHUP.

cater In current American usage, the usual preposition after *cater* is *to* <she *caters to* their every wish>. In British usage the usual preposition is *for.*

catsup, ketchup, catchup The spellings *catsup* and *ketchup* are used with about equal frequency; *catchup* is not as common as the other two, but it is used. All three spellings are standard.

cause The noun *cause* may be followed by the prepositions *of* and *for* <a *cause of* concern> <a *cause for* alarm>. Occasionally it is followed by the infinitive <she has no *cause* to interfere>.

Celtic As part of the name of a sports team, such as the Boston Celtics, this is pronounced \'sel-tik\. You will also hear this pronunciation in other contexts, and at times from very well-educated speakers. But the closer you get to circles concerned with Celtic lore and languages, the more likely you are to hear \'kel-tik\.

cement, concrete As a term for a mixture of ingredients that sets hard when combined with water, *concrete* is more frequently used—especially in technical writing—than *cement,* although *cement* is some 500 years older. Both words are common in figurative uses <is not a policy set in *concrete*> <it is the *cement* that holds the two parties together>.

center The intransitive verb *center* (meaning "to focus") is most commonly used with the prepositions *at, in, on,* and *around. At* is favored in mathematical contexts, while the others are found in a broad range of contexts. Some object to *center around* as illogical, though it is a standard idiom; if you want to avoid it, you can use *center on* (or *in*) or try *revolve around.*

certain The use of *certain* to mean "of a specific but unspecified character" <the house has a *certain* charm>, though criticized as ambiguous by some, continues to be widely used.

certainly Usage commentators have occasionally objected to the use of *certainly* as an intensifier <it is *certainly* true> <this is *certainly* something to consider>, but such use is perfectly standard in speech and is common enough in writing.

chair **1.** *Verb. Chair* is a verb formed from the noun. It has been in use since the 1920s and is standard <she *chairs* two different committees>.

2. *Noun. Chair* has been used in the sense "chairman, chairwoman" (see next entry) since the middle of the 17th century and is standard <it is for the *chair* to decide>.

chairman, chairwoman, chairperson *Chairman* is the oldest of these words and the most widely used. It has been and still is used of women. *Chairwoman* is an old and entirely respectable word but it seems not to have been used as often as it might, probably because it has long competed with *chairman* in application to women and has recently had competition from *chairperson. Chairperson* is a recent coinage as a gender-neutral term, and, in spite of the attacks of usage writers, has won fairly wide acceptance. All three of these words are in standard use. See also CHAIR 2.

chance **1.** *Noun.* The preposition used most frequently after *chance* is *of* <his *chances of* winning are good>. *Chance* is also used, in varying senses, with *at, for,* and *on* <she has a *chance at* taking the election>

<there is a *chance for* reaching an agreement> <took a *chance on* the lottery>. And it is used with the infinitive <a *chance* to go to Europe>.

2. *Verb.* The verb *chance* may be followed by the prepositions *on* or *upon* <we *chanced upon* him while crossing the fairgrounds>. It is also frequently followed by the infinitive <I *chanced* to pick up a copy>. Occasionally *into* and *by* are used <the celebrity couple *chanced into* a group of reporters> <I *chanced by* a phone booth>.

character *Character* is sometimes used unnecessarily as padding (as in "the furniture is rather rustic in *character*"). But the vagueness of the word can be useful <the negative *character* of these ads>, and it cannot always be easily replaced. You need not forgo use of the word entirely, but your use should have a purpose.

characteristic In general, when the adjective *characteristic* is followed by a preposition, the preposition is *of* <is *characteristic of* this administration>.

chary *Chary* is often followed by *of* and somewhat less often by *about* <a person very *chary of* compliments> <he remains a bit *chary about* giving advice>. Occasionally, *chary* may be found with *as to, in,* or *with* <*chary as to* their prospects> <*chary in* his expression of optimism> <*chary with* financial matters>.

chastened When *chastened* is used with a preposition, it is usually *by* <we left *chastened by* her neg-

ative comments>. *For* is often used to indicate the reason for the chastening <*chastened for* our lack of effort>.

chauvinism, chauvinist The use of *chauvinism* and *chauvinist* to mean "male chauvinism" and "male chauvinist" is often disapproved, since the words do have other meanings (including the original meaning, "excessive patriotism or nationalism"). It is generally advisable to be sure that either your context or your modifiers (e.g., *male chauvinism, female chauvinism, economic chauvinism, literary chauvinism, culinary chauvinism*) make your meaning plain.

cheap 1. It is sometimes possible for the neutral sense of *cheap,* "inexpensive," to be taken as pejorative, particularly when used directly in front of the noun it modifies <a *cheap* sofa>. The likelihood of the pejorative connotation creeping in is greatest when the noun denotes a physical object—no one is confused about *cheap electric power* or *cheap travel rates*. If you mean to say that an object is not expensive by using *cheap,* you need to be sure your wording makes your meaning unmistakably clear.

2. *Cheap* is an adverb as well as *cheaply.* The adverb *cheap* is most frequently found in contexts of buying and selling, and it regularly follows the word it modifies <he got it *cheap*>. *Cheaply* is used in a wider range of meanings and may either precede or follow the word it modifies <*cheaply* produced movies> <it was all done rather *cheaply*>.

check *Check* as a verb is used with a number of common English particles. *Check into* means "investigate" <*check into* these rumors>. *Check out* is not reserved to a single meaning <*check out* the competition> <*check out* his story> <*check* it *out* with Barbara>. *Check on* is also common <*check on* the infant> <*check on* his progress>, as is *check up on* <*check up on* them for me>. (*Check up* followed by a clause is chiefly British.) And there are also *check over* <*check over* the invitation lists> and *check around* <*check around* to see where he might be>. These usages are all standard idioms.

Chicano *Chicano* first entered American English in the late 1940s, applied by some Mexican-Americans to themselves. It was first used by politically active groups and hence was a term considered offensive by those Mexican-Americans of different or opposed political views. But with wider application, especially since the 1960s, it has become a less politicized term, and objection to it has largely subsided. It is usually capitalized.

childish, childlike *Childish* usually implies a quality such as immaturity or lack of complexity. *Childlike* usually connotes some good quality such as innocence, trustfulness, or ingenuousness; it is also used in neutral description.

choice The notion that *choice* has but a single meaning—namely, "the act of choosing" <I have only one *choice*: A or B> as opposed to "a person or thing chosen" <I have two *choices,* either A or B> —is a false one. You can use the "thing chosen" sense if you need to; it is standard.

circle Some decry the use of the verb *circle* with *around* (or *round*) as redundant. But the historical evidence shows that these words, along with *about,* have been used with *circle* for several centuries <*circle around* the leader> <*circle about* the airport>. Note that *around* (or *round*) can suggest cautious avoidance of or failing to come to grips with something <*circled around* the problem rather than tackling it head-on>.

circumstances Is it better to use *under* or *in* as the preposition that goes with *circumstances* <*under* the *circumstances*> <*in* certain *circumstances*>? The historical evidence shows that both are in good repute and in standard use.

cite, site, sight These three verb homophones should not be confused. *Cite* means "to quote" or "to summon"; *site,* "to place in position"; and *sight,* "to get sight of." The last are also nouns.

civilian The use of *civilian* to distinguish a civilian from a member of a uniformed force (such as the military, the police, or the fire department) is standard. Some have objected to the use of *civilian* to distinguish ordinary people from members of any group, regardless of whether the group is uniformed or not <tax board officials say they have plans to make use of *civilian* volunteers next year>. Our files indicate that such usage is several decades old and is by now standard.

claim In spite of the disapproval of various usage commentators from the 19th century on, *claim* is regularly used to mean "assert, contend, maintain" <they *claim* their study was the first> and not just in the sense "to ask for as a right" <they *claim* the copyright>. The advantage *claim* can have over any of the oft-mentioned substitutes (*contend, assert, maintain,* etc.) is that it regularly introduces a connotation of doubt or skepticism.

clandestine *Clandestine* need not be limited in application to things that are illicit. It is indeed used of things kept secret because they are unlawful, but it is commonly used to suggest simple secrecy, often implying an underlying fear of discovery <a *clandestine* affair>.

classic, classical *Classic* is used in preference to *classical* in two recently established applications, namely, sports <a *classic* defense> and fashion <in *classic* colors>. *Classical* is used of science <*classical* physics> and is also usual in music <*classical* music>. In reference to the civilization of the ancient Greeks and Romans, *classical* is usual but *classic* is not unknown <*classical* [*classic*] Greek sculpture>. In the senses of "serving as a standard of excellence," "memorable," and "typical," *classic* is more common but *classical* is also used <a series of *classic* poems> <made a *classic* error> <in truly *classical* style>.

clean, cleanse Although *clean* is the more common verb, the older *cleanse* continues to be used. It is often used of the human body <*cleanse* the wound>; but mostly *cleanse* is used figuratively <*cleanse* them of their sins>.

clear, clearly Both *clear* and *clearly* are adverbs, but in recent use they do not overlap. *Clear* is most often used in the sense "all the way" <you could see *clear* across the bay>. *Clearly* is used in the sense "in a clear manner" <she writes very *clearly*>.

cliché *Cliché* is in origin a French word for a printing surface, but in English it came to mean "a trite phrase or expression." Since its introduction into English it has been extended from words to ideas to visual images to things of various kinds <his designs make deliberate use of architectural *clichés*>. The unaccented *cliche* is sometimes used, but the accented *cliché* is much more common.

client, customer One difference between these two words is that a customer buys goods whereas a client buys services from a professional (and perhaps especially from a lawyer). In recent use, however, *professional* tends to be construed broadly, so that the difference between goods and services is often blurred. The upshot is that you have some discretion in choosing *client* where in the past *customer* may have been preferred <the broker's *clients*> <the bookie's *clients*>.

climb 1. *Climb,* although originally an irregular verb of the same class as *sing* and *begin,* developed regular inflections, so that its principal parts are *climbed* (past) and *climbed* (past participle). Surviving forms of the old inflections, *clim, clomb,* and *clum,* are dialectal.

2. *Climb down, climb up.* Some usage commentators have attempted to do away with the particles *down* and *up* in combination with *climb,* claiming that *down* is wrong since *climb* means "to go up," and that *up* is simply redundant. Both *climb up* and *climb down,* however, are in perfectly good use as standard idioms.

cling *Cling* is an irregular verb that used to have a past tense and past participle similar to those of *ring*—namely, *clang* and *clung.* For the past two hundred years, however, both past and past participle have taken the form *clung.*

clique The anglicized pronunciation \'klik\ for this French loanword is firmly established but it is less frequent than \'klēk\.

close proximity See PROXIMITY.

coalesce When *coalesce* is used with a preposition, *into* is the one used most often, whatever the sense of the verb <the clouds *coalesced into* a threateningly dark mass>. Less frequently, *coalesce* may be followed by *with* or *in* <our plans *coalesced with* their ideals> <the separate decisions *coalesced in* one grand strategy>. When *coalesce* is used to mean "to unite for a common end," it may be also used with *around* <rep-

resentatives of those interests *coalesced around* the candidate>.

coed The noun *coed,* once an acceptable word for a female student at a coeducational institution, is now in disfavor and is rarely used. The adjective *coed* continues to be used, most often in the sense "open to or used by both men and women" <a *coed* dorm>.

cohort *Cohort* is in standard use to mean "companion, colleague, follower" <her *cohorts* came along to the game>, though some still claim it should only be used with its older meaning, "band or group" <a *cohort* of medieval enthusiasts>.

collaborate *Collaborate* is frequently used with *in, on,* and *with* <*collaborated in* its development> <*collaborating on* a book> <*collaborating with* the authorities>. *With* is often used with either *in* or *on* in the pattern "collaborate with someone in (or on) something" <she *collaborated with* her husband *on* the project>.

collectable, collectible *Collectible* is the more frequent spelling for both the noun and the adjective.

collide Some believe that *collide* can only be used when both objects in the encounter are moving, but there is little historical basis for this belief. Our evidence for the literal sense of *collide* shows that it is used standardly both when all bodies are in motion and when one object is stationary <the two planes

collided in midair> <the car *collided* with the railing>. *Collide* is most often used figuratively—in connection with ideologies, politicians, nations, and the like—and in these uses relative motion is not a consideration.

come and See TRY AND.

comic, comical *Comic* is a much more common word than *comical.* It can be used of anything that is funny <a *comic* character>, and in particular it may stress thoughtful amusement <his plays advance a *comic* perspective on the fate of the author>. *Comical* is not used in that way; it tends to stress spontaneous, unrestrained hilarity <you looked *comical* in that awful dress and silly hat>.

commence Some critics have complained that *commence* is too formal or affected a word and have recommended using *begin* or *start* instead. But *commence* has been in regular use since the 14th century, and has been used by writers of every stripe in all kinds of contexts. You need not routinely change it to *begin* or *start.*

commend When *commend* means "praise," it is usually used in the pattern "*commend* someone *for*" or "*commend* someone *on*" <they *commended* him *for* his effort> <we want to *commend* all of you *on* the diligence you have shown>. When it means "entrust" or "recommend," the pattern is usually "*commend* someone or something *to*" <she *commended* her beloved dog *to* her closest friend> <the group *commends* the book *to* all its members>.

commensurate *Commensurate,* when followed by a preposition, usually takes *with* <an objective *commensurate with* the candidate's own>. It is sometimes also used with *to* <proposed legislation *commensurate to* the expectations of the time>.

commiserate *Commiserate* used intransitively (a use more common now than the transitive use) is most often followed by *with* <sought to *commiserate with* her>. It is also used with *over* <*commiserated over* the bill's failure>, and sometimes both *with* and *over* phrases appear <*commiserated with* them *over* the loss of their house>.

commitment There is only one *t* in the middle of *commitment,* which contrasts with the spelling of *committed, committing, committal,* and *committee.* Take note.

commune The verb *commune,* in its modern usage, is almost always intransitive and followed by *with* <*commune with* nature>.

communicate *Communicate* is usually followed by *with* <she *communicated with* him>, but *to* is standard when there is a direct object <to *communicate to* him the wishes of her government>.

comparatively Some commentators have tried to argue that this adverb should not be used when no comparison is stated or implied. Judging from our evidence, the use is nevertheless standard <a *comparatively* wide outer margin allows for note taking>.

compare to, compare with The conventional rule is this: when you mean "to liken," use *compare to* <shall I *compare* thee *to* a summer's day?>; when you mean "to examine so as to discover the resemblances and differences," use *compare with* <these results *compare* favorably *with* those of 10 years ago>. The rule is usually followed when *compare* is used as an active verb (as it is in the examples above). There is still considerable variation, however, partly because in some contexts either sense of *compare* may apply <he *compares* them *to* [*with*] laws passed in the last century>. Thus, the rule is best regarded as a general guide. When *compared* is used as a detached participle, sometimes introduced by *as,* the prepositions *with* and *to* are equally common <*compared with* [*to*] last year's crop> <as *compared to* [*with*] someone who is self-employed>.

comparison 1. For a discussion of grammatical comparison (as distinct from the word *comparison,* which is treated below), see ABSOLUTE ADJECTIVE; DOUBLE COMPARISON (in Glossary).

2. The word *comparison* is frequently followed by *with* <hardly bears *comparison with* the riches of Holland> <meager findings in *comparison with* those revealed earlier>. It is less frequently followed by *to* <in *comparison to* other cities>. *Between* is used in sentences where both items being compared appear after *comparison* <a *comparison between* Freud's and Jung's versions of psychoanalysis>.

compatible When *compatible* is used with a preposition, it is usually *with* <a view *compatible with* reformist goals> <a device *compatible with* most existing systems>.

competence, competency *Competence* is more frequently used in general than *competency*; *competence* is used in a technical sense in linguistics; and *competency* (or *competencies*) is similarly used in the fields of education and law.

complacent When *complacent* is used with a preposition, the preposition is most likely to be *about* <rather *complacent about* the outcome>. Less frequently used are *with, of,* or *to* <*complacent with* the status quo> <*complacent of* his high standing>. Occasionally *complacent* is used in the sense "complaisant, disposed to please," in which case it may also be used with *to* <less *complacent to* the media than to her own fans>.

complement, compliment *Complement* ("something that completes") is sometimes misspelled as *compliment* ("flattering remark"). Watch that middle vowel. The same caution applies to the adjectives *complementary* and *complimentary*.

complete, completely *Complete* is one of those words some people think are absolute adjectives—adjectives that cannot be modified by *more, most,* or *less*. The word is, however, quite frequently so modified, and you need not worry about using it thus <the most *complete* record yet compiled>. The adverb *completely* is similarly modified, despite occasional objection.

complex Figurative use of this noun, derived from its psychological sense (as in *Oedipus complex*), has been criticized by some but nevertheless remains in frequent modern use <she developed a tennis prodigy *complex*>. It is not used very often in highly serious writing.

compliance The standard pattern in current English is *compliance with* (something) and *compliance of* (something) <in *compliance with* state statutes> <required the *compliance of* car manufacturers>.

compliment, complimentary See COMPLEMENT, COMPLIMENT.

comply The preposition most frequently used with *comply* is *with*, and *with* is always used when the agent is human <you must *comply with* the court order>. When the agent is mechanical, however, either *with* or *to* may be used <permits the bearing mounts to *comply to* the reduced shaft diameter>.

comprise The sense of *comprise* meaning "to compose or constitute" <the branches that *comprise* our government> rather than "to include or be made up of" <our government *comprises* various branches> has been attacked as wrong, for reasons that are unclear. Until recently, it was used chiefly in scientific and technical writing; today it has become the most widely used sense.

concensus See CONSENSUS 3.

concept Some commentators complain of a fad use of *concept* in a sense approximating *idea* <selling the *concept* to them> <a *concept* album>—a usage that has been around since the 16th century but which is prevalent nowadays mostly in the fields of business and entertainment, where it is standard. Our evidence suggests that *concept* is currently not in extensive literary use, but seemingly unfaddish general uses can be found <his *concept* of strategy was to wait and see what the other guy did>.

concern When the noun *concern* means "an uneasy state of interest or anxiety," it is used especially with the prepositions *over, for,* and *about* <*concern over* these issues> <*concern for* her safety> <*concern about* quality>. *With* is also used with this sense <a *concern with* city government>. When *concern* denotes marked interest or involvement, the usual preposition is *with* or *in* <his *concern with* achieving lasting peace> <her *concern in* the matter>.

concerned When the adjective *concerned* suggests worry or anxiety, it can be followed by any of several prepositions. The most frequent are *about* and *for* <*concerned about* public health> <*concerned for* the little tyke>. *Over, at,* and *by* are also used <*concerned over* their unwillingness> <*concerned at* the increasing pressures> <*concerned by* Mr. Roper's attitude>. When *concerned* conveys the notion of interested engagement, *with* is the most common preposition <*concerned with* winning approval>. *In* is also used; it tends to suggest involvement <has long been *concerned in* economic affairs> and is the preposition of choice when something criminal is suggested <he is suspected of being *concerned in* the Dutra murder>. When *concerned* suggests interest or care, it can also be followed by *to* and the infinitive (though this is more common in British English than in American) <is *concerned* not *to* appear weak>.

conciseness, concision *Concision* is currently used about as frequently as *conciseness* <has achieved greater *concision* [*conciseness*] in this rewriting>.

concrete See CEMENT, CONCRETE.

concur *Concur* may be used with various prepositions, primarily *with, in,* and *on* <we *concur with* his opinion> <they have *concurred in* finding him responsible for the mishap> <the two of them *concur on* this one point>. The infinitive can also follow *concur* to mean "to happen together, coincide" <this set of events *concurred* to produce the Industrial Revolution>.

condition Lamented by some as a euphemism (because of its time-honored application to pregnancy), *condition* is nevertheless standard in medical contexts where the precise ailment is unknown or not understood <a troublesome heart *condition*>.

conducive *Conducive* is almost always used with *to* <circumstances *conducive to* scholarly debate>.

confess The intransitive *confess* is often followed by the preposition *to* and either a gerund <*confesses to* having murdered her> or a noun <*confessed to* the crime>. The transitive *confess* is used with a direct (and possibly also an indirect) object <*confessed* his sins to the priest>.

confidant, confidante *Confidant* usually refers to a male, though it is also used of females <he [she] was my friend and *confidant*>. *Confidante* is usually applied to females, but it is also used of males <my wife [husband] and *confidante*>. (Though these gender endings seem to reflect French usage, the French words are actually spelled *confident* and *confidente*.)

confide *Confide* in its intransitive sense, is often used with *in* <they haven't *confided in* me>. *Confide* may also be followed by a dependent clause <she *confides* that no one has yet questioned her about it>. In its transitive sense *confide* may be followed by *to* and the indirect object, which may precede or follow the direct object <*confided to* her psychiatrist the nature of her anxiety> <*confided* his problem *to* his mother>.

confident When the adjective *confident* is followed by a preposition, *in* and *of* are the ones most likely to be used <*confident in* her ability> <*confident of* the ad's success>. Less frequently, *about, as to,* or *on* may be used <*confident about* the market> <*confident as to* the validity of her findings> <*confident on* the issue of wage increases>. Very often, of course, *confident* is followed by a dependent clause <we are *confident* that an agreement will be reached>.

conform When *conform* is followed by a preposition, it is most likely to be *to* <does not *conform to* the usual pattern>. *With* is also frequently used <this *conforms with* our understanding>.

conformity When followed by a preposition, *conformity* usually takes *to* or *with* <its *conformity to* standards of wear> <in *conformity with* international law>. When both related entities follow *conformity,* the first preposition may be *between* or *of* <*conformity between* past and present methods> <*conformity of* his principles with mine>.

congenial When *congenial* is used with a preposition, the preposition is usually *to* <a schedule *congenial to* her work habits>.

congruence For pronunciation, see INFLUENCE 2.

connect *Connect* is used with the prepositions *with* and *to*. Some commentators have tried to limit the use of *with* to figurative senses <he had been *connected with* a secret organization> and of *to* to concrete senses <the white wire *connects to* switch A>; this restriction is generally, but not always, followed in practice. Two things may also be connected *by* still another thing <these items are *connected by* their relation to a third>.

consensus 1. *Consensus of opinion.* It is thought by some that the phrase *consensus of opinion* is redundant and that *of opinion* should be dropped. But since there are various other types of consensus (e.g., consensus of views, of experts, of values), *consensus of opinion* is really not a redundancy. You must decide whether you want to use *consensus of opinion,* and make your meaning perfectly clear while perhaps running the risk of being censured, or use *consensus* alone and perhaps risk less than full clarity. In any case, you are safe in using *consensus* alone when it is clear that you mean consensus of opinion, and most writers in fact do so.

2. *General consensus.* Whereas *consensus of opinion* is not necessarily a redundancy, *general consensus* in fact seems to be one, since generality is already part of the meaning of *consensus*. You can safely drop *general* and use *consensus* alone.

3. *Concensus.* This misspelling of *consensus* often turns up in publications where it should have been corrected. Resist the tempting influence of *census* when you spell the longer word; the two are not related.

consequent When *consequent* is used with a preposition, the preposition is usually *on* or *upon* <*consequent on* [*upon*] the cessation of hostilities>.

consequential Though *consequential* in the sense "important" is objected to by some, this use has a long history <the most *consequential* of her works>.

consider **1.** *Consider* in the sense "believe to be" can be used with several kinds of complements. It may be followed by a noun <he is *considered* a heavyweight>; an adjective <a river not *considered* dangerous>; an adjectival prepositional phrase <a poet once *considered* of some importance>; two nouns (or a pronoun and a noun), one the direct object and the other its complement <*considers* the effort puffery and no more> <*considers* it blasphemy>; a noun (or pronoun) and an adjective <*considered* the act irresponsible>; or a noun and a phrase introduced by an infinitive <they *consider* an early decision to be unlikely>.

Consider is also used in many of the same constructions with *as*: with a single noun <it had been *considered as* a means to an end>; with an adjective <ended up *considering* it *as* less than desirable>; or with two nouns, or a pronoun and a noun <*considers* liberty *as* a given> <has *considered* it *as* a liability>. It may also be followed by a participle <*considered as* stolen>. Our evidence suggests that the *as* constructions are perfectly idiomatic but are not as common as they once were.

Consider may also be followed by an infinitive phrase <is *considered* to appeal especially to elder voters>. And, finally, it may be followed by a *that* clause <they *considered* that little would come of the arrangement>.

2. In the sense "to think about with regard to taking action," *consider* can also be used with *for* <they *considered* her *for* the post>.

considerable **1.** The adjective *considerable* most commonly follows a determiner, a word like *a, the, his, one,* or *any* <the play was a *considerable* success> <her *considerable* fortune>. These uses are standard in both British and American English. When *considerable* modifies a mass noun, however, with no determiner, there is a slight difference between British and American usage. Both allow *considerable* to be used with nouns for immaterial things <offers the viewer *considerable* pleasure>. But the use of *considerable* with nouns for material things <found *considerable* dirt there> is American and tends to occur in works of a general but not a literary nature.

2. The adverb *considerable* is still alive in speech (as in "the circular saw speeded the work up *considerable*") but is seldom used in edited prose other than fiction. See also FLAT ADVERB (in Glossary).

consistent When *consistent* is used with a preposition, *with* is by far the most common <books *consistent with* the child's language abilities>. Other prepositions are used less often; the choice depends on the intended meaning <should be *consistent in* giving praise> <findings *consistent across* several disciplines> <remained *consistent throughout* this period> <*consistent as to* their purpose>.

consist in, consist of Many writers draw a distinction between *consist in,* "lie, reside (in)" <the painting's originality *consists in* its perspective>, and *consist of,* "to be composed or made up (of)" <the team *consists of* one senior and three junior debaters>. Although the distinction is generally observed, some variation occurs.

consonant When used with a preposition in contemporary English, the adjective *consonant* is followed by *with* <a practice *consonant with* our beliefs>.

constitute See COMPRISE.

contagious, infectious The standard medical distinction is this: Contagious diseases are spread by contact, and infectious diseases are spread by infectious agents. Thus, all contagious diseases are also infectious, but not all infectious diseases are contagious.

In figurative uses, there is no implied distinction between infection and contagion. But a difference in the use of *contagious* and *infectious* is observed: *Contagious* is used of both pleasant and unpleasant things <the idea that terrorism is *contagious*> <an enthusiasm that is *contagious*>, whereas *infectious* is almost always used of pleasant things <an *infectious* smile>.

contemporaneous See CONTEMPORARY.

contemporary *Contemporary* in the sense "present-day, modern," though objected to by some, has been fully established since the late 1940s <*contemporary* literature>. But because *contemporary* can also mean "existing at the same time," some commentators recommend the use of *contemporaneous* if the use of *contemporary* might cause confusion <Byron's *contemporaneous* critics>. *Contemporaneous* is in fact increasingly replacing *contemporary* in such contexts, while *contemporary* is being used chiefly in its "present-day" sense.

contemptible See CONTEMPTUOUS 1.

contemptuous **1.** *Contemptible, contemptuous.* Though in earlier centuries these two words were used interchangeably, in current usage they are distinguished. *Contemptible* means "worthy of contempt" <a *contemptible* act>, while *contemptuous* means "showing contempt" <is *contemptuous* of the effort>.

2. When *contemptuous* is used in the predicate position and is followed by a prepositional phrase, the preposition is always *of* <have grown *contemptuous of* the public they are supposed to serve>.

contend The word *contend* is very commonly followed by a clause <she *contends* that she was out at the time>. *Contend* is also used with prepositions, usually *with* <had difficulty *contending with* the traffic>. Less frequently, *contend* is used with *against* <forces *against* which they could not successfully *contend*>. When the object of the preposition is the source of contention, *for* is the choice <*contended for* the Triple Crown in 1992>.

continual, continuous The conventional distinction between these two words is this: *continual* means "steadily recurring" <*continual* skirmishes>, and *continuous* means "continuing without interruption" <*continuous* driving>. The choice of word often seems to depend on whether a given writer perceives the activity as uninterrupted or not <*continual* [*continuous*] progress> <*continuous* [*continual*] crying>. You will have to rely on your own best judgment in the more problematic cases.

continually, continuously *Continually* is used where stress is laid on an uninterrupted flow that continues for an indefinite period of time <have the idea of freedom *continually* before you> <*continually* humid> <*continually* high spirits>. *Continually* is also the adverb of choice when repetition is emphasized <we *continually* reminded them>. *Continuously* is used where stress is laid on a prolonged succession of discrete time periods <the oldest *continuously* published newspaper in the United States> or ongoing recurrence <during that 18-month period, meetings were held *continuously* in the mayor's office>. The two words, however, are sometimes used as if they were interchangeable <*continually* beset by nightmares>; this is hardly surprising, since the standard distinction between the adverbs partially reverses the distinction between the adjectives *continual* and *continuous* (see entry above).

continue on Some dismiss *continue on* as a redundancy, the *on* supposedly being superfluous. Travel writers, on the other hand, find the phrase useful <we *continued on* to Tunis>. It is also used in other contexts <he *continued on* this way for many years>. There seems to be no good reason to avoid it.

continuous See CONTINUAL, CONTINUOUS.

continuously See CONTINUALLY, CONTINUOUSLY.

contrast **1.** As a noun, *contrast* is used with the prepositions *between, with,* and *to* <the *contrast between* old and new> <makes a *contrast with* her earlier style of writing> <offers a *contrast to* his own efforts>. When preceded by *in, contrast* may be followed by either *to* or with; *to* is somewhat more common in American English <in *contrast to* the relatively loose organization> <in *contrast with* other disciplines>.

2. As a verb, *contrast* is used with the prepositions *with* or *to*; *with* is used more frequently <*contrasted* her clean apartment *with* her boyfriend's messy digs> <*contrasting* their production methods *to* those of their rival>.

convenient As a predicate adjective, *convenient* can be followed by the infinitive <it is more *convenient to* order directly>. It can also be followed by prepositional phrases introduced by *for* or *to*. *For* is used mostly for persons or their activities <a *convenient* way *for* you to access it> <*convenient for* storing stationery>. *To* is used for persons <a decision *convenient to* them politically> but also for places <a location *convenient to* the mall>.

conversant *Conversant* usually takes the preposition *with* <is *conversant with* Sanskrit>. It also takes *in,* but less frequently <must be *conversant in* such matters>.

convict When the verb *convict* is followed by a preposition, the preposition is usually *of* <*convicted of* perjury>. Less frequently, *convict* is used with *on* <*convicted on* two counts of armed robbery>.

convince, persuade Earlier usage writers tried to maintain a rigid distinction between these two words, arguing that *convince* meant simply "bring about mental acceptance" and *persuade* meant "bring about mental acceptance followed by action." Such commentators thus rejected the use of *convince* followed by an infinitive <sought to *convince* them to halt the bombing>, claiming that only *persuade* could be used in such cases. For most people born after the 1920s, however, this use of *convince* sounds entirely standard. Also standard is the use of *convince* followed by a phrase beginning with *of* <*convinced of* the need> or a clause usually beginning with *that* <*convinced that* they can win>.

Persuade, for its part, has indeed long been used to imply action <was *persuaded* to bring her daughter home early>. But it also has been and is still used in the purely mental sense in which no action is implied <I wasn't *persuaded* of the innocence of it all>. In short, *convince* and *persuade* have moved into each other's sphere of influence over the years, and in many cases can be used more or less interchangeably.

cop The use of *cop* for "police officer" has gained respectability. *Cop* is used regularly in newspapers and magazines in the United States, Great Britain, and other countries using British English; it is common in novels and occasionally turns up in collections of essays, although it does not appear often in the most formal kinds of writing.

cope *Cope* in the sense "to deal with difficulties" has long been used with the preposition *with* <she was having trouble *coping with* her mother>. Around the middle of this century *cope* began to be used absolutely, with no preposition and no following object <he could no longer *cope*>. The latter usage, though objected to by some, is by now established as standard.

correct *Correct* is on some lists of ABSOLUTE ADJECTIVES (see Glossary). It has, however, been used in the comparative <his version seems more *correct* than hers> and superlative <recommends his own as most *correct*>.

correspond *Correspond,* in the senses meaning "to be in conformity or agreement" or "to compare closely, match," may be followed by either *to* or *with*; *to* seems to be more frequent <a reference that does not *correspond to* any published source>. When meaning "to write to someone," *correspond* is used with *with* exclusively <we *correspond with* them frequently>.

could care less, couldn't care less The negative *couldn't care less* is the older form of the expression. No one knows how the positive form developed. Some critics disparage it as illogical, but it is used nonetheless. Defenders of *could care less* point out that it is meant to be sarcastic. But it is easier to convey sarcasm by the spoken word than by the written word, so more writers choose the clearer *couldn't care less*.

could of See OF 2.

council, counsel These two words are sometimes confused, especially *council* for *counsel*. *Council* generally stands for some sort of deliberative or administrative body, while *counsel* is used for advice or for a lawyer and as a verb meaning "to advise" or "to consult."

counterproductive If *counterproductive* is a vogue word, as some critics have charged, its vogue has lasted for more than a quarter of a century and shows no sign of abating. You can use it if you need it.

couple, *noun* **1.** *Agreement. Couple* is a singular noun but it often takes a plural verb <the *couple* have been known to be extravagant>. Usually the plural verb appears when the sentence also has a pronoun referring to *couple* <the young *couple* were driving to their new home> since the pronoun will almost always be *they, their,* or *them*. The governing principle here is notional agreement: If the writer is thinking of two people as individuals, the verb is plural; if the writer is thinking of them as a unit, the verb is singular <the *couple* has two children> <the *couple* owns a house in Del Mar>. *They, their,* and *them* have been used to refer to nouns and pronouns that take singular verbs for centuries <the *couple* plans to relocate their business>, though many newspaper editors seem not to realize it. Use of the plural verb may work in some instances <the *couple* plan to relocate their business>, but in others you may have some complicated rewriting to do. British English generally prefers the plural verb.

2. *A couple of.* Some handbooks call *a couple of* colloquial or informal, but the phrase has been in use for 500 years <*a couple of* lost children>. Others have objected to the use of the phrase to mean "a small but indefinite number"<in just *a couple of* years>, but many notable writers have used it in that sense.

couple, *adjective* The adjective use of *a couple,* without *of,* has been called nonstandard, but it is not. In both British and American English it is standard before a word (such as *more*) indicating degree <a *couple* more tricks>. Its use before an ordinary plural noun is an Americanism, common in speech and in informal writing <they live a *couple* houses down the street> <their first *couple* recordings>. It is most frequently used with periods of time <a *couple* weeks> and numbers <a *couple* hundred> <a *couple* dozen>.

course *Course* as used in such phrases as *in the course of* or *during the course of,* is sometimes considered redundant for *during, while, at,* or other shorter alternatives. But phrases like these are often used for rhythm or space in a sentence—to keep other, important words from becoming too tightly packed to be immediately understood. In addition, these phrases can add emphasis to the notion of duration. Depending on their context, they can be either useful <when *in the course of* human events> or unnecessary (as in "were consolidated *during the course of* 1995"). You need not avoid them on principle, but you should weigh their use carefully.

craft Some usage commentators have turned thumbs down to *craft* used as a verb <her skill at *crafting* agreements>. But *craft* is well established in current American use both as a verb and as a participial adjective <finely *crafted* stories>. It is also sometimes used in British English.

credence, credibility The problem here involves the phrases *give credence to* and *lend credence to*. When the subject of the phrase is a person, the meaning of *credence* is the familiar one of "belief" <no one could *give* any *credence to* these ridiculous reports>; this sense is present even when the sentence is passive and the person understood <we question whether the stories should be *lent* any *credence*>. When the subject of these phrases is inanimate, we get a use closer in meaning to *credibility*, "trustworthiness" <a trend that *lends credence to* the view> <such findings *give credence to* earlier theories>. This use, which is sometimes criticized, is of 20th-century origin and seems to be increasing, especially in *lend credence to*. It is standard in both British and American English.

credibility See CREDENCE, CREDIBILITY; CREDULITY, CREDIBILITY.

credit **1.** A view is sometimes asserted that the verb *credit* should not be used to attribute something unfavorable or discreditable <insiders *credit* terrorists for the explosion>. This view overgeneralizes what is usually done into what must always be done. *Credit* is indeed usually used in a positive sense <have *credited* the show with creating the television news magazine format>, but not always. You may want to be credited with something I find reprehensible (as in the explosion example above). And *credit* is also used for things that fall between the laudable and the blameworthy <the difference was *credited* to timing> <the shortage of paper must be *credited* as a significant factor>.

2. *With* is the preposition most commonly linked with *credit,* but it is by no means the only one. The examples above also show *for, to,* and *as.*

credulity, credibility *Credulity* and *credibility* come close in meaning only when used with such verbs as *strain, tax,* or *stretch.* Even here, their use is quite straightforward in most instances. *Credulity* is used of the receiver <such lame dialogue taxes the audience's *credulity*>. *Credibility* is used of the sender <the

author's *credibility* as a journalist is stretched to the limit in this book>.

creep The predominant form of both the past tense and past participle is *crept* <the cat *crept* toward its victim> <a rate that has recently *crept* up>. But, like *leap, kneel,* and *dream, creep* has also developed the more regular past and past participle *creeped. Creeped* is generally heard in speech; in print, *crept* is still the usual form.

criterion, criteria The usual plural form of the singular *criterion* is *criteria* <the ability to communicate effectively was identified as the most important *criterion*> <several *criteria* were advanced>. *Criteria* is in fact more common than the singular *criterion,* and it is undoubtedly this frequency that has led to its perception by many as a singular. Although the singular *criteria* is found mostly in speech (as in "that's the main *criteria*"), it is not entirely absent from print, to the dismay of language commentators and editors. It has not yet reached the point of unquestioned acceptability, however. See also LATIN PLURALS.

criticize There is a neutral use of *criticize* that implies measured judgment or evaluation <the students' performance was favorably *criticized* by their professor>. But the most common use in recent years is the one implying censure <*criticized* the police for using violence>. It is probably the relatively high frequency of this "censure" sense that has caused the neutral sense to begin to carry connotations of disfavor and be increasingly replaced by *critique* as a verb (see CRITIQUE).

critique *Critique* has, despite grumbling from some critics, become firmly established as a verb. The negative overtones of *criticize* (see preceding entry) seem to have led to the revival of *critique* (which has been in intermittent use as a verb since 1751). In a headline like "Betty Friedan Critiques the Women's Movement" (*N.Y. Times*), you can see the usefulness of *critique*. *Criticize* would be interpreted as "censure," and *review* would suggest more of a historical overview than a critical examination.

culminate **1.** When *culminate* is used with a preposition, the choice is usually *in* <a depression that *culminated in* suicide>. *Culminate* is also occasionally followed by *with* <the celebration *culminates with* the sounding of the gong>.

2. The transitive use of *culminate* is no longer as rare as it once was <these summit talks *culminate* a long period of rapprochement>.

cum *Cum* was taken over into English from Latin in the 19th century. It is used in English primarily as a sort of combining word attached to the preceding and following nouns or adjectives by hyphens <her friend-*cum*-psychoanalyst Mary> <a tough-*cum*-innocent quality>. *Cum* is used mainly in writing and is standard in a considerable variety of contexts. It is fairly often italicized.

cupful The common plural is *cupfuls*; the variant *cupsful* is only occasionally found. See also -FUL.

cured When *cured* is followed by a preposition, it is usually *of* <he was *cured of* the habit>, though *from* was formerly also used in such cases.

curriculum *Curriculum* has two plurals: *curricula* and *curriculums*. *Curricula* is quite a bit more frequent, but both are standard. For other foreign plurals, see LATIN PLURALS.

customer See CLIENT, CUSTOMER.

cute *Cute* has been deplored by some commentators, who seem to find it too cute a word. It continues to be used, of course, but mostly in speech (real or fictional) and in informal writing.

D

dais The usual pronunciation is \ˈdā-əs\, rhyming with *pay us*. The second most common pronunciation is \ˈdī-əs\, as though the word were spelled (as it is, in fact, sometimes misspelled) *dias*.

dare *Dare* is both an ordinary verb and an auxiliary verb. As an auxiliary verb, *dare* is regularly followed by an infinitive phrase without *to* <no one *dared* say a word>. It has in its present tense the uninflected third-person singular *dare* <he *dare* not do anything upset-

ting now>. As a regular verb, *dare* has *dares* in the present third-person singular, and can be followed by an infinitive phrase with *to* <she *dares to* criticize me>. When preceded by other auxiliaries (such as *might, would,* and *do*), *dare* is followed by the infinitive without *to* <I wouldn't *dare* ask them> <do we *dare* call it quits?>.

daresay, dare say The one-word styling of this compound verb is slightly more common. It is used in the first-person singular of the present tense <I *daresay* your claim is a weak one>. In its transitive use (as in the example above), *daresay* is followed by a clause. Formerly the clause would never have been introduced by *that,* but in recent use *that* occurs <I *daresay that* your claim is a weak one>.

dastardly *Dastardly* is still alive and well in the language. Once meaning "cowardly," it has for the past hundred years or so been used to suggest underhandedness and treachery <a *dastardly* scheme to eliminate the opposition>. This use has spawned another heavily rhetorical use of *dastardly* that simply expresses disapproval, as of something considered villainous <a *dastardly* speech promoting white supremacy>.

data *Data* has become quite independent of *datum,* of which it was originally the plural. It occurs in two constructions: (1) as a plural noun (like *earnings*), taking a plural verb and plural modifiers (such as *these, many, a few*) but not cardinal numbers <these *data* show that

we're out of the recession>; and (2) as an abstract mass noun (like *information*), taking a singular verb and singular modifiers (such as *this, much,* or *little*) <much *data* on the subject is available>. Both constructions are standard. The plural construction is more common in print, evidently because the house editorial style of several publishers mandates it. See also LATIN PLURALS.

date When the verb *date* is used to point to a date of origin, it may be used with *from, back to,* or *to* <these vases *date from* the early Ming period> <the poem *dates back to* 1843> <the dispute *dates to* Japan's annexation of the islands>.

datum See DATA.

days See ADVERBIAL GENITIVE (in Glossary).

dead Sometimes considered to be an ABSOLUTE ADJECTIVE (see Glossary).

deal **1.** *Deal* belongs to a class of regular verbs including *feel, creep, kneel,* and *mean* in which the past tense and past participle have a short vowel (\e\) contrasting with the long vowel of the infinitive (\ē\). Some of these (see KNEEL; CREEP) have alternative forms, but *deal* has only *dealt* <*dealt* out two sandwiches apiece> <*dealt* him a blow>.

2. Use of the noun *deal* in the senses "transaction," "bargain," or "arrangement, agreement" has been thought slightly vulgar or infelicitous in the past, but these uses are now standard <a done *deal*> <what a

deal!> <the *deal* between the governor and the legislature>.

3. When the intransitive verb *deal* means "concern oneself" or "take action," its usual preposition is *with* <the book *deals with* education> <trying to *deal with* her son's death>.

When *deal* is used in relation to selling—literally or figuratively—the usual preposition is *in* <*deals in* insurance>.

dear, dearly The adverbs *dear* and *dearly* are interchangeable only in contexts dealing with cost <has cost us *dear* [*dearly*]>. *Dearly* is used in other contexts <loves him *dearly*>.

debacle This word was borrowed from French and is its second syllable is normally stressed as in that language: \di-ˈbä-kəl\ or, less often, \di-ˈbak-əl\.

debar When it is used with a preposition, *debar* most often appears with *from* <*debarred from* further negotiations>.

debut The verb *debut,* disapproved of by some, is standard in newspaper and magazine articles, since newsy writing often discusses first appearances of people, products, and the like. It seems to have almost no use in literature and other more formal writing. Intransitive uses <the show *debuted* in 1986> have been around since 1830, but transitive uses <*debuting* their fall line>, which have a more jargonish flavor, only since the 1950s.

decide Intransitive *decide* is used with several prepositions, of which *on, upon, for,* and *against* are the most common <*decided on* the latter> <*decide upon* it soon> <*decided for* the defendant> <*decided against* the proposition>. Sometimes a phrase may replace *for* <*decided* in favor of the defendant>. *Between* and *about* are also used <must *decide between* A and B> <still *deciding about* the house>.

deem A few commentators have labeled *deem* "pretentious." But the word is in wide literary and journalistic use and has been for generations <*deemed* it wise to go slow>. You may use it with impunity.

defect When *defect* is followed by a preposition, either *in* or *of* is chosen <the grave *defects in* [*of*] our foreign policy>.

defective, deficient The modern tendency is to use *defective* to emphasize a flaw <a *defective* pane of glass> <*defective* eyesight>, and *deficient* to emphasize a lack <*deficient* in judgment> <*deficient* strength>. See also DEFICIENT.

defend *Defend* may be followed by *against* or *from* <playing deep to *defend against* a pass> <*defended* herself *from* criticism>.

deficient When *deficient* is used with a preposition, the preposition is almost always *in* <a panel *deficient in* expertise>. See also DEFECTIVE, DEFICIENT.

defile When used with a prepositional phrase expressing means or agent, *defile* is followed by *by* or *with; by* occurs a little more frequently than *with* <the countryside *defiled by* billboards> <boots *defiled with* blood>.

definite **1.** This word is sometimes misspelled *definate.* Watch out for that second *i.*

2. *Definite, definitely.* Some commentators have objected to the use (or overuse) of these words as intensifiers <the quarterback was a *definite* hero today> <they were *definitely* ill at ease>. The use is established in general prose, but it seems to have made few inroads in literature and virtually none in any sort of formal writing.

degree The phrase *to a degree* originally meant (and still does in older literary English) "to the last degree" or "to a remarkable extent" <she is in most things sharp *to a degree,* but in others quite dull>. In current American usage, however, it means "in a moderate measure" or "in a small way" <*to a degree,* you are justified in complaining>. The newer sense has been objected to by some older critics, but it is established as standard. Standard, too, are phrases of the form *to a . . . degree,* <*to a* considerable *degree*> <*to an* extraordinary *degree*>.

déjà vu **1.** *Déjà vu* is a psychological term brought into English from French just after the turn of the century. It was used for an illusory feeling of having previously experienced something that was in fact happening for the first time. When it began to appear in popular writing it took on an additional meaning: "something overly or unpleasantly familiar" <I'm getting a strong sense of *déjà vu* from this movie>. And this popular use has produced an adjective <there was something *déjà vu* about the food there>. Both noun and adjective are now well established in professional writing.

2. The most common form of *déjà vu* has both accents and no hyphen. The word is still italicized about half the time.

delectable *Delectable* has been regarded variously as ironic, gushy, and arch by its critics, but you need not give a passing thought to the criticism. If the word fits, use it <a *delectable* dish> <*delectable* illustrations>.

delusion, illusion *Delusion* and *illusion* are often used in ways that overlap in meaning. *Delusion* is the stronger word; it denotes a longer lasting, more tenacious, and sometimes more harmful or dangerous notion <paranoid *delusions*> <*delusions* of grandeur>. *Illusion* seldom implies mental derangement, or even an inability to distinguish between the true and the false <artistic *illusion*> <a lover's *illusions*>. *Illusion* is the more common word in general contexts.

demand The noun *demand* is commonly used with the prepositions *for, on* or *upon,* and *of* <the *demand*

for lawyers> <*demands on* [*upon*] our time> <the *demands of* her career>.

demise Some feel that *demise* is a pretentious term for *death* or that it should not be used in a sense close to *decline.* Nevertheless, in current use (of a nonlegal sort) *demise* most often means "death" <met his *demise* on a cliff face>, or "a cessation of existence or activity" <bad business decisions caused the company's *demise*>. These uses are standard.

depart **1.** Quite a number of prepositions are used with *depart;* the choice is determined by the meaning and purpose of the prepositional phrase. The most common prepositions are *on, in,* or *at* for the time <*departed on* June 19> <*departed in* late December> <*departs at* 3:30>; *on* for the nature of the activity <*departing on* a visit home>; *for* for the destination <*departing for* Los Angeles>; and *from* for the point of departure, whether physical or nonphysical <*departed from* Denver> <*departs from* convention>.

2. Transitive use of *depart,* if once perhaps uncommon, is now standard <we *departed* San Francisco at noon> <he *departed* this life Saturday, Oct. 3>.

depend In most senses *depend* is followed by *on* or *upon* <life *depends on* [*upon*] food> <you can *depend on* [*upon*] me>. *Depend* is also used absolutely, though chiefly in conversation <Can I come? It *depends*>.

dependent **1.** *Adjective.* Like the verb *depend,* the adjective *dependent* is frequently used with *on* or *upon*

<the child is *dependent on* [*upon*] his parents>. The spelling *dependant,* once in use for the adjective, is no longer current.

2. *Noun.* The noun is usually spelled *dependant* in British English and *dependent* in American English.

deprive *Deprive* is usually used in the construction "*deprive* (someone or something) *of* (something)" <the painting deliberately *deprives* its subject *of* its individuality>.

de rigueur *De rigueur* is occasionally misspelled. There is a *u* both before and after the *e.*

derisive, derisory *Derisive* and *derisory* are sometimes used as synonyms in contemporary writing, but most often writers use *derisive* in its original sense, "causing or expressing derision" <*derisive* laughter>, and use *derisory* when they mean "worthy of ridicule" <a *derisory* sum>.

derive *Derive* is usually used with a prepositional phrase, which nearly always begins with *from* <a French loanword ultimately *derived from* Latin>.

derogate In its intransitive senses, *derogate* is used with *from* <some are trying to *derogate from* his reputation as a leader>.

derogation *Derogation,* when followed by a complement, usually takes *of* <a serious *derogation of* his influence and prestige>.

desert, deserts, dessert The problem here is one of spelling. There are two nouns spelled *desert.* The first of these is the barren *desert,* which, perhaps because of its distinct pronunciation, is infrequently mistaken for the others. The second *desert* is related to *deserve* and is pronounced like *dessert.* It is frequently used as a plural, especially in the phrase *just deserts.* The most common error is the substitution of *desert* for *dessert* ("sweet food"). Care, perhaps assisted by a dictionary, is all that is needed here.

design, intend Some maintain that *design* is overused and that *intend* is usually preferable. While there are indeed contexts in which the two words are nearly interchangeable <an event *designed* [*intended*] to show off the candidate's popularity> <moves *intended* [*designed*] to get his goat>, the automatic substitution of *intend* will not make you a better writer. Rather, stop and think (and consult your dictionary) when you go to write *design;* sometimes *intend* will be the better choice.

desirous While *desirous to* is sometimes still used <was *desirous to* gain her respect> *desirous of* is the more common modern construction <*desirous of* her respect>.

desist When *desist* takes a complement in the form of a prepositional phrase, the preposition is usually *from* <the city has been ordered to *desist from* further

levies>. Less frequently, *desist* is followed by *in* <has *desisted in* his effort to acquire the company>.

despair The verb *despair,* when used with a preposition, is usually used with *of* <*despaired of* winning>.

despoil When *despoil* is used with a preposition, it is *of* <*despoiled* the Aztecs *of* their wealth>.

dessert See DESERT, DESERTS, DESSERT.

destined *Destined* is almost always used with a preposition, either *to* or *for. Destined to* is most common when it is followed by an infinitive <a relationship *destined* to last>. When *destined* is used with *for,* it is followed by a noun or noun phrase <the younger son was *destined for* the priesthood>.

destruct, self-destruct *Destruct* is an old (17th-century) verb that reappeared as part of aerospace jargon in the 1950s <the missile will *destruct* upon impact>. It is seldom found outside technical contexts. *Self-destruct* was popularized by its use in the television series *Mission Impossible* <this tape will *self-destruct* in five seconds>. This verb rapidly established itself and is now standard. *Self-destruct* is also used as an adjective <a *self-destruct* mechanism>.

destructive When it is used with a preposition, *destructive* is most often used with *of* or *to,* with *of* occurring more frequently <*destructive of* firmly established ideas> <*destructive to* the animal's habitat>.

detract, distract The issue here is whether *detract* may replace *distract* in the phrase "*distract* (the) attention." The fact is that while "*distract* (the) attention" is far more common, "*detract* (the) attention" (which makes use of an older sense, "to divert") is also found in the works of standard authors <all the publicity *detracts* attention from the real accomplishment>.

When *detract* is used with a preposition, it is used with *from* <I didn't want to *detract from* your enjoyment>.

deviate When *deviate* is used with a preposition, it is most often used with *from* <she never *deviated from* her story>.

device, devise *Devise* is sometimes mistakenly used where *device* is expected. Mind your spelling.

devolve When used with a preposition, *devolve* usually appears with *on* or *upon* <his estate *devolved on* a distant cousin> <after the general fell, command *devolved upon* the colonel>. Less frequently, *devolve* is used with *to* or *into* <authority on this matter *devolves to* the states> <the peaceful protest *devolved into* skirmishes with police>. *Devolve* followed by *from,* at one time relatively rare, is becoming a little more frequent (perhaps influenced by *evolve*) <higher import taxes, which have *devolved from* years of trade imbalances>.

diagnose Complaints have been lodged against use of the verb *diagnose* with a person, rather than a condition or problem, as its object <*diagnosed* the patient>. But the usefulness of this sense of *diagnose* is obvious, and its use may well increase.

dialogue **1.** The spelling *dialogue* is much more commonly used than *dialog.*

2. Some commentators seem concerned about the sense of *dialogue* that means "an exchange of ideas and opinions" <the need now is for Palestinians and Israelis to hold a meaningful *dialogue*>. However, it is now standard.

3. The verb *dialogue* (which was formed from the noun as discussed above) is also standard <our attempt to *dialogue* with them proved a failure>, though deplored by many.

dice See DIE *noun,* DICE.

dichotomy *Dichotomy* is used in standard prose to mean "division" or "split" <a *dichotomy* between practice and theory> <a *dichotomy* between written and spoken evidence>. *Dichotomy* is also sometimes used to mean "paradox" or "problem," often in a rather vague way that suggests the writer is simply using a fancy, academic-sounding word for effect. If you want to use *dichotomy,* it would be best to stick to the "division" sense.

dictum While the plurals *dicta* and *dictums* are both in standard use, *dicta* is quite a bit more commonly used. See also LATIN PLURALS.

die, *verb* *Die* in various senses is used with a number of different prepositions. *Of* seems to be the most commonly used <*dying of* embarrassment>. *From* is also common <*dying from* fatigue>. *For* is frequently used <*dying for* a cigarette>. Other prepositions are also possible <the bill *died in* committee> <the secret *died with* him> <their anger *died at* these words>. *Die* is often used with the adverbs *away, down,* and *out* <criticism *died away*> <the storm *died down*> <the species *died out*>.

die *noun,* **dice** The use of the singular *dice,* rather than *die,* for one of the small cubes thrown in various games is objected to by some. Dice players use *dice* in speech, but in print the singular is usually *die.*

differ When *differ* means "to be unlike" and is followed by a preposition, it is followed by *from* <the laws of this state *differ from* those of neighboring states>. When *differ* means "to disagree," it is usually followed by *with* <*differs with* the Pentagon on the use of preemptive strikes>. *Among* is also found with the "disagree" sense <they *differ among* themselves>.

Several prepositions—*on, over, in, as to, about*—are used to indicate the subject of the difference <we *differ on* [*over, in*] religious matters> <they *differ as to* [*about*] the dating of the site>.

When *with* follows *differ* in its "be unlike" sense, *with* means something like "in the case of" <dietary preferences *differ with* each culture>.

different The use of *different* after a number <at least three *different* speakers>, is sometimes objected to on the ground that it is unnecessary. But this use of *different* is simply for emphasis. See also DIFFERENT FROM, DIFFERENT THAN.

different from, different than Both of these phrases are standard, in spite of some critics' disliking *different than.* Each form has its particular virtues. *Different from,* the more common, works best when followed by a noun or a pronoun <the new proposal is very *different from* the old one> <her view is so *different from* his>. *Different than* works best when a clause follows <expecting a *different* result *than* to be left penniless> <she looks little *different* now *than* we remember her from our school days>. *Different than* is also used in place of *different from* before the noun or pronoun <*different than* the old proposal> <*different than* mine>, though some editors may change it to *different from.* See also THAN.

British English allows *different to,* but the phrase is rare in American English.

differentiate When *differentiate* is used with a preposition, it is most often *from* <one of the things that *differentiated* a gentleman *from* a commoner>. Less frequently, *differentiate* is used with *between* <to *differentiate between* prose and poetry>.

dilemma Some insist that *dilemma* can only denote a choice between two or more unpleasant alternatives

<presents this *dilemma:* raise taxes or reduce services>. While this use is standard, *dilemma* is equally common in instances where no clear alternatives are expressed or implied <the traditional *dilemma* of how to secure campaign financing>. In this use the word becomes very close in meaning to *problem, difficulty, predicament.* Though objected to by some, the use is standard.

direct, directly These adverbs are sometimes interchangeable <flew *direct* [*directly*] to Chicago> <buy *direct* [*directly*] from the manufacturer>. *Directly* is used more often than *direct,* having uses and meanings that it does not share with *direct.* An important exclusive use of *directly* is to precede the word or phrase it modifies <*directly* relevant> <the road runs *directly* east and west>.

disagree When *disagree* is used with a preposition, the preposition is usually *with* <he *disagreed with* me on every point> <fried food *disagrees with* me>. Other prepositions are also used <they *disagreed about* [*over*] the exact nature of the conflict> <*disagreeing on* virtually every topic>.

disappointed When *disappointed* is used with a preposition in contemporary writing, it may take *about, at, by, over,* or *with* <*disappointed about* [*at, by, over, with*] the decision>. *Disappointed in* is also prevalent <*disappointed in* himself>.

disapprove When used with a preposition, *disapprove* is generally used with *of* <*disapproves of* the practice>. When the object of the preposition is the one disapproving, however, *by* is used <*disapproved by* the school board>.

disassociate See DISSOCIATE, DISASSOCIATE.

disburse, disperse Don't confuse *disburse,* "to pay out," with *disperse,* "to scatter."

discontent The noun *discontent* may be followed by *with* <workers' *discontent with* the new management>. Less frequently, *discontent* is used with *over* <expressed *discontent over* Congress's activities>.

discourage When *discourage* is used with a preposition, it is usually *from,* which in turn is often followed by a gerund phrase as its object <was *discouraged from* pursuing a literary career>. Occasionally *discourage from* is followed by a noun phrase <*discouraged from* the use of medications>.

discreet, discrete The history and spelling of *discreet* and *discrete* are closely intertwined, but in current usage they are distinguished. *Discreet* means "capable of keeping a secret" <very *discreet*> while *discrete* means "individually distinct" <*discrete* components>.

disinterest, disinterestedness *Disinterest* is used primarily to mean "absence of interest" <acknowledged voter *disinterest* in the issue>. It is also used, less frequently, as a synonym of *disinterestedness,* meaning "impartiality" <his methods reflect a studied *disinterest* in the outcome>. *Disinterestedness* is more common in this sense. See also DISINTERESTED, UNINTERESTED.

disinterested, uninterested In current use, *disinterested* has basically two meanings: "unbiased" <a *disinterested* decision> <*disinterested* intellectual curiosity>, and "not interested" <seemed *disinterested* in her work>, of which the latter is also the basic meaning of *uninterested.* Some critics object to the second use, but it is standard, and may even be chosen for purposes of emphasis or to suggest a loss of interest <became *disinterested* in the subject>.

disinterestedness See DISINTEREST, DISINTERESTEDNESS.

dislike 1. *Noun. Dislike* can take the prepositions *of* and *for* <a *dislike of* salty food> <expressed *dislike for* the new teacher>. The phrase *take a dislike* usually takes *to* as its preposition <*took a* strong *dislike to* the man>.

2. *Verb.* The verb *dislike* can take, besides a noun object <*dislikes* the ocean>, a participial phrase <*dislikes* having to take the subway> or, less commonly, an infinitive phrase <I *dislike* to disturb you at home>.

dismayed *By* is the usual preposition after *dismayed* <*dismayed by* his girlfriend's refusal>. *With* and *at* may also be used <*dismayed with* their negative attitude> <*dismayed at* the size of the job>. *Dismayed* can also be followed by the infinitive <*dismayed* to discover that she had lost>.

dispense *Dispense* is often used in the fixed expression *dispense with,* which means "to set aside, discard" <*dispensing with* the usual introduction> or "to do without" <could *dispense with* such a large staff>. When *dispense* is used in any of its senses involving portioning out or administering, and the phrase denotes the receiver, *dispense* is naturally used with *to* <*dispensing* medicines *to* the sick>.

disperse See DISBURSE, DISPERSE.

dispossess *Dispossess* is sometimes used with the preposition *of* <was *dispossessed of* his property>.

disqualify When used with a preposition, *disqualify* is used with either *from* or *for* <a conviction for perjury *disqualified* him *from* being a witness> <he was *disqualified for* cheating>.

disregard The noun *disregard* may be followed by *for* or *of* <a *disregard for* the safety of the passengers> <a *disregard of* legal restraints>. The phrases *with disregard for* and *with disregard of* are both quite common <*with disregard for* [*of*] the truth>; however, when *disregard* is preceded by *in,* it is followed by *of* <*in disregard of* the realities>.

dissatisfied, unsatisfied Though *dissatisfied* and *unsatisfied* appear to be synonyms, there are distinctions to be made. *Unsatisfied* is more frequently used to modify nonhuman terms (such as *ambition, debts, curiosity, demands, claims*) than human ones, and the meaning is generally "unfulfilled" or "unappeased" <their demand was left *unsatisfied*> <our curiosity went *unsatisfied*>. *Dissatisfied,* in contrast, is used primarily with respect to persons or groups in the sense of "not pleased or gratified" <these *dissatisfied* workers voted with their feet> <the tenants were *dissatisfied* with the repairs>.

While both *dissatisfied* and *unsatisfied,* when used with a preposition, are usually followed by *with,* both words may be followed by *by* <*dissatisfied with* the working conditions> <*unsatisfied by* the last-minute effort>.

dissent When *dissent,* as a noun or verb, is followed by a preposition, the preposition is usually *from* <*dissenting from* the prevailing opinion> <wrote in *dissent from* the majority opinion>.

dissimilar Some insist that *dissimilar* should be followed by *to* when it needs the complement or a prepositional phrase <were not *dissimilar to* those we identified previously>, but in actual usage *dissimilar* is just as likely to be followed by *from* <the defense's list was markedly *dissimilar from* the prosecution's>.

dissociate, disassociate *Dissociate* and *disassociate* share the sense "to separate from association or union with another," and both words, when used with a preposition, most often take *from* <*dissociated* [*disassociated*] himself *from* the business>. Both are in current good use, but *dissociate* is more common.

distaff *Distaff* has been disparaged as old-fashioned or mildly offensive to women (it originally denoted a staff for holding flax for spinning, and later came to mean "woman's work or domain"). But the adjective use of *distaff* shows no sign of waning. The word is used primarily as an alternative to *maternal* <the *distaff* side of the family> or *female* <*distaff* executives>. (It is also applied to horses with some frequency.)

distaste When used with a preposition, *distaste* overwhelmingly takes *for* <a *distaste for* opera>.

distill, distil *Distill* and *distil* are variant spellings, but *distill* is by far more common. *Distill* is used with a variety of prepositions, occuring most frequently with either *from* or *into* <a short volume *distilled from* a large mass of writings> <many years of thought *distilled into* a single powerful statement>. Other prepositions used with *distill* are *out of, through, to,* and *of* <*distilled out of* her experience in the foster care system> <*distilled through* the lens of a camera> <*distilled to* a single proposition> <*distilled of* a variety of red wines>.

distinguish When *distinguish* is used with a preposition, the preposition is most likely to be either *between* or *from* <to *distinguish between* truth and falsehood> <features which *distinguish* the language *from* Old Norse>. Less often, *distinguish* is used with *among* <*distinguishes among* several different shades>. In using *among,* writers seem to be influenced by the notion that *between* can be used only of two items and that *among* must be used for more than two. For a discussion of this issue see BETWEEN, AMONG.

distract See DETRACT, DISTRACT.

distrustful *Of* is the preposition used with *distrustful* <*distrustful of* their motives>.

dive, dived See DOVE.

divest When followed by a prepositional phrase, *divest* appears with *of* <the firm plans to *divest* itself *of* its foreign holdings>. *Divest* may also take as a direct object the thing that is given up <will *divest* several properties>.

divide **1.** The verb *divide* is used with a large number of prepositions, most frequently *into* and *in* <*divided into* equal portions> <*divided in* half>. *Divide* is also used with *between* and *among, between* occurring far more often <*divides* her time *between* home and the office> <to be *divided* equally *among* the partners>. (See also BETWEEN, AMONG.) The use of *divide* with *from* is also common, especially when both divisions are mentioned and one is the direct object <*divides* diehards *from* dilettantes>. In addition to the common mathematical use of *divide* with *by, divide by* is used in other contexts <the community was *divided by* the new freeway> <*divided by* several generations>. *Divide* may be used with *on* or *over* when the matter that causes the division is the object of the preposition <remain *divided on* [*over*] the issue>. *Divide with* occurs, but not very often <*divided* duties *with* her sister>. We also find occasional instances of *divide* being used with *as to, to, against,* and *toward.*

2. *Divide up.* This phrase is sometimes criticized as a redundancy, but it continues to be used by good writers <*divided up* the proceeds>.

divorce The verb *divorce* is almost always used with *from* when followed by a prepositional phrase <a solution *divorced from* any domestic considerations>.

dominate, domineer *Dominate* is used far more often than *domineer.* If either word is used intransitively with a complement, the preposition used is *over* <he *dominated* [*domineered*] *over* the proceedings>. When *dominate* is used in the passive voice, the agent is named in a phrase beginning with *by* <the debate was *dominated by* the Republicans>. *Domineer* occurs most frequently now as its present participle, *domineering,* which has taken on adjectival status <never imagined having such *domineering* in-laws>.

done *Done* in the sense "finished"—especially when used with a form of *be*—has been subject to a certain amount of criticism over the years, yet its use in this sense has long been standard <the job is finally *done*> <we're *done* with you now>.

don't seem See CAN'T SEEM.

don't think The placement of the negative in such sentences as "I don't think it will rain tonight" and "I don't think they have a chance" is a characteristic English idiom that is sometimes objected to on the grounds of logic. Such sentences exemplify a phenomenon known as "raising," the shifting of a negative (or other element) from a subordinate to the "higher" clause it is dependent on. See also CAN'T SEEM.

dote When *dote* is used with a preposition—and it almost always is—*on* is the usual choice <*doted on* her only grandchild>.

doubt, *verb* The transitive verb *doubt* may take a clause as its object. The clause may be a sort of CONTACT CLAUSE (see Glossary) without a conjunction, or a clause introduced by *that, whether,* or *if.* (In the past, *but* and *but that* were also used.) *That* is preferred when the main clause is negative <I wouldn't *doubt that* such a thing exists> <We never *doubted that* they would come>; *that* also tends to be used with a third-person subject <he *doubts that* the settlement will last>. When the subject is in the first person, which it very often is, most writers choose *if, that,* or *whether* by no other criterion than personal preference <I *doubt if* [*that, whether*] we'll ever know>. All are standard.

doubt, *noun* **1.** The noun *doubt,* when followed by a clause, may take a clause introduced by the conjunctions used for the verb (see DOUBT, *verb*), including the older *but* and *but that* <there is little *doubt that* [*but,*

but that] they will succeed> <the usual *doubt whether* the thing will succeed>.

2. *Doubt,* whether as a singular or a plural, is followed idiomatically by a number of prepositions <*doubt about* the outcome> <*doubt of* his authority> <*doubt over* the proposal> <*doubt as to* their motives>.

doubtful *Doubtful* is usually not followed by a clause, but when it is the clause can begin with *that, whether,* or *if* <It is *doubtful that* [*whether, if*] the deal will go through>. See also DUBIOUS, DOUBTFUL.

doubtless, no doubt, undoubtedly *Doubtless* and *no doubt* are often used to mean "probably" <seeing and *doubtless* believing it all> <dismayed, *no doubt,* by the recent announcement>; *undoubtedly* tends to carry more conviction <*undoubtedly* interested in retrieving her property>.

Ways of expressing greater certainty include the sometimes maligned *indubitably, without (a) doubt* and *beyond a doubt,* and even longer phrases such as *there can be no doubt* or *there is no doubt at all.*

dove The verb *dive* has the past tense *dived* or *dove.* Although *dived* is somewhat more common in writing in the U.S., and is usual in British English, *dove* is used in many regions of the U.S. and may even be spreading its range. You may use whichever is more natural to you.

dozen *Dozen* has two plurals: *dozen* (just like the singular) and *dozens.* When a number is put before the noun, *dozen* is used <three *dozen* lobsters>. When the number is not specified, *dozens* is usual <performed in *dozens* of off-Broadway plays>.

draft, draught In British English *draft* is used for a preliminary sketch and for the corresponding verb, and also for an order for payment (a bank draft); but *draught* is used for beer, horses, and a current of air. American English uses *draft* in all cases.

drank See DRINK.

drapes, draperies *Draperies* used to be preferred for the decorative fabric hung as curtains, and is still insisted upon by some, but *drapes* has established itself as a standard alternative.

draught See DRAFT, DRAUGHT.

dream 1. The verb *dream* has the past and past-participle forms *dreamt* and *dreamed.* Both forms are many centuries old and both are flourishing in current American use. You may use whichever one feels more natural to you.

2. *Dream* may take either *of* or *about* before a gerund or a noun object <*dreamt of* [*about*] riding an elevator> <*dreamed about* [*of*] the trip to her grandmother's>.

drench *Drench* is often used with a complement introduced by *in* or *with* <*drenched in* blood> <*drenched with* wealth>.

drink The usual past tense of this verb today is *drank* <we *drank* from the well>. The usual past participle is *drunk* <the guests had already *drunk* several bottles>. The past tense *drunk* was formerly common, but has mostly dropped from use. The past participle *drank* is still used in some Northern areas of the U.S. and in some areas of Canada, but chiefly in speech. It seldom appears in print.

drown It is a convention of newspaper writers and editors that *drowned* should be used for an accidental drowning, and *was drowned* for a murder or other intentional drowning. Unless you are reporting an intentional drowning, you probably don't need to use the passive.

drunk, drunken **1.** *Drunk* is normally used as a predicate adjective <he was *drunk* when he left the bar>, whereas *drunken* is usual when the adjective precedes the noun <stopped to pick up a *drunken* couple>. One key exception is that *drunk* is commonly used before the words *driver* and *driving* <a *drunk* driver>.

2. For use of *drunk* as an inflected form of *drink*, see DRINK.

dubious, doubtful Is it permissible to say that you are dubious about something? Some critics have tried to limit *dubious* to the person or thing that is the object of doubt, and *doubtful* to the person who questions. *Dubious* is indeed most frequently used in the sense of "giving rise to uncertainty" <felt that our plan was a little *dubious*>, but many good writers have used *dubious* to mean "doubting, unsettled in opinion, suspicious" <she was *dubious* about the truth of the claim>. Similarly, both *dubious* and *doubtful* are frequently used to refer to the object of doubt. *Doubtful* may imply a simple lack of conviction or certainty <the outcome of the election remains *doubtful*>, while *dubious* usually implies suspicion, mistrust, or hesitation. In many contexts, however, either word can be used.

due to When the *due* of *due to* is clearly an adjective <absences *due to* the flu> no one complains about the phrase. When *due to* is a preposition <*due to* the holiday, our offices will be closed>, some people object and call for *owing to* or *because of.* Both uses of *due to* are entirely standard, but in formal writing one of the alternatives for the prepositional use may be less likely to be criticized.

due to the fact that This phrase often can be replaced by the shorter *because* or *since,* but not always <the lower numbers are *due to the fact that* the test scores have been averaged>. Adding *the fact that* to *due to* allows a clause to be used as the object, which sometimes comes in handy.

during the course of See COURSE.

dwell **1.** Although there are two spellings—*dwelt* and *dwelled*—for the past tense of *dwell, dwelled* has steadily lost ground over the centuries, and *dwelt* is now found far more often <she *dwelt* on her plans for the future>.

2. *Live* is the more commonly used word for "reside," but *dwell* has by no means disappeared <*dwelt* beside the river>.

3. *Dwell* may take any number of prepositions. In addition to *behind, on, within, in,* and *at,* it is used with *among, beneath, outside, over, under, upon,* and with.

dying, dyeing You will want to take care not to use *dying,* the present participle of *die* <*dying* of cancer>, when you mean to use *dyeing,* the present participle of *dye* <*dyeing* it a shade of blue>.

E

each There are several problems about *each* and its agreement with either verb or pronoun. These problems are taken up separately below. See also AGREEMENT: INDEFINITE PRONOUNS (in Glossary).

1. When the pronoun *each* is the simple subject, the rule of thumb is that it takes a singular verb <*each is* ready to accept the terms> <*each holds* a secret for the discoverer>. Sometimes, NOTIONAL AGREEMENT (see Glossary) interferes with the singular construction when *each* has a plural antecedent <a number of

proposals; *each have* been reviewed>. Since this use may be criticized, it is safer to use the singular.

2. When the adjective *each* modifies a singular noun subject, the singular verb is normally used <*each* car *displays* the corporate logo> <*each* intern *is* trained in the technique>.

3. *Each of* is followed by a plural noun or pronoun and notional agreement is strong. Singular and plural verbs are about equally frequent <*each of* the animals *was* placed in a shelter> <*each of* his paintings *are* exercises in self-mockery>. Sticklers will insist on the singular.

4. When the adjective *each* follows a plural noun subject, the plural verb and the plural pronoun commonly follow <they *each have their* own constituencies> <we *each have our* stake in the outcome>.

5. *Each* shares with many indefinite pronouns the tendency to take a plural pronoun in reference <*each* of the waiting moviegoers pulled out *their* ticket>, even though this use is sometimes censured. And *each,* like other indefinite pronouns, often takes a singular verb but a plural pronoun <*each* branch library *strives* to provide superior service to *their* patrons>. The principle of notional agreement is strong in these instances.

each and every *Each and every* is an emphatic form of *each* or *every.* It is sometimes criticized as jargon or worse, but it remains in good use <*each and every* offer has been rebuffed>. You may use it if it seems to be called for, but be careful not to overdo it.

each of See EACH 3.

each other, one another **1.** A traditional rule calls for *each other* to be used in reference to two <the two girls looked at *each other* in surprise> and *one another* to be used in reference to three or more <there will be time for people to talk with *one another* after the meeting>. In fact, however, *each other* and *one another* are employed interchangeably.

2. The possessive is normally *each other's, one another's.* The following noun can be either singular or plural <invading *each other's* sphere of influence> <moving in *each other's* circles>.

eager When *eager* is used with a preposition, the preposition is usually *to* and it is followed by an infinitive <officials are *eager to* shut the operation down>. *Eager for* is also frequent in contemporary writing <they were *eager for* any news>.

early on *Early on,* having arisen in British English in the 1920s, came into frequent use in American English in the 1960s and is now well established on both sides of the Atlantic <*early on* in the process>. It cannot always be easily replaced by *early,* as some critics have claimed it can.

earth The names of planets other than our own are invariably capitalized, but *earth* is usually not. When the other planets are also being referred to, there is some tendency to capitalize *Earth* and to omit the article *the* which normally precedes it. Both treatments are perfectly acceptable. Choose whichever styling seems more natural to you in a particular context and use it consistently in similar contexts.

easy, easily *Easy* as an adverb has many uses, most of which have a somewhat informal quality <he was told to go *easy* on them> <his illness forced him to take it *easy*>. *Easily* is the more common adverb, and it has a wider range of applications <not *easily* fooled> <is *easily* the best place in town>. In situations where both adverbs are possible (such as "Laughs come *easy*" or "Laughs come *easily*"), you should choose whichever seems more natural and appropriate to the tone of your writing.

economic, economical *Economic* usually refers to economics or an economy, whereas *economical* usually means "thrifty" or "not wasteful." Some crossover does occur, however.

educationist In British English, *educationist* is an ordinary word synonymous with *educator.* But in American English, *educationist* most often serves as a term of disparagement for a stereotypically muddleheaded educational theorist.

educator *Educator* is more often used of administrators in education than of actual teachers. Its application to an actual teacher usually carries implications of responsibility or achievement outside the classroom.

effect See AFFECT, EFFECT.

e.g. See I.E., E.G.

either **1.** *Either* as an adjective meaning "each" is still in common use, though it is not as common as *each* <a long straight path lined on *either* side by robust sycamores>.

2. *Either* is rarely used of more than two items when it is a pronoun <in *either* of the two buildings> or an adjective (see 1 above); but the conjunction *either* is commonly so used <it was sent by *either* Rachel, Lindsay, or Marisa>.

3. In *either . . . or* constructions, *either* should be placed where it will provide parallelism. Thus, the sentence "the sum will be donated *either* to the college, the public library, *or* the state education fund" should be altered to "the sum will be donated to *either* the college, the public library, *or* the state education fund" or "the sum will be donated *either* to the college, to the public library, *or* to the state education fund." Correction will result in greater elegance of expression, but the nonparallel sentence is just as easily understood. See also, in Glossary, AGREEMENT; PARALLELISM.

4. When the pronoun *either* is the subject of a clause, it takes a singular verb <Wilma and Betty are closer to each other than *either is* to Maud>. A plural verb is often used when *either* is followed by *of* and a plural noun or pronoun <*Are either of* you going?> <it would seem that *either of* them *are* acceptable>. This pattern of agreement seems to be more common in speech than writing.

5. In *either . . . or* constructions, if both subjects are singular the verb is traditionally singular <*either* the cable *or* the connector *is* not functioning>. Because of the strength of NOTIONAL AGREEMENT (see Glossary), however, a plural verb is not uncommon <*either* the House committee *or* the Senate subcommittee *are* to review the matter>. When both subjects are plural, or the first is singular and the second plural, a plural verb is expected <*either* the rings *or* the satellites usually *obscure* the planet's surface> <*either* Maria *or* her cousins *are* bringing the salad>.

either . . . or See EITHER 3, 5.

elegy, eulogy An *elegy* (from the Greek *elegos,* "song of mourning") is a sorrowful or melancholy song or poem; a *eulogy* (from the Greek *eulogia,* "praise") is a formal statement or oration expressing praise. A funeral oration is called a *eulogy* because it praises the accomplishments and character of the person who has died. Sometimes *elegy* is mistakenly used to mean "a funeral oration, eulogy" because funerals are occasions for mourning. Use your dictionary if you are still in doubt.

elicit, illicit *Elicit,* "to draw forth," and *illicit,* "unlawful," are occasionally confused because of their similar pronunciations. Take care to use the right word.

eligible *Eligible* may be used with a prepositional phrase, and *for* or *to* are the prepositions used most often <she is *eligible for* tenure>. When *eligible* is used with *to,* an infinitive usually follows <he is *eligible to* retire>.

else In contemporary English, compound pronouns with *else*—such as *anybody else, somebody else,* and *who else*—take the *-'s* of the possessive on the *else* <nobody *else's* problem>.

elude See ALLUDE 2.

emanate *Emanate* is usually used with the preposition *from* <radio signals *emanating from* outer space>.

embark *Embark* may be used with a few different prepositions, but the usual choice is *on* (or *upon*) <*embarked on* a new career>. *For* is used when the object is a destination <*embarked for* Constantinople>. And *from* is occasionally used to indicate the point of departure <*embarked from* San Francisco harbor>.

embellish *Embellish* is most often used with *with* when it takes a complement <*embellished with* metalwork>. It is also used with *by* <*embellished by* many fine photographs>.

emend See AMEND, EMEND.

emerge When *emerge* is used with a preposition, the choice is most often *from* <they *emerged from* behind the curtain>. It is also very frequently used with *as* <*emerged as* the victor>. Other prepositions commonly used with *emerge* include *at, in, into, on, onto, out of, through, upon,* and *with. Emerge* is also sometimes followed by a *that* clause <it *emerged that* he had been receiving bribes>.

emigrate, immigrate *Emigrate* means "to leave a country," *immigrate* "to come into a place." Distinguishing between the two is easy if you remember that *emigrate* usually takes the preposition *from* <*emigrated from* Russia>, while *immigrate* usually takes *to* or *into* <*immigrated to* Canada>. Get the prepositions right, and you will be right.

eminent, imminent *Eminent* means "prominent" <an *eminent* author>; *imminent* means "soon to occur, impending" <in *imminent* danger>. Use of one word for the other does occur from time to time. Be careful.

emote The normal uses of *emote* are facetious <*emoting* all over the place>. Use of *emote* without humorous intent is generally only in reference to actors <learning how to *emote* before the camera>.

employ *Employ* and *use* are often interchangeable, but *employ* is most appropriate when the conscious application of something for a particular end is being stressed <the scene *employs* exotic costumes to good effect>.

emporium *Emporium* has two plurals, *emporiums* and *emporia,* both of which are in good use. *Emporiums* is the more common of the two.

enamor *Enamor* is used most often in the passive, and when used with a preposition usually takes *of* <we became *enamored of* the young boy>. Less frequently, it is followed by *with* <was *enamored with* foreign films>.

encroach When used with a preposition, *encroach* usually appears with *on* (or *upon*) <*encroaching upon* her territory>. Occasionally it is used with *into, onto,* and *to* <*encroaching into* domestic air space> <*encroaching onto* their neighbor's property> <*encroaching* ever closer *to* the city limits>.

end When *end* is used intransitively with a preposition, the preposition is often *by* <he *ended* the concert *by* playing Chopin>, or somewhat less frequently *as, at,* or *on* <the paper *ended as* a monthly with wide circulation> <the duty-free zone *ends at* the fence> <the session *ended on* a positive note>. See also END UP.

endeavor *Endeavor* is used as a somewhat formal synonym for *attempt* or *try.* It tends to connote a continuing and earnest effort, as in attempting to enact a long-range policy or to achieve a lasting result <the committee *endeavored* to settle all grievances>.

endemic *Endemic* can be followed by either *in* or *to* <a condition *endemic in* [*to*] the region>.

endow *Endow* is very often used with a preposition, and usually the preposition is *with* <*endowed with* political acumen>. *Endow* is used with *by* when the sense is "furnish with funds" <a hospital *endowed by* a local philanthropist>.

end result, end product Some people find *end* in these two phrases superfluous and advise that you should use only *result* or *product.* This is largely a matter of personal preference, though you probably will not want to overuse either phrase.

end up **1.** Although *end up* is sometimes criticized as too informal and is occasionally changed to *end* by copy editors, it is useful when you want to emphasize the notion of everything that led up to a certain result <after all the wrangling, they still *ended up* producing nothing>. *End* is often not only an awkward synonym for *end up* but sometimes no synonym at all.

2. When *end up* is followed by a preposition, the preposition is usually *with, in, as, by,* or *at.*

enervate To *enervate* is "to lessen the vitality or strength of" or "to reduce the mental or moral vigor of" <completely *enervated* following a hectic weekend>. Some people use this word without really knowing what it means, or confuse it with *invigorate* or *energize.* Don't be misled by the superficial resemblance of *enervate* to these other words.

engage *Engage* may be used with several prepositions. It most often takes *in,* which is usually followed by a gerund or a noun <*engaged in* trade for a number of years>. Less frequently, it is used with *with* <*engaged with* his old publisher at the time> or, in British English, *on* or *upon* <*engaged on* a series of novels>. It may also be used with *by* <he was *engaged by* the local paper>, *for* <he *engages for* the honesty of his brother>, *as* <*engaged as* a manservant>, and *to* <*engaged to* be married>.

enormity *Enormity,* some people insist, is improperly used to merely denote large size. They insist on *enormousness* for this meaning, and would limit *enormity* to the meaning "great wickedness" <the *enormity* of his crimes>. In actual practice, however, it regularly denotes a considerable departure from the expected or normal <the *enormity* of their situation suddenly dawned on them>. When used to denote large size, either literal or figurative, it usually suggests something so large as to seem overwhelming <the *enormity* of the sea bottom> <the *enormity* of the task>. It can also emphasize momentousness <the *enormity* of the collapse of Communism>.

enquire See INQUIRE, ENQUIRE.

enquiry See INQUIRY, ENQUIRY.

en route This French phrase was first used in English in the 19th century. Its assimilation into our language was completed long ago, and there is no longer any need to underline or italicize it as a foreign term. It is used as both an adverb <he reads *en route*> and an adjective <arrived early despite *en route* delays> and is usually written as two words.

ensure, insure, assure *Ensure, insure,* and *assure* are interchangeable in many contexts where they indicate the making certain or inevitable of an outcome <will *ensure* [*insure, assure*] correct usage>, but *insure* sometimes stresses the taking of necessary measures beforehand <to *insure* safe passage> and *assure* distinctively implies the removal of doubt and suspense from a person's mind <*assures* them that the vehicle is perfect>.

enter *Enter* may be used with many prepositions, but most often it is used with *into* <*enter into* an agreement>. Less often, it is used with *upon* or *on* <*entering upon* a career>. It is also used with complements introduced by *in, for, as, at, by,* and *with* <ten were *entered in* the race> <*entered* purely *for* symbolic reasons> <she *entered as* a standby> <*entered* the building *at* 3 PM> <*entered by* another door> <*entering with* the rank of lieutenant>.

enthrall When *enthrall* is used with a preposition, it is usually used with *by* <*enthralled by* the mix of cultures>. Less frequently *enthrall* is followed by *with* <*enthralled with* the campaign>.

enthuse *Enthuse,* an apparent Americanism that has been disapproved since the late 1800s, is nonetheless flourishing on both sides of the Atlantic, especially in journalistic prose <*enthusing* over the food>.

entitle *Entitle* has two common meanings: "to give a title to, title" <a work *entitled* "Penance"> and "to give a right to" <this ticket *entitles* the bearer to free admission>. Both are standard.

envelope The two pronunciations \ˈen-və-ˌlōp\ and \ˈän-və-ˌlōp\ are used with about equal frequency and are both fully acceptable.

envisage, envision These two words are, in many respects, interchangeable. When, however, the thing envisaged or envisioned is an abstract concept rather than a mental image, *envisage* tends to be chosen <*envisages* an entirely new system of education>. When a specific picture is in mind, *envision* is more often chosen <*envisions* a career in the law>.

equal **1.** When *equal* is used with a preposition, it is used most often with *to* <bored with work not *equal to* his abilities>. Occasionally it is used with *with* <a level more or less *equal with* that of the previous year>.

2. *Equal* is one of those adjectives that some insist are absolute and therefore incapable of comparison (as in "*more equal*"). (See ABSOLUTE ADJECTIVE in Glossary.) This opinion, however, fails to recognize the common use of *more* to mean "more nearly" <perhaps we are *more equal* now than were citizens of the antebellum period>. This use has been in existence at least since the 17th century and remains standard.

equally as This innocuous phrase has drawn criticism because of its supposed redundancy, in that either *equally* or *as* can usually stand alone in place of it. Indeed, "The old show was awful, and the new show is *equally as* bad" can be revised to ". . . the new show is *equally* bad" or ". . . the new show is *as* bad" with no change of meaning. What will change, though, is emphasis. The point of the *equally* in *equally as* is to make it clear that the comparison is unqualified.

Equally as, then, is an idiomatic phrase equivalent to *just as.* It occurs commonly in speech, but it has been criticized enough to make it relatively rare in edited prose, where *just as* is more common.

equivalent 1. When the adjective *equivalent* is used with a preposition, the choice is usually *to* <*equivalent to* one year's pay>.

2. When the noun *equivalent* is used with a preposition, it is usually used with *of* <the *equivalent of* religious heresy>.

equivocal, ambiguous These two words are essentially synonyms, but *equivocal* may suggest intent to deceive or evade <*equivocal* actions that no one knew how to interpret>. Often, though *equivocal* suggests no more than *ambiguous* <an *equivocal* translation of the original>. See also AMBIVALENT, AMBIGUOUS.

erotica *Erotica* has the form of a Greek plural, but it is now usually understood as a mass noun meaning "erotic material" and is treated as a singular <such *erotica* is now off-limits to Internet users>. Treatment of *erotica* as a plural still occurs, however, and is not incorrect <these *erotica* are quite revealing of the culture>. For other foreign plurals, see LATIN PLURALS.

err In current English, the standard pronunciation of this word is \'er\, rhyming with *air.* It was, however, traditionally pronounced \'ər\, rhyming with the last syllable of *prefer,* and some people still favor the latter pronunciation.

escape Does a prisoner escape jail or escape from jail? *Escape from* is the usual idiom, but *escape* is also occasionally used as a transitive verb in such a context, without *from* <we *escaped* the mortar attack only to run into snipers> <*escaped* the earth's gravitational field>.

espresso, expresso The strong brew made by forcing steam through finely ground coffee is known in Italian as *caffé espresso,* or just *espresso* for short. Contrary to a popular belief of English-speakers, *espresso* means not "fast" but "pressed out"—it refers to the process by which the coffee is made, not the speed of the process. The idea that *caffé espresso* means "fast coffee" may have contributed to the occurrence in English of the spelling *expresso,* which also more closely resembles a familiar English word than does *espresso.* In any case, *espresso* is the more common form, at least in writing.

Esquire (Esq.) *Esquire* (abbreviated *Esq.*), which in British English is used as a respectful title in addressing correspondence to a man, is in American English used mainly among attorneys, who likewise use it when referring to or addressing each other in writing. There is still some controversy about using *Esq.* after the name of a woman lawyer. Some lawyers are all in favor of such usage, while others are strongly opposed to it. Indications are that the pros are gradually winning out over the antis. Note that when *Esq.* is used as a title following a name, no other title or term of address is used before the name. You can write *Mr. John Smith* or *John Smith, Esq.*, but you should not write *Mr. John Smith, Esq.*

-ess Many so-called feminine nouns—*empress, duchess, princess, lioness, abbess, goddess,* and so forth—have never stirred up much controversy. But others—*authoress, poetess, sculptress*—have been decried in recent decades. You will have little need for them. And what about *waitress?* Is it really being displaced by the genderless *waitperson* or *waitron?* Perhaps not. As an informal verb, *waitress* has even become more common in print over the last 20 years or so. In British English, the word *manageress* continues in frequent use. Clearly this portion of our vocabulary is still evolving.

essential, *adjective* **1.** *Essential* is used most often with the preposition *to* when the phrase requires a preposition <*essential to* one's health>. Sometimes it is used with *in* <*essential in* hot climates>. Less often it is used with *as* <*essential as* a means of prevention>.

2. Some hold *essential* to be an absolute adjective that cannot be qualified by adverbs such as *more* or *most.* The use of such adverbs with *essential* is, however, common among writers. *Most essential* is used for emphasis <it is *most essential* that you attend>. So are *absolutely essential* and *so essential. More* and *most* are both used for comparison <observed that this action is *more essential* to

the peace process> <the *most essential* part of the book is the last one>.

essential, *noun* When the noun *essential* is used with a preposition, it is used most often with *of* <the *essentials of* astronomy>. Less frequently, it is used with *in, for,* or *to* <one of the *essentials in* this game> <an *essential for* visitors to Montreal> <an *essential to* the maintenance of proper form>.

estimate 1. When the verb *estimate* is used with a preposition, it is usually *at* <*estimated* the crowd *at* two hundred>. There is also scattered use of *as, by, for,* and *from.*

2. The noun *estimate* is often used with *of* <an *estimate of* the firm's worth>.

estimation The use of *estimation* to mean "opinion, judgment" <in my *estimation,* it is sound> is entirely reputable, despite the disapproval of some critics. The use dates back to the 14th century and can be found in the works of many standard authors.

estrange When used with a preposition in contemporary English, *estrange* is used with *from* <*estranged from* her husband>.

et al. This Latin abbreviation means "and others" or "and the others." The most frequent use of it is in citing (as in a footnote or bibliography) a publication that has several or many authors <Ruth I. Anderson *et al., The Administrative Secretary*>. Some discourage the use of *et al.* in regular prose, but it is commonly so used <we have Shelley, Byron, Wordsworth, *et al.* to thank>. The period is generally retained after *al,* and regular roman type is normally used.

etc. **1.** This abbreviation of the Latin *et cetera* means literally "and others of the same kind." *Etc.* thus should not be preceded by *and* (as in ". . . *and etc.*") and it should not be used at the end of a list introduced by *for example* or *such as* (as in "*such* photographic material *as* lenses, filters, *etc.*"). *Etc.* now appears commonly in ordinary prose, though some critics feel it is inappropriate in formal writing. If you need an alternative, you can use *and so on, and so forth,* or *and the like.*

2. *Et cetera* is often mispronounced \ek-ˈset-ər-ə\, and *etc.* is often misspelled *ect.* Remembering that the phrase begins with the Latin *et,* "and," should prevent you from committing either the mispronunciation or the misspelling.

eulogy See ELEGY, EULOGY.

even *Even* is an adverb whose placement can affect its meaning. In speech, a natural place for *even* to fall is just before the verb <they *even* do windows>. In writing, where stress cannot be as clearly signaled and where complex sentences may more often occur, you should put the *even* directly in front of the word or phrase it qualifies <faithful *even* unto death>. See also ONLY.

event The phrase *in the event that* serves as a somewhat formal substitute for *if* <*in the event that* an actual emergency occurs>. The *that* is often omitted <*in the event* a parent or guardian cannot pick up the child>. Both versions are sometimes criticized for wordiness or pomposity, and there are certainly contexts in which neither would be appropriate ("*In the event that* I had a hammer, I'd hammer in the mornin'"). But their distinctive tone and rhythm make them useful in other contexts. In elevated writing, for instance, they are entirely at home.

eventuate *Eventuate,* meaning "to result, come about," is used primarily in scholarly writing, textbooks, and reference works. It has also had some use in popular magazines and newspapers, but it is not the best choice when you are aiming for simplicity, informality, or forcefulness in your style <*eventuating* in a kind of serendipitous euphony>.

every **1.** *Subject-verb agreement.* Since *every* normally modifies a singular noun, a singular verb usually follows <*every* page *contains* some new revelation>. When *every* modifies two or more nouns joined by *and,* the singular verb is common <*every* man, woman, and child *is* going to benefit>. But the plural verb is not rare <*every* plant, *every* rock, and *every* inhabitant of the garden *were* planned before we started>.

2. *Pronouns with every.* Since *every* modifies a singular noun, it would seem logical that it would be followed by singular pronouns. But it often is not; the effect of notional agreement and considerations of gender often result in plural pronouns. For instance, when there is no problem about males or females, the singular pronoun is usually used <*every* woman attorney knows *she* faces an uphill battle> <*every* man in the village can offer *his* opinion at the council meeting> <*every* knickknack was in *its* proper place>. But when inanimate objects are involved, notional agreement often causes a plural pronoun to be used <*every* doctor, *every* lawyer and *every* drugstore was on his route, and he visited *them* regularly>, though in edited prose the plural pronoun may often be changed to singular. Finally, when the reference is to both men and women or when the gender is unknown, the plural pronoun is almost always used <*every* man and woman of voting age should ask *themselves* that question> <*every* recipient was requested to write *their* answers on the back>.

everybody, everyone *Everyone* and *everybody* regularly take a singular verb but a plural pronoun—specifically, *they, their,* or *them* <*everyone* was on *their* best behavior> <*everybody* at the picnic had brought *their* assigned dishes>. You can use a singular pronoun if you want to (and you are more likely to use a singular with *everyone* than with *everybody*) <*everyone* had *his or her* ticket>, but the plural pronoun seems to sound more natural to most people. See THEY, THEIR, THEM; NOTIONAL AGREEMENT (in Glossary).

everyday, every day The single word *everyday* is an adjective <an *everyday* occurrence> <part of *everyday* life>; the two-word phrase *every day* functions either as a noun <*every day* is new> or as an adverb <I see her *every day*>. The adverbial phrase is increasingly written as a single word <*everyday* a new scandal is reported>, but the two-word styling is still more common.

everyone See EVERYBODY, EVERYONE.

everyplace *Everyplace* is a somewhat informal synonym of *everywhere* <we went here, there, and *everyplace* in between>. It is not highly regarded by some. See also ANYPLACE; SOMEPLACE.

everytime, every time *Every* and *time* form a common adverbial phrase that is normally written as two words <they'll do it *every time*> <*every time* it rains, the roof leaks>. There is, however, a persistent tendency to treat this two-word phrase as a single-word adverb, especially when it occurs at the beginning of a clause and means "whenever" <*everytime* a jet flies over, the house shakes>. Such usage seems to be slowly increasing, but the two-word styling is still more widely preferred.

every which way This expressive Americanism is perfectly standard <we chased him *every which way*>, despite the doubts of some critics.

evidence *Evidence* has been used as a transitive verb for many centuries <certificates *evidencing* stock ownership>. The word has, however, retained a formal quality. If the audience, tone, and subject of your writing make formality suitable, then *evidence* is as good a verb as any other.

evidently See APPARENTLY, EVIDENTLY.

evoke, invoke *Evoke* (from the Latin, *evocare,* "to call forth") is usually used to mean "to elicit," "to bring to mind," or "to recreate imaginatively" <a smell that *evokes* images of his childhood>. *Invoke* (from the Latin *invocare,* "to call upon, to appeal to") is usually used to mean "to appeal to or cite" or "to implement" <*invoke* the death penalty>. *Evoke* is sometimes used in place of *invoke* in the sense "to appeal to or cite" (as in "*evoked* the authority of the Bible"), but it is preferable to use *invoke* in such cases.

ex- The use of *ex-*, a hyphenated prefix meaning "former," to modify a noun phrase <*ex-*Chicago Bulls star> <*ex-*postal worker> is standard in general prose but is largely avoided in formal or literary writing.

exact same This phrase is sometimes criticized as faulty or redundant, but it is frequently used by educated speakers and writers <found in the *exact same* place>. Its use is especially common in speech. See also REDUNDANCY (in Glossary).

exception When *exception* takes a preposition, the preposition is usually *of* or *to* <with the *exception of* Randy> <she takes *exception to* Brand's characterization>.

exclude When *exclude* is used with a preposition, it is usually *from* <*excluded from* consideration>.

exclusive When *exclusive* is used with a preposition and the object is what is excluded, the preposition is *of* <all land *exclusive of* the state utility access road>. When *exclusive* means "limited," the preposition is *to* <a view *exclusive to* these houses>.

excuse When the verb *excuse* is used with a preposition, it ordinarily is used with *from* <*excused from* jury duty>, less often with *for* <*excused for* believing it>.

exhilarate, exhilaration Spell these words with caution, noting that each contains two *a*'s the first of which can easily turn into an *i* or an *e*. It may help to remember that they are related to *hilarious.*

exhorbitant See EXORBITANT.

exhuberance, exhuberant See EXUBERANCE, EXUBERANT.

existence, existent *Existence* is sometimes misspelled *existance,* and *existent* (perhaps because of confusion with the word *extant*) is sometimes misspelled *existant*. Be careful.

exonerate *Exonerate,* when used with a preposition, is usually used with *from* or *of, from* being more common <managed to *exonerate* himself *from* the charges> <was *exonerated of* all wrongdoing>.

exorbitant Note that there is no *h* following the *x* of *exorbitant.*

expatriate The misspelling *expatriot* occurs relatively frequently in print and should be guarded against.

expect **1.** Using *expect* to mean "suppose" or "think" in sentences such as "I *expect* you were sorry to hear that" is now far less controversial than it once was, although the use still has its detractors. *Expect* in this "suppose" sense is almost invariably used in the first person, and it therefore appears most often in speech and in the kinds of writing which make use of the first person—correspondence, dialogue, and informal prose. Whenever *I* is appropriate in a written context, the "suppose" sense of *expect* is likely to be appropriate also.

2. *Expect* is very often followed by the infinitive <researchers *expect* to find clues to the planet's origin>. Less often, but still very commonly, *expect* is used with *from* or *of* <what would you *expect from* the likes of Grady?> <little was *expected of* us>.

expel **1.** When *expel* is used with a preposition, the choice is almost always *from* <*expelled from* college>.

2. Do not misspell *expel* as *expell.*

experience When the verb *experience* is used with a preposition, the form is usually the past participle and the preposition is usually *in* <highly *experienced in*

foreign affairs>. Less frequently, *experience* is used with *as* <had *experienced* severe hardships *as* a child>.

expert **1.** When the adjective *expert* is used with a preposition, it is usually *in* <is *expert in* dealing with trauma> and sometimes *at* <quite *expert at* judging the stock market>.

2. The noun *expert,* when used with a preposition, is most often used with *on* <an *expert on* civil procedure>, sometimes with *in* <an *expert in* education>, and less frequently with *at* <an *expert at* juggling knives>.

exposé *Exposé* can be written with or without an acute accent. Both forms are widely used. The accented form is the more common, perhaps because it clearly indicates how the word is pronounced \ˌek-spō-ˈzā\.

expressive When it takes a complement in the form of a prepositional phrase, *expressive* is used with *of* <*expressive of* our inner longings>.

expresso See ESPRESSO, EXPRESSO.

exquisite Stressing the second syllable—\ek-ˈskwiz-ət\—is about as widespread as stressing the first syllable—\ˈek-skwiz-ət\. Either way is correct.

extemporaneous, impromptu *Extemporaneous* in its oldest sense is synonymous with *impromptu,* and its use in describing off-the-cuff remarks is common and correct <some *extemporaneous* observations>. *Extemporaneous* is also, however, used to describe a prepared speech given without notes or text <the press secretary's somewhat *extemporaneous* summary>, while *impromptu* is almost always used in describing speech that is truly unprepared <these *impromptu* remarks came back to haunt him>.

extract When the verb *extract* is used with a preposition, the choice is almost always *from* <*extracted* a piece of shrapnel *from* his leg>.

exuberance, exuberant The same spelling error that occurs with *exorbitant* also occurs with *exuberance* and *exuberant*—an *h* slips in following the *x*. Watch out for it.

exude *Exude,* when used with a preposition, is usually used with *from* <pus *exuding from* the eye>.

F

faced When *faced* is used as an adjective with a preposition, the preposition is usually *with* <he was *faced with* ruin>. As a verb meaning "to cover a front or surface," *face* is used equally with *with* or *in* <*faced* the building *with* [*in*] marble>.

fact A few phrases built around *fact*—e.g., *the fact that, in point of fact,* and *the fact is*—are occasionally criticized as unnecessarily wordy, and they undoubtedly are in many cases. But such phrases can also help the writer get a sentence organized or make an awkward transition. You should not use these phrases in every other paragraph, but if you need them for emphasis or to make a smooth transition, you may use them. See also TRUE FACTS.

fact that See FACT.

factor It is all right to use *factor* when there is no need to be extremely precise, but it is used a great deal, and many critics think it overused. You do not want to depend on it too heavily.

fail When *fail* is used with a preposition, it is often *to* and the infinitive <*failed to* lock the door>. *Fail* is also sometimes used with *in* or *at* <*failed in* his duty> <*failed at* selling insurance> and occasionally with *as, by, for, from, on,* or *with.*

famed *Famed* is used today both as a predicate adjective, often with *for* <*famed for* great chili>, and as an attributive adjective <Johnson's *famed* companion, Boswell>. Both uses are perfectly standard, though *famous* is the word used more often.

familiar The usual prepositions used with *familiar,* when it is a predicate adjective, are *with* and *to* <*familiar with* the facts of the case> <her face looked *familiar to* him>.

farther, further *Farther* and *further* have long been used more or less interchangeably, but have for some time been diverging. As adverbs they continue still to be used interchangeably when distance in space or time (either figurative or literal) is involved <traveled *further* [*farther*] today than yesterday> <taking the principle one step *farther* [*further*]>. But where there is no notion of distance, *further* is used <our techniques can be *further* refined>. *Further* is also used as a sentence modifier <*Further,* the goals they established were unrealistic>, but *farther* is not. As adjectives they also appear to be diverging: *farther* is taking over the meaning of distance <the *farther* shore>, and *further* the meaning of addition <needed no *further* training>.

fascinated *Fascinated* is more often used with *by* than with any other preposition, and *by* can take either a human or nonhuman object <is *fascinated by* her> <was *fascinated by* carnivals>. *Fascinated with* takes only nonhuman objects <*fascinated with* power>.

fascination When used with a preposition, *fascination* is most often used with *for, of,* or *with* <a moth's *fascination for* the flame> <they experienced the *fascination of* the wild West> <a *fascination with* numbers>.

fatal, fateful There are a number of distinctions to be made between these two adjectives. *Fatal* has more meanings and is more common. It has long had the sense of "involving momentous consequences, portentous," though some critics prefer to restrict this meaning to *fateful* alone <that *fatal* day> <the *fatal* letter>. *Fateful* is also used in about the same way <a *fateful*

remark> <his *fateful* decision>, but it is sometimes has a more neutral (if not quite positive) tone. *Fatal* has some meanings not shared with *fateful*: it can mean "deadly," <a *fatal* accident>, "disastrous" <a *fatal* misstep>, or "powerful and dangerous" <*fatal* charms>.

favorable When *favorable* is followed by a preposition, the preposition is usually either *to* or *for*. When the meaning of *favorable* is "feeling or expressing support or approval," *to* is used <the committee was *favorable to* accepting such applications>. *For* is the usual choice when *favorable* means "suitable" <weather that was *favorable for* our yacht trip>. Both *to* and *for* are used when *favorable* means "advantageous," though *to* is more common <a provision *favorable to* homeowners>. An alternative preposition is *toward* <taking a *favorable* attitude *toward* our request>.

February Despite admonishments to pronounce this word as \'feb-ru̇-ˌwer-ē\, the most widespread pronunciation among educated speakers is \'feb-yə-ˌwer-ē\. A succession of *r* sounds within a single word presents a challenge to many speakers, and often one gets transformed or dropped. Thus *caterpillar* is often pronounced \'kat-ə-ˌpil-ər\, and the first *r* sound of *governor, surprise,* and *thermometer* is often dropped without bothering anyone. On the other hand, pronouncing *library* as \'lī-ˌber-ē\ is generally disapproved (except when it comes from the mouths of children).

feed *Feed,* when used with a preposition, is most often used with *on* <he *feeds on* newsmagazines and opinion columns>. It is also used with *upon* and *off* <such groups *feed upon* the unwary consumer> <she *feeds off* all the attention>. Less frequently, it is used with *into* and *from* <this line *feeds into* the main switch> <the holding tank is *fed from* the well>.

feel bad, feel badly The choice between *feel bad* and *feel badly* is related to the choice between *feel good* and *feel well* (see GOOD 1). Those who make a distinction use *feel well* for health and *feel good* for emotion; many make the same distinction with *bad* and *badly* <if you *feel bad* you should lie down> <we *felt badly* about forgetting to invite them>. Usage is divided, however. Some people do not observe these distinctions and use *bad* for the emotional state and (more rarely) *badly* for health.

feel good, feel well See GOOD 1.

feet See FOOT.

feisty A few critics call *feisty* slang or colloquial, but it is in standard use <the *feisty* new assistant D.A.>.

fell swoop Although this phrase has become a bit of a cliché, it has a fine pedigree. It was used by Shakespeare, for whom *fell* meant "cruel, savage, ruthless" (the image is of a hawk swooping down on defenseless prey). If you use the phrase, be sure to get it right and not write *fell stroke, full swoop, felt soup,* or some other approximation.

female The noun *female* used to be used widely in literature. It is from the French word *femelle,* and is unrelated to the word *male* except through a deliberate spelling change that made *male* and *female* rhyme. In the mid-19th century it began to be criticized as demeaning (since it classed people with nonhuman animals), and the criticism continued well into the 20th century. Various humorous and mildly negative uses persist, as does an indefinite or indeterminate use—describing a group or class of women or girls whose age is unknown or irrelevant <the term "police officer" includes *females* as well as males>. The latter usage is the most common, and is still common in literature.

female forms See -ESS; see also PERSON 2.

ferment, foment Among the figurative senses of *ferment* is "to work up" (as into a state of agitation) <discontent *fermented* by government inattention>. This sense comes close to *foment* when it means "to promote the growth and development of" <*fomenting* dissent>. One difference is that things that one fermented can be good or bad; things that are fomented are usually bad. *Foment* is, in any case, much more common in this context.

fewer See LESS, FEWER.

field The phrase *the field of,* as in "He is majoring in *the field of* physics," is often unnecessary and may be omitted—particularly before the name of a well-known field. It is sometimes useful, however, when the field of study is uncommon or is something not ordinarily thought of as a field <*the field of* credit-card fraud>.

figure *Figure* meaning "conclude, decide, think" is sometimes thought to be rural, slang, or unsophisticated. But it is in fact standard, though rarely used in formal writing <*figured* there was no use in pursuing the matter>.

final *Final* is sometimes used with words like *end, destination,* or *outcome* to emphasize the notion of finality <we reached our *final* destination>. Such use is entirely standard, though occasionally criticized.

finalize Though avoided by many writers, *finalize* is used frequently in business and government writing <the budget will be *finalized*>, where it is regarded as standard. It is usually not found in more literary writing.

fine **1.** The adjective *fine,* meaning "good" or "superior," is sometimes thought to be empty or overused, but it continues to be employed by experienced writers <a *fine* day> <a *fine* wine>.

2. The adverb *fine,* meaning "very well, excellently," is sometimes considered colloquial or overly casual, but it is common in published prose as well as in speech and friendly correspondence <she looked *fine*> <it seemed to suit them *fine*>.

finished In British English, sentences such as "He wasn't *finished* yet" (in which *finished* is an adjective) are often disapproved in favor of the form "He hadn't *finished* yet" (where *finished* is a participle). Both are common in British and American speech, but less common in standard prose. When *finished* has an impersonal subject <the work is *finished*>, its use with forms of *to be* is never criticized. See also DONE; THROUGH.

fire off *Fire off* has been disparaged as journalistic or worse, but it is in quite widespread use to denote the idea of sending in haste or anger. Memos are the thing most commonly fired off.

firm **1.** The noun *firm,* in the technical sense, means a partnership of two or more persons not recognized as a legal person distinct from its members. A firm thus contrasts with a corporation, which is a body with the legal rights and liabilities of a person, although constituted by one or more persons. *Firm* is nonetheless frequently used to mean simply any business unit or enterprise, especially when the precise legal basis on which the business is established is irrelevant to the reader. Such use is entirely standard.

2. The adverb *firm* is usually found in just a few fixed phrases, such as *hold firm* and *stand firm. Firmly* serves for other adverbial uses <she held the child *firmly* in her arms>.

first and foremost This phrase has become a cliché as an introduction to a speech (as in, "*First and foremost,* let me thank the good people of this fair city"). It is, however, still in good standing as an occasional alternative to *primarily* or *primary* <what he wanted *first and foremost* was a good assistant>.

firstly When *firstly* is used to begin an enumeration, it is commonly followed by *secondly, thirdly,* and so on. Most writers and editors, however, prefer *first, second, third,* etc. The principle of consistency is preached, whichever series you use. But history shows that many fine writers have been more interested in making their point than in being consistent with *first* or *firstly*. Consequently many mixed enumerations can be found. It is nice to be consistent, but good writers sometimes mix their enumerating words and even phrases (such as *first of all, in the second place,* etc.).

fit, fitted Both *fitted* and *fit* are used for both past and past participle in the United States <he was *fitted* [*fit*] for a new suit> <the theory *fit* [*fitted*] all the facts>; only *fitted* appears to be used in British English. *Fit* seems to be somewhat more common in speech, *fitted* more common in print.

fix **1.** *Fix* in the senses "repair" and "prepare" is sometimes disapproved, but it is standard in less-than-formal prose <*fix* my watch> <*fix* some supper>.

2. The intransitive sense of *fix* meaning "to get set, be on the verge" (as in "we're *fixing* to leave soon") is used mostly in the South, though it occasionally finds its way into a national publication.

flack See FLAK, FLACK.

flair, flare Be careful with your spelling here. *Flair* is a noun meaning "talent" or "style," while *flare* is both a noun meaning "bright light" or "a spreading outward" and a verb meaning "to shine," "to break out," or "to spread outward."

flak, flack *Flak* was originally antiaircraft fire, and more recently hostile or unfriendly criticism. *Flack* was originally a press agent. Although *flack is* established as a variant spelling of *flak,* and *flak* is occasionally used for *flack,* we recommend that you use the original and still dominant spellings for each word.

flammable, inflammable These two words are synonyms. *Flammable* seems to be less common in British English than it is in American English. *Flammable* is always used literally <*flammable* liquid>; *inflammable* is occasionally used this way (to the chagrin of safety inspectors), but mostly it is used figuratively <his *inflammable* temper>.

flare See FLAIR, FLARE.

flaunt, flout *Flaunt* acquired its meaning "to treat with contempt" <*flaunting* the rules> from confusion with *flout,* which has always had this same meaning <*flouting* the rules>. If you use *flaunt* as a synonym of *flout,* you should be aware that many people will consider it a mistake. Conversely, *flout* is sometimes used to mean “to display ostentatiously” (as in “*flouted* their wealth”), but the standard term in such contexts is actually *flaunt*.

flautist, flutist Both *flautist* and *flutist* are used in American English for a musician who plays the flute, but *flutist* is by far the more common choice. British English favors *flautist*.

flounder, founder A person *flounders* by struggling to move or obtain footing <seemed to be *floundering* onstage), while a ship *founders* by filling with water and sinking <the ship *foundered* off the coast of Maine>. Extended senses are also in use <the firm had been *floundering* for some time> <it finally *foundered* in 1992>. Confusion of the two words sometimes occurs; be careful to keep them distinct.

flout See FLAUNT, FLOUT.

fluorine, fluorescent *Fluorine* and words derived from or related to it (like *fluorescent*) are often misspelled by transposing *uo* to *ou*. Watch out for this mistake.

flutist See FLAUTIST, FLUTIST.

folk, folks Either *folk* or *folks* can be used as an alternative to *people* in an appropriate context. *Folks* is used of people generally <but seriously, *folks*> and for one’s family <her *folks* weren’t home>. It is also used, although not as often as *folk*, for people of a particular class or kind <old *folks*>. *Folk* is somewhat more frequent in this sense <media *folk*> <country *folk*>. These uses are standard, although *folks* seems to be a tad breezier or more informal than *folk*.

following *Following* can be used as a preposition <*following* the lecture, tea was served>. Sometimes, however, it is used in such a way as to leave its meaning unclear: for example, "In March 1863, *following* the manifest intention of the British ministry to enforce the Foreign Enlistment Act more strictly, he went to Paris" (*Dict. of Am. Biog.*, 1929). If you use *following* as a preposition, make sure it cannot be misread as a participle.

foment See FERMENT, FOMENT.

fond *Fond*, when it is used with a preposition, is most often used with *of* followed by a noun phrase <*fond of* rice pudding> or a gerund <*fond of* traveling abroad>.

fondness *Fondness* is usually used with the preposition *for*, followed by a noun <had a *fondness for* argument> or a gerund <his *fondness for* carousing at night>.

foot *Foot* has two common plurals. The usual one is *feet*, the less usual is *foot*. The most common use of the plural *foot* is when it means a unit of measure; it normally occurs (where *feet* would not) joined to a number with a hyphen <an eight-*foot* ladder>. Both *feet* and *foot* occur between a number and an adjective; *feet* is more common in print <he was six *feet* nine inches tall>, *foot* occurring chiefly in speech (as in "a board about twelve *foot* long").

forbid When *forbid* is used with a preposition, *to* followed by the infinitive is the commonest choice <her mother *forbids* her *to* go>. *Forbid* is also used, although less often, with *from,* in which case it is followed by a gerund <the law *forbids* them *from* selling to minors>. *Forbid* is also occasionally used with a gerund not preceded by *from* <the rules *forbid* talking between partners>.

foreign plurals For a list of those most frequently disputed, see LATIN PLURALS.

foreword, forward Don't muddle these words. A *foreword* is a preface in a book; *forward* is a direction.

forget The past tense of *forget* is *forgot*; the past participle is *forgot* or *forgotten.* Both past participles are used in American English. *Forgotten* is more common, especially in print <we had *forgotten* the address>; *forgot* is somewhat more colloquial <he'd almost *forgot* how small the town was>. British English uses only *forgotten.*

formally, formerly There is no reason to confuse these words, although they are likely to sound pretty similar in dictated material. *Formally* means only "in a formal manner" <*formally* signed the bill into law>. *Formerly* means "at an earlier time" <*formerly* of this city>. If you are in doubt about meaning, check your dictionary.

former **1.** An old rule states that *former* refers to the first of two and *latter* to the second of two, and that neither should be used when three or more things are being discussed. In actual usage, however, we see a different pattern. *Former* and *latter* are certainly used when two items are being discussed, but they are also often used when three or more items are mentioned <delivered speeches in Denver, Fort Worth, and Memphis, accepting the nomination at the *latter* site>. The old rule is too restrictive. You may choose to use alternatives (such as *last* or *last-named* instead of *latter*) or repeat the word or phrase that *former* or *latter* might replace, and many writers do so. But as long as your meaning is clear and you do not interrupt the reader's train of thought, you should not feel compelled to substitute something else for *former* or *latter* just because more than two items are involved.

2. See EX-.

formerly See FORMALLY, FORMERLY.

formula The two plural forms, *formulas* and *formulae,* are both common and correct. You may use whichever one you prefer.

formulate *Formulate* is occasionally criticized as a pretentious substitute for *form* or *make*. It is, however, standard when the object is to imply greater complexity or more deliberate intent than *form* or *make* implies <*formulate* a policy>.

forte The noun *forte,* meaning "one's strong point," is commonly pronounced \ˈfȯr-tā\ or \ˈfȯr-tē\ (the last like *forty*), even though these pronunciations are considered by some less correct than \ˈfōrt\ or \ˈfȯrt\ (which are supposed to be closer to the French but are not). The adverb or adjective *forte,* meaning "loud," as used in music, is pronounced \ˈfȯr-tā\ or \ˈfȯr-tē\ and provokes no criticism.

fortuitous The sense of *fortuitous* meaning "lucky" <coming at a *fortuitous* time for us> is sometimes objected to but is nevertheless standard. A newer sense, "coming by a lucky chance" <our chances were improved by the *fortuitous* failure of our chief competitor>, is halfway between the "lucky" sense and the original "occurring by chance" sense. Only the original sense is likely to occur in a negative sentence <could not have been merely *fortuitous*>.

forward See FOREWORD, FORWARD.

founded *Founded,* when used with a preposition, is used most often with *on* <*founded on* high principles>. It is also used frequently with *in,* often to signify a date or place <*founded in* 1772>.

founder See FLOUNDER, FOUNDER.

freedom *Freedom* is used with a number of prepositions, but most often with *of* <*freedom of* choice>. Among the others are *for, from, in,* and *to* with the infinitive.

friend The preposition used with *friend* is most often *of* <a *friend of* mine>, less often *to* <a *friend to* young people>. *With* occurs in the phrases *be friends with* and *make friends with.*

friendly When *friendly* is used with a preposition, it is used most often with *to* <*friendly to* the administration>. Less frequently, it is followed by *with* <*friendly with* her> or *toward* <*friendly toward* Egypt>.

frightened The prepositions used after *frightened* are *of* and *by* <*frightened of* being left alone> <*frightened by* loud noises>, and less frequently *at* and *about* <*frightened at* the sound> <nothing to be *frightened about*>.

from whence *From whence* is a very old phrase (going back at least to 1388) that is still alive in both British and American English. Critics have argued that *from* is redundant, since the notion of *from* is already present in *whence* itself. The phrase is not as frequent as it was a century ago, but you can still use it if it sounds right <*from whence* they came>.

frown Of the prepositions used with *frown, upon* and *on* are the most frequent <critics *frowned upon* [*on*]

the idea>. Less often, *frown* is used with *at* <she *frowned at* her lover>.

fruitful When *fruitful* is used with a preposition, it is most often *of* <*fruitful of* meaningful debate>, less often by *in* <*fruitful in* that instance>, and occasionally *for* or *to* <*fruitful for* the novelist> <proved *fruitful to* pursue it>.

-ful Nouns ending in *-ful, such as cupful, spoonful,* and *capful,* normally form the plural by adding *-s* at the end: *cupfuls, spoonfuls, capfuls,* though variants such as *cupsful* and *teaspoonsful* are occasionally used.

full *Full* is very often followed by *of* <*full of* remorse>. The phrase *to have one's hands full,* however, is followed by *with* when it takes a preposition and is being used metaphorically <she *had her hands full with* her in-laws>.

fulsome The adjective *fulsome* can present a problem of ambiguity: two of its most frequently used senses mean very different things. In expressions such as "*fulsome* praise" or "a *fulsome* tribute," it can be hard to tell whether *fulsome* means "generous in amount, extent, or spirit" or "excessively complimentary or flattering." To avoid misinterpretation, be sure that the context in which you use the word makes the intended meaning clear or choose a different word.

further See FARTHER, FURTHER.

G

gage See GAUGE.

gainsay This synonym for *deny* is a somewhat literary word that usually occurs in negative contexts <his expertise cannot be *gainsaid*>.

gait, gate You should not misspell *gait,* "manner of walking," as *gate,* "door or opening in a wall or fence."

gambit A *gambit* is, in the original sense, a chess opening entailing the sacrifice of a minor piece. Although some insist on retaining this "sacrifice" aspect of its meaning even when the word is used outside of chess, *gambit* is most often used to mean "a calculated move" or "stratagem," with no implication of sacrifice <a legislative *gambit* to ensure the bill's passage>. The phrase *opening gambit,* felt by some to be redundant, is in frequent use and is standard.

gamble, gambol *Gamble,* "to play a game for money," and *gambol,* "to skip about," sound alike but are spelled differently.

gamut *Gamut,* meaning "an entire range or series," is often used in the phrase *run the gamut* <*ran the gamut* from praise to contempt>. Some caution against confusing it with *run the gauntlet* (see GAUNTLET, GANTLET), but such confusion does not appear to be widespread.

gantlet See GAUNTLET, GANTLET.

garb The noun *garb* in its literal sense most often denotes a highly distinctive outfit <in formal *garb*>. The verb *garb* occurs most often as a past participle <*garbed* in T-shirt and blue jeans>. Both uses are standard, despite the criticism that more straightforward words, such as *clothes* (noun) or *dress* (verb), are available.

gate See GAIT, GATE.

gauge Note the spelling of *gauge*. A common error puts the *u* before the *a*. The older spelling *gage* is now rarely used.

gauntlet, gantlet *Gauntlet* (from the French for "glove") is the usual spelling in the phrases *throw down the gauntlet* and *pick up the gauntlet*. Both *gauntlet* and *gantlet* (an early spelling variant), however, are used in the phrase *run the gauntlet* (*gantlet*), meaning "undergo a severe trial or ordeal" <*ran the gauntlet* of criticism and censure>. *Gauntlet* is more common in this usage, though purists claim—on mistaken etymological grounds—that *gantlet* is more correct. British English uses only *gauntlet* for all three phrases.

gay Ever since *gay* became the word of choice for homosexuals, many have bemoaned the loss of the traditional senses "merry," "bright," and "lively." The older senses, however, are still in regular use

<abandoned a sober traditional style for something more timely and *gay*> <*gay* sunny meadows>. Nevertheless, because of the more frequent use of *gay* in the "homosexual" sense, you may sometimes have to exercise care when using it in the traditional senses, and particularly when applying it to humans.

gender *Gender* meaning "sex" has become increasingly common in standard writing <has no relation to the writer's *gender*>. It is most frequently used as an attributive adjective where *sexual* might otherwise appear <*gender* identity> <*gender* roles>.

genealogy Most speakers pronounce *genealogy* \ˌjē-nē-ˈäl-ə-jē\, as though it were spelled *geneology*. Sometimes inattentive writers even spell it that way. Those whose pronunciation is more influenced by spelling (or who appreciate the word's Greek root *genea*) will tend to say \ˌjē-nē-ˈal-ə-jē\ (rhyming with *analogy*) or sometimes \ˌje-nē-ˈal-ə-jē\.

general consensus See CONSENSUS 2.

genuine The usual pronunciation of this word among educated speakers is \ˈjen-yə-wən\ or \ˈjen-yə-win\. But pronunciation with a long final vowel, \ˈjen-yə-ˌwīn\, is also found in most regions of the Unites States, especially in less educated speech.

get **1.** The past tense of *get* is *got* <she *got* a pencil from the desk>. The past participle is either *got* or *gotten* <they hadn't *got* the word> <he'd *gotten* up to leave>; you may pick whichever form seems more natural to you in a given context. The phrase *have gotten,* however, usually means that something has been obtained <the play has *gotten* good reviews>, while *have got* denotes simple possession <we haven't *got* the money>. See also HAVE GOT TO.

2. The pronunciation \'git\ has been a part of some American (and British) dialects since at least the 16th century and remains in widespread use, especially when *get* helps form the passive <he should *get* married> or is an imperative <*get* up!>. Nevertheless, some disapprove of this pronunciation.

get hold of, get ahold of The usual written form is *get hold of* <*get hold of* the representative>. When the phrase is written with the article *a,* the article may be separate from *hold* <*get a hold of* him> or attached to it <*get ahold of* him>. *Get ahold of* is more conspicuous with *ahold* as one word; the phrase is widespread in dialect, and is more common in speech than in writing.

gibe See JIBE, GIBE.

gift Use of this verb in the sense of "present" <*gifted* her with a necklace> is detested by many commentators, perhaps because gossip columnists use it. It has been in use since the 17th century and is standard, but is not very commonly used.

give credence to See CREDENCE, CREDIBILITY.

glamour, glamor The spelling *glamour* is much more common than *glamor,* though the latter remains a respectable variant in the U.S.

glance, glimpse *Glance* is a noun meaning (among other things) “a quick look” <a mere *glance* at the manuscript>; it is also a verb meaning (among other things) “to give a quick look” <*glanced* at his watch>. *Gimpse* as a noun means “a fleeting view or look” <caught a *glimpse* of a boat in the fog>; as a verb it means “to get a brief look at” <*glimpsed* them in the shadows>. When in doubt, see your dictionary.

glow When the verb *glow* is used with a preposition, *with* is the most common choice <the children *glowed with* excitement>. *Glow* is less frequently used with *about, at, from, in, into, of, over,* and *to* in various senses and constructions.

go and *Go and* is often used to emphasize a following verb <why did you have to *go and* do that?> without implying any actual motion, or *going* anywhere. It can be used without *and* as well <*go* jump in a lake!>. It has the flavor of speech and is seldom used in standard writing. See also TRY AND.

goes without saying Some critics advise writers that if something truly goes without saying, there is no need to say or write it at all; and if you do need to say it, the phrase *goes without saying* is inaccurate. Nevertheless, the phrase (first recorded in the late

19th century) continues in common and reputable use. See also NEEDLESS TO SAY.

good **1.** *Feel good, feel well.* The phrase *feel good* <I *feel good*> can express good health alone, or it can suggest good spirits in addition to good health. *Feel well* <yes, she *feels well*> tends to express good health. Somewhat similarly, *look well* <they both *look well*> suggests good health; but *look good* <he *looks good*> <it *looks good* on paper> refers not to health but to appearance. See also FEEL BAD, FEEL BADLY.

2. Use of *good* as an adverb (as in "we got 'em *good*!" or "listen *good*!") has been criticized since the 19th century. It is primarily a spoken form; in writing it occurs only in dialogue or in very informal contexts. The adverb *well* is used much more frequently in standard writing <the orchestra played *well* this evening>.

3. *Good* used as an intensifier in phrases like "a *good* 20 years" or "a *good* many soldiers" is entirely standard, though it has been questioned by some.

4. See as GOOD AS.

good and *Good and* functions as an intensive adverb <when I'm *good and* ready> <I can see you've been *good and* busy>. It is not found in formal writing. See also NICE AND.

goodwill, good will *Goodwill* can be spelled either as one word or as two. *Goodwill* occurs more frequently, but *good will* is also common.

grateful *Grateful* in its sense "appreciative" may be used with the prepositions *for* or *to*. In general, *grateful for* is used with benefits received <*grateful for* the advice>, *grateful to* with people <*grateful to* her>.

gray, grey Both spellings are correct and common. In American English, the preference is for *gray*, but *grey* is also widely used. The British have a very definite preference for *grey*.

grill, grille The word for a cooking surface that resembles a grating is spelled *grill*; the word for a grating that forms a barrier or screen, such as on the front end of an automobile, is spelled either *grille* or *grill*.

grisly, grizzly The adjective that means "inspiring horror or disgust" is usually spelled *grisly* <a *grisly* scene>; the adjective that means "somewhat gray" is spelled *grizzly* <the *grizzly* old combat veteran>, though it is often supplanted by the past participle *grizzled* <a *grizzled* beard>.

groom A prejudice against the use of *groom* to mean "bridegroom" exists in some quarters, the apparent reason being that *groom* has associations with the stable. Nevertheless, the "bridegroom" sense of *groom* is recognized as standard by all dictionaries, and there is no sensible reason to avoid its use.

grope *Grope* is used most often with *for* <*groped for* the light switch>. Less frequently, it is used with *after* <*groping after* something>, *into* <*groped into* the matter>, *through* <*groped* our way *through* the dark>, *to* <*groped* closer *to* a solution>, and *toward* <*groping toward* an understanding>.

grow Some still occasionally object to the "become" sense of *grow,* especially in the phrase *grow smaller* <the town had *grown smaller*>. This usage is nevertheless completely standard. Standard too is the "cause to develop" sense of *grow* <*grow* wheat>, though when applied to nonliving things <*grow* the economy> it has the ring of jargon.

guarantee, guaranty Some writers and critics formerly preferred *guaranty* for the noun and *guarantee* for the verb, but *guarantee* is now the usual choice for both.

guerrilla, guerilla Both spellings of this word for a type of soldier are reputable, though *guerrilla* (the spelling of the original Spanish word) is the more common form.

guts The sense of *guts* meaning "courage" is over a hundred years old, but it still makes some people uneasy. If you want to use an alternative you might choose *courage, mettle, pluck, spirit,* or *resolution.*

guttural This word is frequently misspelled *gutteral.* If you use it, remember that there are two *u*'s and no relation to *gutter.*

guy *Guy* has gained respectability over the years and is currently in common use in standard journalism. It can mean "man, fellow" or, when used in the plural, "persons, members of a group" (regardless of sex) <saw her and the rest of the *guys*>.

gynecology The most widespread pronunciation of *gynecology* among both physicians and laypeople uses the hard *g*: \ˌgī-nə-ˈkäl-ə-jē\.

gyp *Gyp,* which means "to cheat or swindle," is derived from a noun that is probably short for *Gypsy*. Its use may be offensive to some, though we have no evidence of ethnically derogatory use.

H

had better See BETTER 2.

had ought, hadn't ought These two phrases are regionalisms and are largely confined to speech and fictional dialogue. See also OUGHT 1.

had rather *Had rather* is a perfectly respectable English idiom dating from the 15th century <I *had rather* you not call me at work>. You can use it or the alternative *would rather* as you like.

hail, hale The spelling *hale* is the choice for the verb meaning "to compel to go" <he was *haled* before the court>. *Hale* is also the spelling used for the adjective meaning "healthy" (see HALE AND HEARTY). The spelling *hail* is correctly used for the noun and verb relating to icy lumps of precipitation and for the verb meaning "greet or call for" <*hailed* a cab> or "acclaim" <was *hailed* for her efforts>. It also occurs in the idiom "hail from" <*hails from* Maine>.

hairbrained Most often this word is spelled *harebrained* (after the long-eared mammal), but since the 16th century *hairbrained* has remained a regular if less frequent variant.

hale See HAIL, HALE.

hale and hearty If you use this cliché, mind its spelling—the final word is not *hardy*. See also HAIL, HALE; HARDY, HEARTY.

half **1.** When *half,* either noun or adjective, is followed by a singular noun it takes a singular verb <*half* of the balcony was unfilled> <a *half* share is to be granted>. When followed by a plural noun, *half* takes a plural verb <*half* of their assets go to charity> <*half* smiles were visible on their faces>. The underlying principle here is NOTIONAL AGREEMENT (see Glossary).

2. The phrase *a half a(n)* is mostly a spoken one that occurs in fixed phrases like *a half an hour* or *a half a dollar.* In writing, the preferred forms are *half a(n)* <in *half an* hour> and *a half* <found *a half* dollar in change>.

handful *Handful* has two plurals, *handfuls* and *handsful.* The first is the more common and the one usually recommended.

hands-on *Hands-on* (first recorded in 1969) has become part of the standard vocabulary <*hands-on* experience>, though some still consider it jargon. Our only recommendation is that you avoid it in contexts where it may raise a smile by suggesting physical groping more than practical involvement (as in "a *hands-on* feel for the customer").

hanged, hung *Hanged* (as the past and past participle of *hang*) is usually preferred when the verb has the sense "to hang by the neck until dead," and *hung* is the correct choice for all other senses of the word. Nevertheless, *hung* for execution by hanging has been in use for a couple of centuries, even among highly educated speakers and writers.

hangar The name for a building in which aircraft are housed is *hangar*, not *hanger*.

hanker *Hanker,* when used with a preposition, is most frequently combined with *after* <*hankered after* recognition>. Nearly as often, it is used with *for* <*hankered for* some ice cream> or with the infinitive <is *hankering* to be released>.

harass *Harass* is sometimes misspelled with two *r*'s, probably because of its similarity to *embarrass*. It has been pronounced with stress on the second syllable (\hə-'ras\) for quite some time, despite some critics' preference for initial stress (\'har-əs\).

hardly Expressions such as *can't hardly* and *hasn't hardly* are primarily speech forms that should be avoided in writing other than fictional dialogue. (Such expressions are not double negatives, but are the same in meaning as the positive: "could *hardly* stop shaking" and "couldn't *hardly* stop shaking" are essentially synonymous.) The expression *without hardly* sometimes appears in newspaper reporting <*without hardly* a trace of evidence>. See also DOUBLE NEGATIVE (in Glossary).

hardy, hearty These two words sound much alike and are vaguely similar in meaning, but they are not interchangeable. You may refer to "a hardy crop" or "a hardy flower" as against "a hearty soup" or "a hearty endorsement." If in doubt, consult your dictionary. See also HALE AND HEARTY.

hark back, harken back, hearken back *Hark, harken,* and *hearken* all essentially mean "to listen, listen carefully." All three are today used primarily with the word *back* to mean "to turn back to an earlier topic or circumstance." *Harken* is simply the predominant American spelling of *hearken*. Thus, you may use *hark back, harken back,* or *hearken back* and be correct in each case. The use of *hark* by itself to mean "hark back" is becoming more common.

has got See HAVE GOT TO.

hassle Though neither the noun <faced *hassles* from regulators> nor the verb <feared being *hassled*> is used in literary or formal prose, *hassle* is quite frequent in general prose, such as journalism. You may use it, if you need it, in writing of that kind.

have got to This phrase is listed as incorrect by various handbooks, but it has been used by many literary figures, both English and American, and Presidents Truman, Eisenhower, and Carter, among others <I *have got to* lay off the caffeine>. There is no reason to avoid it.

havoc See WREAK, WRECK.

he, he or she Discussion of what third-person singular pronoun to use in referring to a neutral preceding noun <the researcher should take *his or her* time> dates back to the 18th century, and more recently feminists and others have rediscovered the topics. The usual recommendation on how to avoid using *he* to stand for *he or she* is to cast the sentence in the plural <researchers should take *their* time>, to address the reader directly in the second person <you should take *your* time>, or to remove the pronoun altogether <the researcher should take time>. The double pronoun *he or she* works well at times (see the first example above), but using it repeatedly can create awkward prose. See also THEY, THEIR, THEM; AGREEMENT (in Glossary).

headquarter The verb *headquarter* is a relatively recent word, first recorded in 1903. Some still consider it incorrect. But in its usual use as a past participle <is *headquartered* in New York>, *headquarter* is perfectly standard. The rarer intransitive use <will *headquarter* in New York> is more likely to raise your reader's or listeners' eyebrows.

head up A person can either *head* a committee or *head up* a committee. Both uses are standard.

healthy, healthful A conventional distinction between these two words is that *healthful* means "conducive to health" <a *healthful* diet> and *healthy* means "enjoying or evincing health" <a *healthy* complexion>. Since the 16th century, however, *healthy* has been in standard use in both senses <a *healthy* diet can produce a *healthy* complexion>, and *healthful,* the rarer of the two words, has occasionally been used to mean "healthy" <a *healthful* face>. So if you observe the conventional distinction (which was introduced only in the 1880s), you are correct but in the minority; if you ignore it, you are correct and in the majority. *Healthy* is also commonly used to mean "considerable" <a *healthy* respect for statistics>.

heap *Heap* has been used to mean "a great deal" since the 16th century; it usually occurs in writing that has a conversational tone <a *heap* of trouble> <flavored with *heaps* of sugar>. The adverbial phrase *a heap* (as in "thanks *a heap*") strikes most readers as rustic, and is found in writing only as part of fictional speech.

hearken back See HARK BACK, HARKEN BACK, HEARKEN BACK.

hearty See HARDY, HEARTY.

heave In standard English *heave* has two past-tense and past-participle forms, *heaved* and *hove*. In nautical contexts, *hove* is used <they *hove* up the anchor>. A second nautical sense, "to move in an indicated way" <the skiff *hove* into harm's way>, is sometimes used more generally <the diner *hove* into view as we turned the corner>. All other applications generally require *heaved* <*heaved* the dirt into the hole> <the wagon *heaved* back and forth> <we *heaved* at the rope>.

height Although \'hīt\ is the usual pronunciation, \'hītth\ is not all that uncommon and can be found in educated speech. It may have been influenced by the usual pronunciation of *eighth*. If \'hītth\ is your natural pronunciation, you can stick with it, but you may sometimes be corrected. The spellings *heighth* and *highth*, though older than *height*, are no longer used.

help See CANNOT BUT, CANNOT HELP, CANNOT HELP BUT.

hence See FROM WHENCE.

he or she See HE, HE OR SHE.

her See I, ME.

herb Americans usually do not pronounce the *h* in *herb* (\ˈərb\), while Britishers normally do (\ˈhərb\), and Canadians are somewhat divided.

hers Although a few hundred years ago *hers* was frequently spelled with an apostrophe (as in "the book is *her's*"), in present-day use *her's* is considered a mistake.

herself See MYSELF.

hesitant *Hesitant* is often followed by *about* <*hesitant about* calling> or *to* and the infinitive <*hesitant to* get involved>. Less often, it is used with *in* <*hesitant in* asking customers if they need help>.

hiccup, hiccough *Hiccup* is the older and more common spelling, but *hiccough* (originating as a misunderstanding of *hiccup*) is in widespread and reputable use. Regardless of spelling, the word is pronounced so that it rhymes with *stickup*.

him See I, ME.

himself See MYSELF.

hinder When *hinder* is used with a preposition, the choice is usually *from* <wasn't *hindered from* publishing the attack>. Occasionally, *hinder* is used with *in* <was *hindered in* her work>. In the passive voice, *hinder* is often used with *by* <were *hindered by* high winds>.

hindrance **1.** *Hindrance* is sometimes misspelled *hinderance*. Watch out for it.

2. When used with a preposition, *hindrance* is usually used with *to* <a real *hindrance to* them>. Less frequently but still commonly, it is used with *of* <a *hindrance of* market efficiency>.

hint When used with a preposition, *hint* is usually used with *at* <*hinted at* the possibility>. Less frequently, it is used with *of* <*hinted of* things to come>. Occasionally it is also used with *about, against,* or *for.*

his or her See HE, HE OR SHE.

historic, historical *Historic* and *historical* are simply variants of each other; but over the course of more than 200 years they have tended to diverge somewhat. *Historical* is the usual choice for the broad sense "of, relating to, or based on history" <a *historical* perspective> <*historical* preservation>. *Historic* most commonly means "famous, important in history" <*historic* battlefields> <an *historic* occasion>. Note, too, that both *a* and *an* are used before *historic* and *historical,* with *a* being slightly more common. See A, AN.

hitherto *Hitherto,* sometimes thought to be old-fashioned, is in frequent current use. It means "up to this or that time" or "previously" <a treasure of *hitherto* unheard-of proportions>.

hoard, horde A *hoard* is a hidden accumulation <a *hoard* of paper clips>. A *horde* is a throng or swarm <a

horde of holiday shoppers>. Be careful with the spelling of these words.

hold See GET HOLD OF, GET AHOLD OF.

home, house *Home* and *house* are used interchangeably by many reputable writers, despite the admonition of some to avoid using *home* to mean "a building (for human habitation)."

home in See HONE IN.

Hon. See HONORABLE.

hone in Many consider *hone in* a mistake for *home in*. The verb *home* was first used (of homing pigeons) in the sense "to fly back home" in the late 19th century. An extended use of this verb began to occur in the 1920s, and by the early 1950s the phrase *home in* (or *home in on*) was well established. *Hone in* began to appear only in the mid-1960s but is today quite common. If you nevertheless want to play it perfectly safe, use *home in* (or *zero in*) instead.

honor When used with a preposition, the verb *honor* may take *by* or *with* <*honored by* a special dinner> <*honored with* a commemorative plaque>. It is used less frequently with *for, at,* or *in* <*honored for* his contribution> <*honored at* town hall> <*honored in* grand style>.

Honorable *Honorable* is a title of respect in American use. It is usually capitalized, preceded by *the,* and followed by a given name, initials, or some other title <the *Honorable* James P. Scott>. It may be abbreviated to *Hon.* when this seems appropriate. As to the question of who is entitled to an *Honorable* and who is not, we suggest you consult a "Forms of Address" table or a book on etiquette.

hoof Both the plurals *hoofs* and *hooves* are in standard use. *Hooves* is more common, especially in livestock journals, but *hoofs* is not rare.

hope The noun *hope,* when used with a preposition, is usually followed by *of* <no *hope of* a cure> or, a little less frequently, by *for* <our only *hope for* a victory>. Occasionally it is used with *in, on, over,* or *to* and the infinitive <put his *hopes in* them> <shouldn't place your *hopes on* it> <some *hope over* the possibility of reaching an agreement> <their only *hope* was *to* head off a vote>. It may also be followed by a clause <expressed her *hope* that more would participate in the program>. And it is used idiomatically in the phrases *in the hope(s) of, in hope(s) of, in the hope(s) that, in hope(s) that, with the hope(s) of, and with the hope that.*

hopefully The use of *hopefully* as a sentence adverb to mean "I hope" <*hopefully,* they'll reach an accord soon> is often criticized, even though this sense has been in sporadic use since the 1930s (and frequent use since the 1960s) and even though other similar sentence adverbs (such as *frankly, clearly,* and *interest-*

ingly) are accepted by everyone. Despite the objections, this sense of *hopefully* is in standard use.

horde See HOARD, HORDE.

house See HOME, HOUSE.

hove See HEAVE.

how *How* as a conjunction in the sense of *that* <told them *how* he had a job> has a long history of literary use, but in the 20th century it seems to be mostly confined to speech. See also AS HOW.

how come *How come* is a familiar phrase of obscure origin that was first noticed as an Americanism in the mid-19th century. Since then it has been frequently criticized and defended. Writers seem to find it a sassier and more emphatic way of asking *why*? <*how come* no one reported it?>. It is completely standard, at least outside of the most formal prose, and occurs frequently in journalistic writing.

however The main issue with *however* is its placement in the sentence. When used to mean "on the other hand" some critics hold that *however* should not begin a sentence. However, evidence of actual usage puts that view in doubt. The only valid point that one can make about the placement of *however* is that there is no absolute rule; each writer must decide each instance on its own merits, and place the word where it best accomplishes its purpose.

human Even though this noun has been standard for some 450 years <transmitted the virus to *humans*>, many people still believe it is an incorrect or inappropriate shortening of *human being*. You have absolutely no reason to avoid it.

hung See HANGED, HUNG.

I

I, me In informal speech and writing, such phrases as "It's *me* (*him, her*)," "Susan is taller than *me* (*him, her*)," "He's as big as *me* (*him, her*)," "Who, *me*?" and "*Me,* too" are generally accepted. In formal writing, however, it is safer to use *I* (*he, she*) after forms of *be* <it was *I* (*he, she*) who discovered the mistake> and after *as* and *than* when the first term of the comparison is the subject of the sentence <Ms. Williams is more knowledgeable than *I* on the subject> <he is, if the truth be told, as responsible as *I*>. See also BETWEEN YOU AND I; MYSELF; PRONOUN (in Glossary).

idea The belief—expressed mostly in college English handbooks—that *idea* means "mental conception, notion" and that its use in other meanings is vague or imprecise, may be disregarded. *Idea* is a word of many standard meanings and uses. It may apply to a mental image or formulation of something seen or known or imagined <described his *idea* of a ski house> <my *idea* of paradise>, to a pure abstraction <the *idea* of

holiness>, or to something assumed or vaguely sensed <the child's *idea* of time> <innovative new *ideas*>.

identical *Identical* often takes a preposition, usually *with* or *to* <was *identical with* the one found earlier> <were not *identical to* those of their sister villages>. *Identical with* is the older form, dating back to the 17th century. *Identical to* is of this century. Both are used with about equal frequency.

identify When *identify* is used with a preposition, it is usually *with* <groups that are *identified with* conservation>. Formerly the reflexive pronoun was generally used <he *identifies himself* with the lead character>, but today the pronoun is optional <he *identifies* strongly with the lead character>.

idiosyncrasy, idiosyncracy *Idiosyncrasy* is by far the more common spelling, but *idiosyncracy* has been in use for so long (350 years) that it must be considered a legitimate variant.

i.e., e.g. These two abbreviations are sometimes confused with each other. The usual error is the use of *i.e.* in place of *e.g.* To avoid it, remember that *i.e.* (an abbreviation for the Latin *id est*) means "that is"; *e.g.* (an abbreviation of *exempli gratia*) means "for example." Like *that is, i.e.* typically introduces a rewording or clarification of a statement that has just been made or of a word that has just been used <services provided by the government—*i.e.*, the Food and Drug Administration>. Like *for example, e.g.* introduces one or more examples that illustrate something stated directly or shortly before it <services provided by the government, *e.g.*, food and drug testing>. Neither abbreviation is generally italicized today. Both are normally followed by a comma in American texts.

if **1.** *If, whether.* Both *if* and *whether* are standardly used with such verbs as *doubt, see, ask, wonder, decide,* and *know* to introduce a noun clause <see *if* they will agree> <asked her *whether* she minded>. *Whether* tends to be used more often in formal contexts, perhaps because of the persistence of the notion that *if* is wrong. But there is nothing wrong with using *if;* its use after such verbs goes back to Shakespeare. Both *if* and *whether* are also sometimes used after an adjective <it is doubtful *whether* [*if*] it could succeed>.

2. *If* in the sense of "though" <an interesting *if* untenable argument> is sometimes questioned, but the usage is standard and in fact quite common.

3. *If* is often followed by a subjunctive verb, especially when the clause contains a condition that is clearly hypothetical or contrary to fact <*if* there were a simple rule to follow here, life would be easier>. The indicative is called for when the clause is clearly not hypothetical or identifies the truth <*if* there's one person who knows the answer, it's Packard>. The problem is that the dividing line between what is or could well be true and what is hypothetical or not true is not always clear—in fact it can often be an entirely subjective judgment made by the writer <but *if* France was [were] threatened, the situation would be serious>. See also SUBJUNCTIVE (in Glossary).

if and when This phrase has some standing in the legal field, but outside of the law it is frequently attacked as wordy. It nevertheless remains in common and respectable use <*if and when* they decide>, and you may employ it where it seems useful. The construction with *to* and the infinitive (as in "must choose *if and when to* get married") can be criticized on grounds of faulty PARALLELISM (see Glossary); try replacing the *if* with *whether* instead <*whether* and when to get married>.

if worst comes to worst See WORST COMES TO WORST.

illegible, unreadable The distinction to be made between these words is that *illegible* usually means "impossible to read, indecipherable" while *unreadable* usually means "extremely dull or badly written."

illicit See ELICIT, ILLICIT.

illusion See DELUSION, ILLUSION.

illustrate When *illustrate* is used with a preposition, it may be used with *by, in,* or *with* <is *illustrated by* the plight of the refugees> <as *illustrated in* the exchange of letters> <banners *illustrated with* words and images>.

imaginary, imaginative In ordinary use, these words are not often confused. In the context of art and literature, however, the words can sometimes be close in meaning. In such use, *imaginative* is more common, and it stresses what is produced by the imagination <*imaginative* designs> as distinct from what merely exists in the imagination, for which *imaginary* is the usual word <*imaginary* landscapes>.

immigrate See EMIGRATE, IMMIGRATE.

imminent See EMINENT, IMMINENT.

immune When *immune* is used with a preposition, *from* or *to* is usual <are *immune from* arrest> <*immune to* all pleas>; *against* is sometimes used <*immune against* smallpox>.

immunity When *immunity* is used with a preposition, the latter is most commonly *from* <granted *immunity from* further prosecution>. Less frequently, it is used with *against* or *to* <*immunity against* outside attacks> <*immunity to* smallpox>. Occasionally it is found with *in* or *for* <*immunity in* newborns> <*immunity for* past offenses>.

immure **1.** Do not confuse *immure,* "to enclose within walls," with *inure,* "to accustom to something undesirable." See also INURE.

2. When *immure* is used with a preposition, it is usually *in* <*immured in* the recesses of the library>. Less frequently, it takes *behind* or *within* <*immured* *behind* stacks of new orders> <*immured within* those prison walls>.

impact *Impact* as a verb meaning "to have an impact" <how did the news *impact* on the panel?> or "to have an impact on" <the best way to *impact* that market> was already being used in the 1950s, but only came into widespread use in the 1980s. It has been roundly criticized. You need not use this verb if you find it unappealing; another verb such as *affect, influence, impinge,* or *hit,* can usually be substituted. But *impact* with these meanings has become established in journalism and official writing, though not in literary use.

impatient When used with a preposition, *impatient* is most often followed by *of* <*impatient of* delay>. Less frequently, it is used with *for, to,* or *with* <*impatient for* the results> <*impatient to* get home> <*impatient with* the children>.

impeach **1.** When used with a preposition, *impeach* usually takes *for* <*impeached for* malfeasance>. Occasionally it is used with *on* <*impeached on* several counts>.

2. When used in reference to political misconduct, *impeach* in edited prose usually means "to charge (an official) with misconduct" <the vote to *impeach* was the prelude to two months of hearings in which the governor struggled to retain his office>. But in popular—mostly spoken—usage, *impeach* means "to remove from office" <*Impeach* the bum!>. The popular meaning is partly kept alive by the fact that both meanings can be read into many of the contexts that appear in print.

implicit *Implicit* is often used with a preposition, which is usually *in* <it was *implicit in* their demands>. In other senses and contexts, *implicit* is also used with *from, with,* or *within* <*implicit from* the beginning> <always only *implicit with* them> <a criticism *implicit within* the report>.

imply See INFER, IMPLY.

important **1.** *More important, more importantly.* Although opinion is divided as to which of these two phrases is preferable in sentences like "More *important(ly),* there is no time," the evidence from usage shows clearly that you can use either. Both are defensible grammatically and both are in respectable use; the choice is solely a matter of preference.

2. *Important* may be complemented by prepositional phrases beginning with *for, in,* or *to* <are *important for* us> <is *important in* such matters> <have been *important to* her>.

impose When used with a preposition, the transitive verb *impose* most often takes *on* (or *upon*) <*imposed* his views *on* the committee>. Much less frequently, *impose* is used with *against, around, as, between, from, in, into,* or *over.*

impossible This word is sometimes considered to be an ABSOLUTE ADJECTIVE (see Glossary).

impractical, impracticable *Impractical* is a 19th-century word that has, over the decades, outstripped the older (17th-century) *impracticable* in use, perhaps because it is easier to pronounce and spell. It may be applied to what has no practical value <an *impractical* device>. It is also used, as is *impracticable,* for what is not feasible <the logistics of the enterprise are completely *impractical* [*impracticable*]>.

impromptu See EXTEMPORANEOUS, IMPROMPTU.

improve When *improve* is used with a preposition, it is usually *on* or *upon* <it will be hard to *improve on* the first version>.

improvement The chief prepositions used with *improvement* are *on, in, of,* and *to* <an *improvement on* earlier efforts> <an *improvement in* her condition> <some *improvement of* their status> <*improvements to* the design>.

in, into The basic distinction between these two prepositions is simply stated: *into* is used with verbs of motion <moving *into* the light> <backed *into* a parked car>; *in* is used with verbs that show location <found the letter *in* the folder> <hid it *in* the closet>, but it is also used with some verbs of motion <spit *in* the ocean> <split *in* two>. Sometimes you can use either one <put the names *into* [*in*] a hat> <don't go *in* [*into*] the kitchen yet>, and in those instances remember that *into* gives more prominence to the idea of entrance.

in addition to Some disparage *in addition to* as a wordy alternative to *besides,* but *in addition to* is not always replaceable by *besides.* It may be usefully contrasted with another phrase <carried on *in addition to,* rather than as a substitute for, parental involvement> and it may be used to emphasize its literal sense <several new responsibilities, *in addition to* the basic ones>. It is most interchangeable with *besides* when it begins a sentence <*In addition to* relocating, she changed her name>.

in advance of *In advance of* can sometimes be replaced by the more concise *before,* but it can also be more specific then *before* and can carry more force <were urged to implement voting reforms *in advance of* the election>.

inasmuch as Some advise substituting the shorter *since, as,* or *because* for *inasmuch as.* But if you want a longer expression (writers do not always want to be brief), there is nothing wrong with *inasmuch as* <*inasmuch as* musical talent is part nature, part nurture>.

in back of See BACK OF, IN BACK OF.

in behalf of See BEHALF.

incentive When *incentive* is used with a preposition, it is usually *to* <as an *incentive to* finish it>; *for* is also common <the *incentive for* establishing the fund>. It is also occasionally used with *toward* <an *incentive toward* fostering economic cooperation>.

inchoate Some complain that the meaning of *inchoate* has expanded from "being only partly in existence or operation" to include "imperfectly formed or formulated, formless." This extended use is natural and probably inevitable, however: what is just begun is also unfinished, incomplete, and often also disorganized or incoherent.

incident *Incident* in the sense of "an action likely to lead to grave consequences" <a serious border *incident*> is regarded by some as an undesirable extension of the older meaning "a minor or unimportant occurrence." However, *incident* in the first sense has been in standard use since the early part of the 20th century.

incidental The usual preposition with *incidental* is *to* <problems *incidental to* a rapidly expanding economy>.

in . . . circumstances See CIRCUMSTANCES.

incite, insight Don't confuse or misuse these two words. *Incite* means "to urge on," while *insight* means "discernment" or "intuition."

include Contrary to the opinion of many language commentators, *include* may be and frequently is used when a complete list of items follows the verb <the book *includes* the usual preliminary matter, the text itself, and a bibliography and index>.

incongruous *Incongruous* may be used with the preposition *to* or *with* <must seem *incongruous to* his fans> <an attitude that was *incongruous with* what we knew of him>. Less frequently, it is used with *about, in,* or *on.*

in connection with The phrase *in connection with,* though sometimes disparaged as wordy, is in wide use <faced price increases *in connection with* the dollar's declining value>. The phrase can often be replaced by a shorter preposition such as *about, by, from, at, of, or concerning,* but not always.

incorporate When *incorporate* is used with a preposition, it is usually *in* or *into* <*incorporated* it *in* their motto> <*incorporate* the ideas *into* our system>.

incredulous, incredible *Incredible* means "impossible to believe" <an *incredible* story>; *incredulous* means "unwilling to believe, disbelieving" <an *incredulous* audience>. Although *incredulous* is sometimes used where *incredible* is expected, most writers restrict *incredulous* to its "disbelieving" sense, and we recommend that you do so as well.

inculcate When *inculcate* is used with a preposition, and the direct object denotes what is inculcated, the preposition is usually *in* or *into* <to subtly *inculcate in* the students the idea that learning can be fun> <had *inculcated* their values *into* us as children>. Occasionally *inculcate* is used with *with,* but then the sense of the verb is "to cause to be impressed" <tried to *inculcate* the children *with* American ideals>.

incumbent When the adjective *incumbent* is used with a preposition, it is usually *upon* or *on* <is *incumbent upon* us to act responsibly> <*incumbent on* the company's officers>.

independence When used with a preposition, *independence* is used with either *from* or *of* <*independence from* the electorate> <an *independence of* mind>.

independent *Independent,* when used with a preposition, is usually used with *of* <*independent of* the changes at city hall>.

Indian See NATIVE AMERICAN.

indifferent The preposition used with *indifferent* is almost always *to* <*indifferent to* pleas on moral grounds>.

individual Use of the noun *individual* to mean simply "person," where there is no obvious contrast of the person with a larger unit (such as society) or no obvious stress on some special quality, is often discouraged. But the evidence from usage shows that *individual* (noun) is most often used in contexts that do imply such a contrast <are you the *individual* I spoke with on the telephone?> or special quality <an *individual* with a long criminal record>.

indulge When *indulge* (intransitive or transitive) is used with a preposition, it is usually *in* <*indulged in* games> <*indulging* his interest *in* butterflies>. Transitive *indulge* may also be used with *with* <*indulged* myself *with* food>.

indulgent When *indulgent* is used with a preposition, it may be *in, of, to,* or *with* <*indulgent in* its use of color> <*indulgent of* his shortcomings> <*indulgent to* their leaders> <*indulgent with* the child>.

inedible, uneatable *Inedible* is a considerably more common word than *uneatable*. Otherwise, these two words are more or less interchangeable except in scientific contexts, where *inedible* is standard.

infatuated *Infatuated* takes *with* when it uses a preposition <*infatuated with* Italy>.

infectious See CONTAGIOUS, INFECTIOUS.

infer, imply *Infer* is mostly used to mean "to draw a conclusion, conclude" and is commonly followed by *from* <I *infer from* your letter that everything was satisfactory>. *Imply* is used to mean "to suggest" <the letter *implies* that the service was not satisfactory>. The use of *infer* with a personal subject in the sense of *imply* (as in "Are you *inferring* that I made a mistake?") is widely criticized as a confusion, though in any given context, in fact, the meaning is never in doubt. Further, the use is mostly oral and has seldom been a problem in edited prose in recent years. Certainly the recommended distinction is easy enough to observe, and doing so will win you favor.

infested When *infested* is used with a preposition, it is most often *with* <*infested with* lice> and less frequently *by* <*infested by* a new virus>.

infiltrate When *infiltrate* is used with a preposition, *into* is by far the most common <had *infiltrated into* the Mafia>. When the object is the one doing the infiltrating, *with* or *by* is used <*infiltrating* the organization *with* undercover agents> <a language *infiltrated by* foreign loan words>.

infiltration When *infiltration* is used with a preposition, it is usually *of* <the *infiltration of* enemy lines>; *into* is used somewhat less frequently <the *infiltration into* the language of foreign expressions>.

inflammable See FLAMMABLE, INFLAMMABLE.

inflict, afflict If you need to distinguish between these two words, remember that something is usually inflicted *on* (or *upon*) somebody <*inflicted* ethics training *on* employees annually>, whereas someone is usually afflicted *with* or *by* something <grandfather was *afflicted with* [*by*] gout>.

influence **1.** When the noun *influence* is used with a preposition, *of* is the usual choice; it typically introduces the influence itself <a check against the *influence of* television>. When the one influenced is being introduced, *on* or *in* is used <Seneca's *influence on*

English literature> <the *influence* of the Protestant ethic *in* capitalist society>. *Influence* is also used with *over, upon, among, for, from,* and *with.*

2. Pronouncing *influence,* noun or verb, with stress on the second syllable—\in-ˈflü-əns\—is more common in the South than elsewhere. A similar variation is found in *congruence;* some stress the first syllable and some the second, but in this case the variation is not specific to a particular region.

informant, informer An *informer* is usually someone who informs against someone else underhandedly, such as a spy or a police informer who gets paid for information. An *informant* is usually someone who informs in a neutral way or provides cultural or linguistic information to a researcher.

infringe *Infringe* as an intransitive verb is often followed by *on* or *upon* <*infringing upon* our rights>.

infuse When *infuse* is used with a preposition, it is usually *with* <*infused with* her personal vision>. Less frequently, *infuse* is used with *by* <*infused by* the spirit of the times>. When it means "introduce, insinuate," *infuse* can appear with *into* <a new confidence was *infused into* the team>. *Infuse* is also sometimes used with *in* <*infused* new life *in* him>.

ingenious, ingenuous *Ingenious* means "very clever" <an *ingenious* plan>, whereas *ingenuous* means "innocent and candid" <an *ingenuous* rural

friendliness>. Although these words were once synonyms, they are seldom confused today.

in hope(s) of, in hope(s) that See HOPE.

in line See ON LINE.

inoculate *Inoculate* has only one *n* (unlike *innocuous,* which has two).

in order to Writers are often told to shorten *in order to* to simply *to.* But *in order to* has its place in contexts where reduction to *to* would be ambiguous <it may be necessary *in order to* preserve them in a pure state>. In many contexts ambiguity is not a problem <took on the job *in order to* prove his worth> and *in order* could justifiably be dropped. But *in order to* is one of those phrases that many writers find useful for reasons of rhythm and emphasis. It is not good practice to delete *in order* reflexively in every instance.

in point of fact See FACT.

input This fashionable word, which has spread into general use from the world of computers, is sometimes criticized as jargon or bureaucratese. Most of the objections are directed at the noun when used in the sense of "advice, opinion, comment" <she got *input* from her associates>. Despite the objections the word continues to be popular, largely because precise synonyms seem to be lacking (*advice, opinion,* and *comment* included) and a longer phrase may often be the only alternative. Whether you use the word or not may depend on whether its faddishness or its conciseness has more weight with you.

inquire, enquire **1.** *Inquire* occurs more often than *enquire* in American English; when *enquire* does appear, it is usually in bookish or formal contexts. In British English, *enquire* appears about as often as *inquire.*

2. When *inquire* (or *enquire*) is used with a preposition, it is most often *about* or *into* <*inquired about* the horses> <we are *inquiring into* the situation>. Less frequently, *after, for, as to,* or *concerning* is used <*inquired after* his friend's parents> <he continues to *inquire for* any news about her> <*inquired as to* the progress of the talks> <are *inquiring concerning* your health>. When the person asked for information is the object, *of* is the usual preposition <*inquired of* her>.

inquiry, enquiry **1.** Both *inquiry* and *enquiry* are used in American and British English, with the *i* spelling occurring more often.

2. When *inquiry* and *enquiry* are used with a preposition, *into* is most often the choice <an *inquiry into* the cause of the mishap>. Less frequently, they are used with *about, as to, in, of, on,* or *with* in various relations and senses.

in regard to See REGARD.

in respect to, with respect to Both of these phrases are in current good use, mostly in academic writing.

With respect to is the more common <*with respect to* your last letter>. *In respect to* is primarily American, whereas the British tend to prefer *in respect of*.

inroad **1.** *Inroad* is generally used in the plural, but it also may appear in the singular <made little *inroad* into the market>.

2. When *inroad* is used with a preposition, it is most often *into* or *on* <serious *inroads into* Republican strongholds> <made deep *inroads on* cable TV's monopoly>. Less frequently, *inroad* is used with *in, upon, against, among,* or *with.*

insanitary See UNSANITARY, INSANITARY.

insensitive When *insensitive* is used with a preposition, it is generally *to* <*insensitive to* the demands of the public>.

inseparable When used with a preposition, *inseparable* takes *from* <a precept that is *inseparable from* the notion of freedom>.

inside of *Inside of,* most often used with expressions of time <*inside of* two hours>, is a somewhat informal but nevertheless standard preposition. *Inside* without *of* is more common in written English, however. See also OUTSIDE OF.

insight When *insight* is used with a preposition, the choice is usually *into* <*insight into* the matter>. Occasionally *insight* can be used with *about, as to, in, on, regarding,* or *to*. See also INCITE, INSIGHT.

insignia *Insignia* is used both as a plural and as a singular. Some insist on the Latin *insigne* for the singular, but this form is rarely used (and may seem pretentious). The plural *insignias* has also become common.

insist When *insist* is used with a preposition, it is usually *on* or (less often) *upon* <*insisted on* this point>. As a transitive verb, *insist* takes a clause as its object <Mr. Bergin *insists that* he has nothing to cover up>.

inspire When *inspire* is used with a preposition, it generally is used with *by* and the verb form is usually the past participle <was particularly *inspired by* the Romantics>. *Inspire* is also used, and not just as a past participle, with *in, to,* or (less frequently) *with* <to *inspire* confidence *in* him> <were *inspired to* fight it> <*inspiring* her *with* thoughts of becoming a veterinarian>.

instil, instill **1.** *Instill* is more common in American English, whereas British English favors the single *l* (although it is always doubled in the inflected forms *instilled* and *instilling*).

2. When instill (or *instil*) is used with a preposition, it is most often *in* <*instilled* the work ethic *in* him>. Less frequently *into* is used, and even less frequently *with, among, through,* or *without*.

instruct When *instruct* is used with a preposition, the one that occurs most frequently is *to* followed by an infinitive <was *instructed to* contact them>. *Instruct* is almost as frequently used with *in* <were *instructed in* the goldsmith's art>, occasionally with *as to* or *for*.

insure See ENSURE, INSURE, ASSURE.

intend *Intend* may be followed by an infinitive <never *intended* to upset them>. It may be followed by a direct object and an infinitive phrase <apparently *intended* the money to go to charity>. It may be followed by a gerund <the parents *intended* leaving the children with a relative>. It may be followed by a clause, with or without *that*; the verb in the clause will be a subjunctive or the equivalent of a subjunctive <events unfolded the way she *intended* they should>. Finally, *intend* may take a prepositional phrase introduced by *for* <not *intended for* consumer use>. In speech and speechlike writing, it is sometimes followed by *on* and a gerund (as in "I don't *intend on* answering her anytime soon"). See also DESIGN, INTEND.

intensive, intense These two words have evolved along different lines in this century. Today *intense* is generally limited to describing some inherent characteristic <*intense* pleasure> <*intense* heat>. *Intensive,* on the other hand, usually connotes something that is applied from the outside <*intensive* training> <*intensive* screening>.

intent, *noun* See INTENTION 1.

intent, *adjective* When the adjective *intent* is used with a preposition, it is usually *on* <*intent on* their work>. Less frequently, it is used with *upon* <*intent upon* finding them>, and even less frequently with *in* or *to* and the infinitive.

intention **1.** *Intention* and *intent* are often used very nearly interchangeably. But in general *intention* implies simply what one has in mind to do or bring about <announced his *intention* to marry>, while *intent* suggests clearer formulation or greater deliberateness <the clear *intent* of the statute>.

2. When *intention* is used with a preposition, it is most often *of,* which is followed by a gerund or a noun <with the *intention of* signing it later> <the *intentions of* the administration>. Almost as frequently, *intention* is used with *to* and the infinitive <the group's *intention to* halt the action>. *Intention* has also been used with *against, behind,* and *toward.*

in terms of *In terms of* is a compound preposition that emerged in the 1950s and has remained popular ever since <thinks of everything *in terms of* money>. Some say that it is imprecise or overused and that you should substitute a simple preposition for it, such as *by, with,* or *about.* If you seek to do so, however, you will likely find yourself making additional revisions, since a one-to-one exchange is not always available. *In terms of* seems to be one of those expressions whose imprecision is its greatest virtue—writers do not always want to be precise. There will be times when a reworking of your sentence will improve it, but there is no need to make a strict policy of avoiding *in terms of.*

interpretative, interpretive These words are synonyms. *Interpretative* is older by a century or so, but in recent use the shorter *interpretive* has become the more common of the two. Both forms are standard.

intervene *Intervene* is used with a variety of prepositions. It occurs most often with *in* <having authority to *intervene in* such disputes>. Less frequently, it is used with *between* or *with* <a lucidity that *intervenes between* episodes of derangement> <she *intervened with* the school principal to make an exception>. It has also been used with *after, against,* and *into.*

in the course of See COURSE.

in the event that See EVENT.

in the hope(s) of, in the hope(s) that See HOPE.

into **1.** For a discussion of distinguishing between *in* and *into,* see IN, INTO.

2. *Into, in to.* In a sentence such as "Turn this form *in to* your department head," the adverb *in* followed by the preposition *to* is not to be confused with or carelessly replaced by the preposition *into.*

introduce When *introduce* is used with a preposition, it is usually used with *to* or *into* <will serve to

introduce you *to* the subject> <after *introducing* the compound *into* the test material>. It has also been used with *among, at, between, for, in, round,* and *within.*

intrude When *intrude* is used with a preposition, the choice most often is *into* <*into* which *intrudes* a granite dome> or, slightly less frequently, *on* (or *upon*) <*intruding on* the rival gang's turf>. It is also occasionally used with *between* or *in.*

inundate When *inundate* is used with a preposition, *with* is usual <*inundated with* phone calls>. Less often, *inundate* is used with *by* <a scoop of vanilla *inundated by* cherries and sauce>.

inure *Inure,* when used with a preposition, almost always takes *to* <*inured to* pain>. See also IMMURE 1.

invite The noun *invite* has been in use for more than 300 years, but it is criticized by some as slang. It remains standard, though it does tend to have a light or humorous quality and is not used in formal prose <thanks for the *invite*>.

invoke See EVOKE, INVOKE.

involve When *involve* is used with a preposition, it is most often *in* <the right of Congress to *involve* the nation *in* war>. It is also used often with *with* <was *involved with* a married man>.

invulnerable This word is sometimes considered to be an ABSOLUTE ADJECTIVE (see Glossary).

iridescent This is sometimes misspelled *irridescent.* Like its close relative *iris,* the word should have only one *r.*

irregardless This adverb, apparently a blend of *irrespective* and *regardless,* originated in dialectal American speech in the early 20th century. It has continued in spoken use, and occasionally finds its way into edited prose. But *irregardless* is still a long way from winning general acceptance as a standard English word. Use *regardless* instead.

irrelevant This word is sometimes misspelled (and mispronounced) *irrevelant,* where the *l* and *v* are transposed.

is because See BECAUSE 1; REASON IS BECAUSE.

isolate When *isolate* is used with a preposition, the choice is usually *from* <*isolated from* her family>. Occasionally it is used with *in, by,* or *with.*

is when, is where See WHEN, WHERE.

it For *it* in reference to preceding ideas, topics, sentences, or paragraphs, see THIS.

iterate See REITERATE.

its, it's These two forms are sometimes mistakenly interchanged. *It's* is the contraction of *it is* and *it has* <*it's* not enough to simply apologize>. *Its* is a possessive pronoun <the earth and *its* atmosphere>.

it's me See I, ME.

-ize Almost any noun or adjective can be made into a verb by adding *-ize* (e.g., *hospitalize, familiarize, idolize*). Many technical terms are formed this way (*oxidize, crystallize*), as are verbs of ethnic derivation (*Americanize*) and verbs derived from proper names (*bowdlerize, mesmerize*). People have always complained about new words formed this way and they still do: *finalize* and *prioritize* are two fairly recent ones that have been criticized. Remember that some *-ize* words are special or technical terms regularly used in a particular field or profession. No matter how strange these may seem, they should not be avoided in materials intended for the specialists.

J

jealous When *jealous* is used with a preposition, it is usually used with *of* <is *jealous of* her friend's new relationship>.

jewelry This word is sometimes pronounced \'jü-lə-rē\ (a transposed form of \'jü-əl-rē\), but this is not yet a widely accepted pronunciation. See also REALTOR.

jibe, gibe The distinction between *jibe* and *gibe* is not as clear-cut as many seem to think. *Jibe* is the more common spelling. It is used primarily for the verb meaning "to be in accord, to agree" <their views

jibe with ours>. But it is also used as a variant of *gibe* for the verb meaning "to utter taunting words, to deride or tease" <*gibed* [*jibed*] at her about it> and for the noun meaning "a taunting remark, jeer" <a gentle *gibe* [*jibe*]>. Though *gibe* is occasionally used as a variant of *jibe* (as in "the two schedules *gibe*"), most still consider this use an error.

join 1. *Join* is used with any of several prepositions, most often *in, to,* or *with.* When *in* is used, it is followed by a noun <*joined in* marriage> or gerund <*joined in* singing>. *To* and *with* both occur in many situations <her grieving spirit, *joined to* her physical pain, caused her to do it> <a series of images *joined with* narrative captions>. When *join* is being used of persons, *with* is the more common preposition <we *joined with* another group>.

2. Some disapprove the phrase *join together,* considering it a redundancy. It is primarily a spoken rather than a written idiom, in which the purpose of *together* is to add emphasis <let us *join together* in honoring her memory>, but it is nevertheless standard.

judgment, judgement Both spellings have been in use for centuries. *Judgment* is currently more common in the U.S., *judgement* in Britain.

judicial, judicious *Judicial* has to do primarily with judges and the law <the *judicial* branch of the government>, while *judicious* relates to sound judgment of a general kind <a fair and *judicious* critic>. The use of *judicial* in the sense of "judicious," while standard, has been criticized as an error but is rare now.

juncture *Juncture* is used especially to denote an important or critical point brought about by a concurrence of circumstances or events <an important *juncture* in our country's history>, but also often simply to mean "a point in time" <at this *juncture,* the company's prospects look good>. Some criticize the latter use as pompous, suggesting that *point* or *time* would work as well, but the criticism seems to have had little effect on published prose.

junior, senior Unlike *major, minor, inferior,* and *superior,* the adjectives *junior* and *senior* are regularly preceded by *more* and *most* <the *most junior* member> <a *more senior* position>. They function in this capacity as IMPLICIT COMPARATIVES (see Glossary). See also MAJOR.

just As an adverb, *just* has many uses, almost all of which have a somewhat informal quality. It can mean "exactly" <*just* right>, "very recently" <someone *just* called>, "barely" <*just* in time>, "immediately" <*just* west of here>, "only" <*just* a reminder>, "very" <*just* wonderful>, and "possibly" <it *just* might work>. Handbooks on writing occasionally disparage one or more of these senses (the "very" sense, in particular, has often been criticized), but all of them occur commonly in writing that is not especially formal.

justify When *justify* is used with a preposition, it often occurs with *in* or *by.* When *by* is used, it is usually followed by a noun <an action *justified by* customer responses>, less often by a gerund <to *justify* himself *by* claiming ignorance>. Less frequently, *justify* is used with *as* or *to* <forced to *justify* it *as* a viable enterprise> <sought to *justify to* herself her decision>. *Justify* is also frequently followed by *on the ground(s)* <is *justified on the grounds* of states' rights>.

K

ketchup See CATSUP, KETCHUP, CATCHUP.

kick off *Kick off,* once considered slang, now occurs commonly in written English. Its most characteristic use is in describing the beginning—often ceremonial—of large-scale public events or activities <will *kick off* the campaign>. However, its tone is not solemn.

kid The "child" sense of *kid* <the *kid* on the pro golf tour> is sometimes criticized as unacceptable, even though it has been used in print for nearly 400 years. It has an informal quality, which means it is suited to most contexts.

kilometer In North American speech, *kilometer* is most often pronounced with primary stress on the second syllable. This pronunciation is also heard frequently in British speech. Those who object say that the first syllable should be stressed as it is in *centimeter, millimeter,* etc. However, second-syllable stress has a long history of use, and it shows no sign of receding.

kin The usual sense of *kin* is "relatives" <considered them close *kin*>. But it also is occasionally used to mean "kinsman" <he's no *kin* of mine>. The singular *kin* is not new (it was being used in the 13th century), but it is uncommon enough to draw attention to itself. See also KITH AND KIN.

kind 1. *These* (or *those) kind* (or *sort) of.* Most of the standard handbooks and usage books state the following rule: Use *this* or *that* with singular *kind* or *sort* and follow *of* with a singular noun <*this kind of* argument>; use *these* or *those* with plural *kinds* or *sorts* and follow *of* with a plural noun <*these kinds of* warnings>. But this advice presents an unrealistically narrow set of options; real usage is more complex. Both *kind* and *sort* are often found in the singular preceded by a singular and followed by a plural <*the kind of* questions that must be asked> <*any sort of* contingencies>, and in the singular preceded by a plural and followed by a plural <*these sort of* people> <*those kind of* letters>. And *kinds* and *sorts* are followed not only by plurals but also by singulars <*several kinds of* decision making>. Despite these usages, the issue is a bugbear of American handbooks on writing, and you should be aware that any deviation from the common rule may be noticed with disfavor by some critic.

2. See KIND OF, SORT OF; KIND OF A, SORT OF A.

kindly *Kindly* is used both as an adjective <a *kindly* smile> and as an adverb <he smiled *kindly*>. It sometimes serves as a synonym of *please* <would you *kindly* refrain from doing that?>. The "please" sense is sometimes criticized as outmoded, but writers and speakers continue to find it useful and effective.

kind of, sort of *Kind of* and *sort of* appear in print mostly in fictional speech or in prose written in a light or familiar style <we just *kind of* took it on faith> <I always *sort of* liked him>.

kind of a, sort of a This English idiom has been around for a few hundred years but began to be criticized early in this century. Most modern critics advise omitting the *a,* and most writers do so. Still, there never has been a sound reason for questioning the less common idiom. If it is your idiom, there's no need to avoid it, especially in speech or in informal writing <some *kind of a* joke> <what *sort of a* person is she?>.

kith and kin This alliterative phrase—some would label it a cliché—is said by those who know its history to mean not "kinsfolk" but rather "countrymen and kinsfolk." However, the "kinsfolk" sense is now the more common.

kneel The past tense and past participle of *kneel* can be either *knelt* or *kneeled. Knelt* today occurs a little more frequently than *kneeled* <*knelt* [*kneeled*] before the altar>.

knit, knitted The past tense and past participle of *knit* can be either *knit* or *knitted* <a *knit* [*knitted*] shirt> <he *knitted* [*knit*] his brows in concentration>. *Knit* is definitely preferred, however, with such adverbs as *closely* and *tightly* <a closely *knit* family>.

kudo, kudos Some claim that since *kudos* is a singular word (derived from the Greek *kydos,* "fame, renown"), it cannot be used as a plural, and thus the word *kudo* is impossible. But *kudo* does exist, though it is far more often used in the plural than the singular <various *kudos* and other compliments>; it is simply one of the more recent words (*cherry* and *pea* are older examples) created by back-formation from another word misunderstood as a plural. While it is now standard, it has not yet penetrated the highest range of scholarly writing or literature.

L

labor See BELABOR, LABOR.

lack *In* and *for* are the prepositions used with the verb *lack* <*lacking in* decorum>; *for* usually appears in negative constructions <does not *lack for* supporters>. Both are often omitted <*lacking* decorum> <does not *lack* supporters>.

laden When *laden* is used with a preposition, the choice is almost always *with* <*laden with* goods>.

lady *Lady* is one of the fine old words of English. In the 19th century, after perhaps 1100 years of use, it began to be subject to criticism (as vulgar, affected, common, biased as to class, etc.). It has been long used as a polite way of referring to a woman <is the *lady* of the house in?> but many disapprove such use, finding it sexist or condescending. *Woman* is now the safest and usual choice, a notable exception being in the phrase *ladies and gentlemen,* which remains in very common use.

lament The verb *lament,* when used with a preposition, is used with *about, for,* or *over* <was *lamenting about* the situation with her daughter> <they *lamented for* her> <started to *lament over* the flood damage>. *About* and *over* can often be omitted <was *lamenting* the situation>.

last Some writers make the distinction that *last* means "final" and *latest* means "most recent." Others admit that both words can mean "most recent" <his *last* book> <his *latest* book> but insist that only *latest* conveys this meaning unambiguously. The context usually makes clear what sense of *last* is intended; if for some reason that clarity is missing from something you have written, you may want to substitute *latest* (or *final*).

late When should we stop referring to a dead person as *the late*? Ten years? Twenty years? Fifty years? The phrase is in fact generally applied to people whose lives were recent enough to exist within the living memory of the writer or speaker. Other than that, there is no hard-and-fast rule. See also WIDOW, WIDOWER.

Latin plurals The use of the plurals of foreign words—mostly, but not all, Latin—as singulars is a recurrent issue. For discussions of individual cases, see AGENDA; CRITERION, CRITERIA; CURRICULUM; DATA; DICTUM; EROTICA; MEDIA; MEMORANDUM; PHENOMENA; STRATA, STRATUM; TRIVIA.

latter See FORMER 1.

laudable, laudatory Very occasionally these words are confused, with *laudatory* used for *laudable*. *Laudable* means "deserving praise, praiseworthy" <*laudable* attempts to help the poor>, while *laudatory* means "giving praise, praiseful" <a *laudatory* book review>.

lay, lie *Lay* has been used as an intransitive verb meaning "lie" since the 14th century (as in "tried to make the book *lay* flat," or "*lay* down on the job"). By the last third of the 18th century, however, it was being regarded as a mistake. Since then schoolteachers and critics have succeeded in eliminating the use from most literary and learned writing, but it persists in familiar speech and in casual writing. Part of the problem lies in the confusing similarity of the inflected forms of the two words (*lay*'s past tense and past participle are both *laid; lie*'s are *lay* and *lain* respectively). Although many people will continue to use *lay* for *lie,* anyone who has invested effort in maintaining the distinction is likely to judge you unfavorably if you use it.

lead, led The past tense and past participle of the verb *lead* is spelled *led* <*led* his opponent in early returns> <were *led* to believe otherwise>. A common mistake is to spell it *lead*. See also MISLEAD, MISLED.

lean **1.** In British English both *leant* and *leaned* are used for the past tense and past participle. In American English, *leaned* is used almost exclusively.

2. When *lean* is used with a preposition, the preposition is most often *on* <*leaned on* the counter>. *To, toward* (or *towards*), *upon, in, against, into, out of,* and *over* are also common.

leap *Leaped* and *leapt* are interchangeable both as the past tense <he *leaped* [*leapt*] over the ditch> and past participle <the song has *leapt* [*leaped*] to the top of the charts> in American English. In British English, *leapt* is the more common choice.

leary See LEERY, LEARY.

leave, let **1.** Should you say "*leave* me alone" or "*let* me alone"? Our evidence shows that, despite some criticism, the phrases have long been used interchangeably.

2. *Leave* in the sense of "let" followed by a pronoun and an infinitive without *to* <*leave* it be> is a mostly spoken idiom used occasionally in writing for humorous effect. It is not often criticized in British English, but American commentators generally dislike it.

3. See LET.

led See LEAD, LED.

leery, leary **1.** *Leery* and its less common variant *leary* have been in use for nearly 300 years. Perhaps because the word first appeared in thieves' cant, it was long regarded as slang. Today the word is quite common and is completely standard.

2. When *leery* (or *leary*) is used with a preposition, it is most likely to be *of* <*leery of* such pronouncements> or, less frequently, *about* <*leery about* discount offers>.

legitimate, legitimize Some have questioned the need for using *legitimize* (first recorded in 1848) when the older verb *legitimate* (first recorded in 1586) remains available. The use of *legitimize* (and the less common *legitimatize*) has certainly increased in the 20th century <the assault *legitimized* Republicans' call for an arms buildup>, but *legitimate* is still common <serves only to *legitimate* racial intolerance>.

lend See LOAN, LEND.

lend credence to See CREDENCE, CREDIBILITY.

less, fewer The traditional view is that *less* is used for matters of degree, value, or amount, and that it modifies nouns that refer to uncountable things <*less* hostility> <*less* clothing> while *fewer* modifies numbers and plural nouns <*fewer* students> <*fewer* than eight trees>. However, *less* has been used to modify plural nouns for centuries and today is actually more likely than *fewer* to be used of distances <*less* than 100 miles>, of sums of money <*less* than $2,000>, or in certain fixed phrases <in 25 words or *less*>. In other contexts, the traditional rule is a safe guide.

lesser **1.** The adjective *lesser,* sometimes thought to be a double comparative like *worser,* is in fact a standard comparative of *little.* It is used to indicate a difference in value or importance <a *lesser* woman would have caved in> <the *lesser* of the two piano works>. It is also sometimes used of numerical quantities where *smaller* or *lower* is more usual <took the *lesser* amount>. And it is used of size in the names of various plants and animals <*lesser* celandine> <*lesser* yellowlegs>.

2. The adverb *lesser* is today limited to modifying past participles—especially *known*—to which it may or may not be joined by a hyphen <one of the *lesser-known* authors>.

lest This conjunction is almost always followed by a verb in the subjunctive mood <hesitant to speak out *lest* he be fired>. It can also be followed by a *should* clause, though this was more common in the past than it is now <worried *lest* she should be late>. Occasionally a writer follows *lest* with a verb in the indicative mood (as in "*lest* the lesson is lost on us"), but this is liable to be regarded as a mistake.

let **1.** For a discussion of distinguishing between *let* and *leave,* see LEAVE, LET.

2. Is it preferable to say "*Let's* you and I get together" or "*Let's* you and me get together"? Both expressions are justifiable on historical grounds; however, you will probably not need either in anything you write that is more formal than casual speech.

3. The negative of *let's* is formed in three ways: *let's not,* which is widely used; *don't let's,* which is chiefly found in British English; and *let's don't,* which is used in speech and casual writing.

let's See LET 2, 3.

liable, apt, likely Both *liable* and *apt,* when followed by an infinitive, are used nearly interchangeably with *likely. Apt* and *likely,* however, are common in situations having a positive or neutral outcome <he's *likely* [*apt*] to be praised> or a negative outcome <is *apt* [*likely*] to falter>. *Liable,* on the other hand, is generally limited to situations having a negative outcome <is *liable* to get lost>.

liaison With its French origin and unusual sequence of vowels, *liaison* tends to be troublesome to pronounce. The two most common pronunciations are

\ˈlē-əˌzän\ and \lē-ˈā-ˌzän\. The variant \ˈlā-əˌzän\ is well entrenched in the military, but in other circles it is often regarded as an error.

The spelling of *liaison* also gives many people trouble, the tendency being to drop the second *i.* Watch out for it.

library For pronunciation, see FEBRUARY.

lie See LAY, LIE.

lighted, lit Both *lit* and *lighted* are acceptable and standard as the past tense and past participle of the verb *light.* Both forms have been used for centuries and currently appear with about equal frequency <rockets *lighted* [*lit*] up the sky> <a smile *lit* [*lighted*] up her face>.

lightning *Lightning* very often gets an extra *e* (*lightening*). Watch out for this mistake.

light-year Some have criticized the use of *light-year*—a unit of astronomical distance—to mean "a very long time" (as in "that was *light-years* ago"), since in figurative use *light-year* is generally restricted to the sense "a very great distance," with the distance referred to typically being more cultural than physical <we are *light-years* behind the Japanese>.

like **1.** *Like, as, as if. Like* has been used as a conjunction meaning "as" <it was well done, *like* you'd expect> and "as if" <looks *like* it will rain> for more than 600 years, though it was fairly rare until the 19th century, when an increase in use provoked critics to censure it. Though criticism persists even today, the usage has never been less than standard, even if more often spoken than written. Someone writing in a formal prose style may well prefer to use *as* or *as if* or to recast the sentence.

2. *Like, such as.* Should you write "cities *like* Chicago and Des Moines" or "cities *such as* Chicago and Des Moines"? You are in fact free to use either one or to change the latter to "*such* cities *as* Chicago and Des Moines."

liked to See LIKE TO, LIKED TO.

like for *Like for* is fairly common in spoken American English, especially as part of a request (as in "we'd *like for* you to come"), but you will not have much need for it in ordinary prose.

likely The use of *likely* as an adverb <he will *likely* be elected> without a qualifier such as *more, most, very,* or *quite* has been criticized as unidiomatic. But in fact the use is an old one, dating back to the 14th century, and is standard today. See also LIABLE, APT, LIKELY.

liken The verb *liken* takes the preposition *to* <*likened* it *to* putting a fox in charge of the henhouse>.

likes of The phrase *the likes of,* disparaged by many on uncertain grounds, goes back more than 200 years and is standard. It has two principal uses. In one, it takes a single object (often a pronoun) and carries overtones of disparagement <have no use for *the likes of* you>. In the other, it takes a multiple object (usually a list of names), means essentially "such people as" or "such things as," and carries no disparaging connotations <reads *the likes of* Jane Austen and Robert Browning>. *The like of* is also sometimes used, and it is probably a better choice when the reference is to a single object and no disparagement is intended <an achievement *the like of* which we have not often seen>.

like to, liked to Both of these phrases mean "came near (to), almost" (as in "I *liked to* die!"). Though they have had a long and distinguished literary career, since the first part of the 20th century they have been primarily used in speech rather than writing. In the United States in particular, they are associated with uneducated or old-fashioned speech, and you will not need them in ordinary prose.

lit See LIGHTED, LIT.

literally *Literally* means "in a literal sense or manner" <took the remark *literally*> or "actually" <was *literally* insane>. But it is also used as an intensifier to mean "in effect" or "virtually" <she *literally* flew up the stairs> <the performance *literally* brought the house down>. Though the latter use is often criticized as nonsensical, it is not supposed to make sense, but rather only to interject a bit of hyperbole. The word is often used (or overused) in contexts where no additional emphasis is necessary, however.

loan, lend The verb *loan* <*loaned* me the book> came to America with early settlers and continued in use here when it dropped out of use in Great Britain. Various 19th-century commentators decided that the use was improper, and a surprising number of critics still object to it. Nevertheless, *loan* is entirely standard as a verb. You should note that it is used only literally (as in the example above); *lend* is the verb used in figurative expressions, such as "*lend* a hand" or "*lending* a touch of class."

loath, loathe The spelling *loath* is used for the adjective <is *loath* to do it>, while *loathe* is used for the verb <she *loathes* him> and secondarily for the adjective. In pronouncing the adjective, some people rhyme it with the verb, voicing the *th*. This pronunciation causes many people to spell the adjective *loathe*. If you want to play it safe, use *loath* for the adjective and *loathe* for the verb. But if *loathe* represents your pronunciation of the adjective, you may use it.

loose, lose The issue here is faulty spelling. The verb *lose* rhymes with *choose*, and in casual writing it often gets an extra *o*. Be careful not to make this mistake.

lost This word is sometimes considered to be an ABSOLUTE ADJECTIVE (see Glossary).s

lots, a lot These expressions, though often labeled colloquial, have been used in serious but not highly formal writing for a long time <*a lot* of money> <*lots* of friends>. See also ALOT, A LOT.

loud, loudly *Loud* is most familiar as an adjective <a *loud* noise>. When used as an adverb, it always follows the verb that it modifies, and it occurs chiefly with only a few simple and familiar verbs, such as *talk, scream, shout,* or *cheer* <talks *loud*> <shouting as *loud* as she could>. In most other contexts, *loudly* is preferred <*loudly* proclaimed victory> <seagulls squawking *loudly* overhead>.

M

mad **1.** The use of *mad* to mean "angry" (rather than "crazy, insane") has been criticized as slang or colloquial, but the usage is quite old (going back at least to Shakespeare) and remains in good standing <were particularly *mad* about the slow pace>. *Mad* in this sense is found today in fiction, general nonfiction, correspondence, and of course in speech.

2. *Mad* is followed by a number of different prepositions. People who are angry are *mad at* or less often, *mad with* people or things; they are also sometimes *mad about* things. People who are carried away by enthusiasm are *mad about, mad for,* or, if they are British, *mad on* something or someone. People who are frantic or wild are *mad with* something.

magnate, magnet These two words are occasionally confused. A *magnate* is a person of rank, influence, or distinction <publishing *magnate*>. A *magnet* is a body that attracts iron, or simply "something that attracts" <a *magnet* for fashion buyers>.

major **1.** Some complain that the word *major* is overused. It is true that it does appear frequently, and often in contexts where its meaning gets diluted (as in "a *major* motion picture," which is nothing more than a new movie). But you need not stop using a word simply because other people overuse it; just take care not to overuse it yourself.

2. Critics have claimed that *major* is a comparative, like *greater,* and so should not be used as a straight adjective <a *major* campaign speech>. They recommend substituting *important, principal,* or *big.* But *major* is perfectly standard in this use, and often preferable to any of the proposed substitutes. The same claim has been made with regard to *minor,* and the same conclusion applies.

majority **1.** *Majority* is used as a collective noun that takes either a singular or a plural verb, depending on whether the writer views the majority as a single unit or as a collection of individuals. When *majority* stands alone as the subject, it tends to be used with a singular verb <the *majority* has decided to support the mayor>. It also frequently takes a plural verb <the *majority* are unable to make new friends easily>. When *majority* is followed by *of* and a plural noun, a plural verb is usual <the *majority of* the bills have been paid>.

2. The use of *majority* with things that are not countable has been generally discouraged. While it is not as common as use with a plural, it is found in standard sources in scientific, legal, and general contexts <must contain a *majority* of dark matter> <the *majority* of the court> <the *majority* of the world's cocaine>.

male Although there has been controversy over the use of *female* (see entry), the parallel term *male* has escaped criticism. It is generally used as an adjective <a *male* collie>; when used as a noun, it is often paired with *female* <the gang included both *males* and females>.

man *Man* in the generic sense "a human being" <no *man* is an island> or "mankind" <*man*'s natural rights> has come under attack in recent years by people who feel, not unreasonably, that it slights women. *Human* and *human being* are sometimes used as replacements, though *man* is still used. See also MANKIND.

mankind *Mankind* has been open to some of the same objections as the generic use of *man* (see above). If *mankind* is offensive to you, you may substitute *humankind, human beings, humans,* or *people. Humankind,* like *mankind,* is a mass noun that is usually treated as singular <*humankind* worships many different gods>.

mantel, mantle *Mantel* refers to the shelf above a fireplace, *mantle* to a cloak or cover.

many a The phrase *many a* is followed by a singular noun and usually a singular verb <*many a* sprinter has tried>. When a pronoun is used as well, it may be either plural or singular <led *many a* good citizen to put *their* trust in him> <*many a* president has changed *his* mind>. (See NOTIONAL AGREEMENT in Glossary.)

mar When the verb *mar* takes a preposition, it is usually *by* <*marred by* a few gaffes>. Less frequently, *mar* takes *with* <*marred with* errors>.

marital, martial Note that a slip of the finger can easily transpose the *i* and the *t*, changing *marital* to *martial* or vice versa.

marshal, marshall The usual spelling of both the noun and verb is *marshal* <a federal *marshal*> <*marshaling* support>. The two-*l*'d *marshall*, however, is a variant that has been in use for centuries.

martial See MARITAL, MARTIAL.

martyr **1.** When the noun *martyr* is used with a preposition, it is usually *to* <a *martyr to* duty>. Occasionally *martyr* is followed by *for* or *of* <a *martyr for* academic freedom> <a *martyr of* love>.

2. When the verb *martyr* is used with a preposition, it is usually *for* <*martyring* herself *for* her family>.

masterful, masterly *Masterly* means "suitable to or resembling that of a master" <a *masterly* performance>. *Masterful* has several meanings, one of which is "masterly" <a *masterful* performance>. It has been argued that since *masterly* has only one meaning, it rather than *masterful* should be used whenever that meaning is intended. But *masterful* is in reputable use in this sense, so there is no need to prefer *masterly*. The distinction is easily observed, however, if you care to do so.

maximize Though *maximize* is sometimes regarded as jargon, perhaps because it occurs so commonly in business writing <*maximize* distribution>, it is in standard use today.

may See CAN, MAY.

may of See OF 2.

me See I, ME.

means **1.** *Means* in the sense of "something helpful in achieving a desired end" may be treated as either singular or plural <whether or not this is the proper *means*> <these *means* have been tried before>. *Means* in the sense of "material resources affording a secure life" is treated as plural when it takes a verb <the family's *means* were rather modest>.

2. When used with a preposition, *means* almost always takes *of* <a *means of* support>. Much less frequently, it takes *to* <a *means to* increase interest>, *toward* <the *means toward* an end>, or *for* <a *means for* solving these problems>.

3. See BY MEANS OF.

meddle When *meddle* is used with a preposition, the usual choice is *with* <*meddling with* others' work>. It is also used with *in* and *into* <had *meddled in* this matter> <to *meddle into* internal affairs>.

media *Media* is a plural of *medium*. For this reason many insist that it must be used with a plural verb. But a singular *media* (plural *medias*) has been in the advertising business for over half a century, and more recently a singular mass noun (with no plural) meaning "the news media" has become established. But this singular use is not yet as fully established as the mass-noun use of *data* (see entry). Usage in the media is mixed <the *media* have [has] exaggerated the issue> but the plural verb is still more frequent and is the safer choice <the *media* are not to be blamed>.

mediate *Mediate* is most often used with *between* when it takes a preposition <*mediating between* the two parties>. Occasionally it is used with *for* <*mediated for* the combatants>. As a transitive verb, it is also found with *through* <meanings that are *mediated through* the senses>.

mediocre This word is sometimes considered to be an ABSOLUTE ADJECTIVE (see Glossary).

medium See MEDIA.

meet, mete If you use the verb *mete* <to *mete* out punishment>, be sure not to misspell it *meet.*

memento See MOMENTO.

memorandum *Memorandum* is a singular noun with two acceptable plurals: *memorandums* and *memoranda. Memoranda* is sometimes mistakenly used as a singular (as in "wrote the *memoranda* and then quickly reviewed it"), and *memorandum* is sometimes mistakenly used as a plural (as in "circulated these *memorandum*"). Be careful.

mete See MEET, METE.

might could See DOUBLE MODAL in Glossary.

might of See OF 2.

mighty The use of *mighty* as an intensive usually conveys a folksy, down-home feeling <*mighty* satisfying>. It is used especially to create a chatty style or to stress a rural atmosphere. You will not need it in formal writing.

militate, mitigate *Militate* means "to have weight or effect" <conditions *militate* against expansion at this time>. *Mitigate,* which means "to make less severe" <circumstances which *mitigate* their involvement>, is sometimes mistakenly used (with *against*) in place of *militate.* You will want to avoid this use in your own writing.

millennium A common misspelling of this word drops one of the *n*'s. Remember that there are as many *n*'s as *l*'s.

mine See MY, MINE.

miniscule, minuscule This word is derived from the Latin *minusculus* and is related to the word *minus.* If you want to be consistent with etymology, spell it *minuscule,* as a majority of writers do. The spelling *miniscule* is also fairly common, especially for the meaning "very small." Even though some dictionaries recognize the *-i-* spelling, many consider it a misspelling.

minor See MAJOR 2.

minus Use of *minus* as a preposition meaning "without" <*minus* his hat> is sometimes objected to for sounding breezy and unserious. But the word has standard use in both humorous and serious, if not highly formal, writing.

minuscule See MINISCULE, MINUSCULE.

minutia The meaning of *minutia* is "a minute or minor detail." The word is almost always now used in its plural form *minutiae* <all the *minutiae* of daily living>. Using the singular *minutia* itself as a plural (as in "all the *minutia* of daily living") is considered an error.

mischievous The pronunciation \mis-ˈchē-vē-əs\ (rhyming with *devious*) and the consequent spelling *mischievious* are of long standing (going back to the 16th century), but both remain nonstandard.

mishap Some have argued that *mishap* applies only to minor accidents. The word is actually applied to both serious and inconsequential accidents <a mechanical *mishap* nearly caused the plant to shut down>, but it most often tends to downplay the seriousness of what happened.

mislead, misled The spelling error that occurs with the verb *lead* (see LEAD, LED) also occurs with *mislead.* The past tense and past participle, *misled,* is sometimes misspelled *mislead.* Remember: in the past tense or past participle, get the *-lead* out.

misspell *Misspell* is sometimes itself misspelled *mispell,* a mistake that has considerable potential to embarrass the misspeller.

mistrustful *Mistrustful* is usually used with *of* when it takes a preposition <*mistrustful of* them>. Sometimes *toward* is used instead <*mistrustful toward* her colleagues>.

mitigate See MILITATE, MITIGATE.

mix When *mix* takes a preposition, it is most often *with* <*mixes* business *with* pleasure>. Less often, *in* or *into* is used <decided not to *mix in* politics> <*mixing into* this ideological brew some rather silly notions>.

momentarily Despite the wish of some critics to limit the meaning of *momentarily* to "for a moment" <we were delayed *momentarily*>, an equally common meaning is "in a moment" <we'll be departing *momentarily*>. These two senses have coexisted in American English for many decades (in British English, the "in a moment" sense is rare), and both are standard, since the meaning is always made clear by the context.

momento The word *memento* ("souvenir") is spelled *momento* by enough people that the latter can be considered a variant form. If you want to stick to the original spelling, though, as most writers do, remember that *memento* is related to *memory* and *remember* and not to *moment.*

moneys, monies Though *money* has no plural in most of its uses, when the reference is to discrete sums of money obtained from various sources or distributed to various individuals or groups, the plural *moneys* or *monies* is often used <all *moneys* in the slush fund have been seized>. The plural *monies* has occasionally been criticized because it suggests a singular *mony* rather than *money.* It is, however, an old and perfectly respectable variant that is used almost as commonly as *moneys.*

monopoly *Monopoly* is used with several prepositions. Most often it is used with *on* <a *monopoly on* goodwill>. *Monopoly of* is also quite common <a

monopoly of technological know-how>. Less frequently, *monopoly* is used with *in* and *over* <a *monopoly in* that field> <a virtual *monopoly over* exports>.

moral, morale *Morale,* meaning "mental or emotional condition," is sometimes misspelled *moral,* which of course means "the practical meaning (as of a story)."

more important, more importantly See IMPORTANT 1.

more than one The idea of the phrase *more than one* is plural, but since it usually modifies a singular noun, it generally takes a singular verb <*more than one* fake is known to exist>. But sometimes a plural verb is used because the notion of plurality (see NOTIONAL AGREEMENT in Glossary) predominates <*more than one* deer are often spotted here by visitors> or because it is simply required by the context of the whole sentence <if there are *more than one,* they appear in alphabetical order>. When the phrase is followed by *of* and a plural noun, a plural verb is usual <where *more than one of* these problems are liable to turn up>.

Moslem, Muslim *Moslem* is the older spelling, but *Muslim* is more used today both because it is preferred by those of whom it is used and because it more closely represents the Arabic pronunciation.

most Although considered unacceptable by some, *most* in the sense "almost" <can be found *most* anywhere

today> is often used in spoken and, to a lesser extent, informal written English modifying such words as *all, everything, anyone,* and *always.*

mostly The propriety of using *mostly* (meaning "mainly") to modify a verb <they *mostly* just wanted to go home> has been questioned. Although this use may not be especially elegant, there is no question that it is standard and common. *Mostly* is also used at the beginning of a sentence <*Mostly,* the discussion focused on debt control>.

motive *Motive* is often followed by the preposition *for,* which is in turn often followed by a gerund <his *motives for* doing it>. *Motive* is also sometimes followed by *of* or *behind* <the *motive of* self-aggrandizement> <the *motives behind* their actions>, and sometimes by *to* and the infinitive <sufficient *motive to* carry it out>.

Ms. *Ms.*, a blend of *Miss* and *Mrs.*, has over the years become the standard form to use, especially in business correspondence, when addressing a woman whose marital status is unknown or irrelevant to matters at hand <Dear *Ms.* Smith>.

mucus, mucous The noun is spelled *mucus* <a buildup of *mucus*>, and the adjective is spelled *mucous* <*mucous* membrane>.

muse *Muse* is used about equally with *on, upon,* and *over* <started *musing on* [*upon, over*] it>. It also occurs, much less frequently, with *about* <*mused about* her role in the affair>.

Muslim See MOSLEM, MUSLIM.

must *Must* in the sense "something essential" used to require quotation marks around it, but now is so common that the quotes are generally omitted <experience using databases is a *must*>.

must of See OF 2.

my, mine *My* is sometimes combined, especially in speech, with another possessive pronoun to create an expression such as "*my* and her child both went." *Mine* is even occasionally used as well ("*mine* and her child both went"). This type of construction, while understandable in speech, should be recast in writing <*my* child and hers both went>.

myself *Myself* is often used in place of *I* or *me:* as subject <others and *myself* continued to press for the legislation>; after *as, than,* or *like* <paying such people as *myself* to tutor> <was enough to make a better man than *myself* quail> <old-timers like *myself*>; and as object <now here you see *myself* with the diver> <for my wife and *myself* it was a happy time>. Such uses often occur, as in some of the examples above, when the speaker or writer is referring to himself or herself as an object of discussion. (The other reflexive personal pronouns—*herself, himself, themselves*—are less frequently used in this way.) Critics have frowned on these uses since the start of the 20th century, but they serve a definite purpose and are standard.

N

naive, naïve, naïveté The adjective *naive* is spelled at least as often without the diaeresis over the *i* as with one. The noun *naïveté,* however, is most often spelled with both the diaeresis and an accent over the final *e.*

naked, nude *Naked* tends to suggest the absence of clothing in general contexts <*naked* above the waist>, while *nude* tends to refer to the unclothed human figure in the context of art <a *nude* model posing for art students>.

native Use of *native* for a nonwhite person indigenous to some place (as in "we conversed with the *natives* in French") is often considered offensive. In North America, however, especially in Alaska and Western Canada, *native* (usually capitalized) is frequently used nonpejoratively in the sense "Native American" <seminars on *Native* cultures>. It also continues to be used without offense of someone belonging to a particular place by birth <a *native* of Wisconsin>.

Native American *Native American* has become, for many, a term of choice to refer to a member of any of the aboriginal peoples of North America (except, usually, the Inuit, or Eskimo, peoples), but it has by no means displaced *American Indian* or *Indian.* All are in frequent use.

nature Phrases like *of this nature* or *of a . . . nature* (as in "The court does not normally hear cases *of a* probate *nature*") are often considered wordy. Though absolute concision is not necessary in every case, if wordiness or awkwardness is apparent the writer may consider revising (e.g., "The court does not normally hear probate cases").

nauseating, nauseous *Nauseous* is most frequently used to mean "physically affected with nausea" <the ride made me *nauseous*>, while *nauseating* is used to mean "causing nausea or disgust" <the *nauseating* violence on TV>.

naval, navel Watch your spelling here. *Naval* means "relating to a navy," while *navel* refers to the belly button.

near, nearly *Near* in the sense of "almost, nearly" <found *near* dead> <a *near*-perfect score>, though standard in speech and informal writing, may sound just a little old-fashioned to some. You can usually substitute *nearly.*

necessary *Necessary,* when used with a preposition, is most often used with *to* <the force *necessary to* apprehend the suspect>. It is less often used with *for* <is *necessary for* a lasting relationship>, and occasionally with *in* <*necessary in* the training of students>.

necessity When *necessity* is used with a preposition, it is usually either *of* or, less often, *for* <the *necessity of* choosing> <the *necessity for* greater clarity>.

née The literal meaning of this word in French is "born." Its usual function in English is to introduce a married woman's maiden name <Mrs. John Jones, *née* Smith>. Some literal-minded critics have warned against following it with a woman's given name <Peggy Lee, *née* Norma Egstrom>, because a person is born only with a last name—the given name comes later. But *née* in English is closer in meaning to "formerly or originally known as" than to "born," and its use before a woman's given name is standard.

need **1.** *Noun.* The preposition that follows *need* is usually *for* <the *need for* regulations>, but *of* is also a common choice, especially in the phrase *in need of* <*in need of* repair> <the *needs of* the institution>. *Need* is also commonly followed by the infinitive <the *need* to begin a dialogue>.

2. *Verb. Need* as an auxiliary verb is followed by the bare infinitive without *to* <no one *need* know> <all she *need* do is apply>. As a regular verb it requires *to* <he *needed to* contact them>. It can also be followed by a gerund <it doesn't *need* repeating here>.

3. The verb *need* is sometimes followed directly by a past participle (as in "the car *needs* washed"). This is an American regional usage found in the Midland area and especially in Pennsylvania. It is primarily spoken but can be found in local newspapers.

needless to say This phrase is criticized on the same grounds as *goes without saying*. Yet it continues to be used standardly to emphasize that the writer or speaker regards the statement being made as in some way self-evident, and to provide a graceful transition between sentences or paragraphs. See also GOES WITHOUT SAYING.

neglectful *Neglectful* is used with *of* <*neglectful of* her chores>.

negligent When *negligent* is used with a preposition, the choice is usually *in* or *of* <*negligent* in settling the account> <*negligent of* the details>. *About* is also used <*negligent about* writing a note of thanks>.

neither **1.** The pronoun *neither* is traditionally used with a singular verb <*neither is* ideal>, especially in formal writing. However, when a prepositional phrase follows *neither,* a plural verb is common and acceptable <*neither* of those solutions *are* ideal>, especially in less formal contexts.

2. *Neither* as a conjunction is usually followed by *nor* <*neither* high winds *nor* freezing temperatures>, although use with *or* is found in casual writing <*neither* he *or* she knew the answer>.

3. The use of *neither* to refer to more than two nouns, though sometimes criticized, has been standard for centuries <*neither* the post office, the bank, nor City Hall is open today>.

4. *Neither . . . nor* with two (or more) singular subjects is governed by NOTIONAL AGREEMENT (see

Glossary) and may take either a singular or a plural verb <*neither* Johnson *nor* Ruskin *was* bothered by it> <*neither* the soloist *nor* the orchestra *were* in top form>. When the subjects are plural, or the last subject is plural, a plural verb is expected <*neither* local fishermen *nor* environmentalists *are* pleased with the decision> <*neither* you *nor* your associates *have* been forthcoming on the issue>. See also AGREEMENT (in Glossary).

never too See NOT TOO.

nice and Unlike the phrase *good and*, which may be followed by a variety of adjectives, *nice and* is generally restricted to a few approving phrases <*nice and* warm> <*nice and* easy>. Such phrases, though standard, are seldom employed in formal writing.

nickel, nickle *Nickel* is the original and generally accepted spelling. *Nickle* does appear in print, but many regard it as an error.

no See DOUBLE NEGATIVE in Glossary.

nobody, no one These indefinite pronouns for the most part follow the same pattern of notional agreement as the other indefinite pronouns: they regularly take a singular verb but may be referred to by either a singular or a plural pronoun <*nobody* wants to have *his* license revoked> <*no one* cares about how *their* lawn looks around here>. A singular pronoun is generally preferred in formal contexts <*no one* could convince top management of the merit of *his* idea>, but a plural pronoun, even though criticized, has the advantage of not forcing a choice between masculine and feminine singular forms <*no one* could convince top management of the merit of *their* idea>. See also THEY, THEIR, THEM; AGREEMENT: INDEFINITE PRONOUNS (in Glossary).

no doubt See DOUBTLESS, NO DOUBT, UNDOUBTEDLY.

noisome *Noisome* is almost always used to mean "noxious" or "disgusting" <the *noisome* exhaust from the truck ahead of us>. Occasionally someone spells it *noisesome* and uses it to mean "noisy" (as in "*noisesome* children running about"), but this is generally regarded as a mistake.

none *None* may take a singular verb <*none* of us is certain> but it may also take a plural verb <*none* of the questions were answered satisfactorily>; it has been used with both since Old English. Writers generally make it singular when they think of it as singular and plural when they think of it as plural (see NOTIONAL AGREEMENT in Glossary). Both uses are perfectly acceptable.

no one See NOBODY, NO ONE.

nor **1.** For the use of *nor* after *neither,* see NEITHER 2, 4.

2. *Nor* sometimes replaces *or* in negative statements <not done by you *nor* me *nor* anyone> to achieve a more emphatically negative effect than is possible with *or.*

no sooner This phrase is usually followed by *than* <had *no sooner* hung up *than* he realized his mistake>. In speech it is sometimes followed by *when,* but this is nonstandard in written English.

not all that See ALL THAT.

not as, not so See AS . . . AS 1.

not . . . but *Not . . . but* is a somewhat old-fashioned expression <did*n't* take *but* three minutes> found mostly in speech. Writers tend to avoid it in published prose <it took but three minutes> <it took barely three minutes>.

not hardly See HARDLY.

not only . . . but also 1. The *also* in this set of conjunctions is optional and is frequently omitted, especially in shorter sentences <her approach was *not only* awkward *but* badly timed>.

2. As a general rule, identical constructions follow *not only* and *but (also)* <*not only* visited Great Britain *but also* traveled to India> in standard prose (see PARALLELISM in Glossary). However, nonparallel constructions are so common as to often go unnoticed <we were *not only* wined and dined there *but* found ourselves rather liking it>. For the related issue of the placement of *only* in a sentence, see ONLY 1.

not so See AS . . . AS 1.

not too The phrase *not too,* where *too* means "very," is most often used for mild understatement <such competency is *not too* difficult to achieve>. The *too* is also occasionally used with *never* <it was *never too* easy to gain his approval>. Some critics complain about these uses, but they are perfectly standard.

no way *No way,* an American expression that emerged in the 1960s, is now standard in speech and prose of a personal or casual nature <*no way* was I going to do that!>. You will not need it in formal writing.

nowhere near *Nowhere near* is a somewhat informal way of saying *not nearly,* but slightly more emphatic <has *nowhere near* the talent she has>. It is more common in speech than in writing.

nuclear The pronunciation \'nü-kyə-lər\ is used by many educated speakers. Many others, however, insist that the word's spelling dictates the pronunciation \'nü-klē-ər\.

nude See NAKED, NUDE.

number A rule of thumb is that *a number* takes a plural verb <*a* large *number* of inquiries were received> while *the number* takes a singular verb <*the number* of inquiries was high>. An adjective like *increasing* or *growing* used with *a number,* however, tends to emphasize that *number* is singular and may be followed by either a singular or a plural verb <an *increasing number* of workers are dissatisfied> <*a* continually *growing number* of cases is undermining the court's ability to function>. *The number,* on the other hand, is less subject to variation of this kind. See also AMOUNT 1; AGREEMENT (in Glossary).

O

obedient When *obedient* is used with a preposition, it is *to* <*obedient to* their masters>.

object When the verb *object* takes a preposition, it is usually *to.* What follows *to* may be a noun <didn't *object to* the proposal>, pronoun <has never *objected to* it>, or gerund <*objected to* going>. *Object* may also be followed by a clause <*objected* that the statement was misleading>.

objective Some critics prefer *object* or *aim* to *objective,* but *objective* is certainly in current good use. *Objective* tends to be found more often in serious prose <our *objectives* were fourfold> than in lighter writing.

obligated, obliged In the sense of being bound or constrained legally or morally, *obligated* and *obliged* are essentially interchangeable <felt *obligated* [*obliged*] to report the incident> <is not legally *obliged* [*obligated*] to respond>. When the constraint is applied by physical force or by circumstances, however, *obliged* rather than *obligated* is used <passengers were *obliged* to suffer a minor loss of cabin pressure>.

oblivious *Oblivious* is usually followed by the preposition *to* <*oblivious to* the complaints>, though *of* is not at all uncommon <*oblivious of* the noise>.

observance, observation The distinction between these two words is as follows: *Observance* is most often used in the sense "an act or instance of following a custom, rule, or law" <*observance* of the Sabbath>; *observation* is used in the sense "an act or instance of watching" <*observation* of a lunar eclipse>. However, *observance* is also sometimes used to mean "an act of watching" <in the *observance* of the child's behavior>.

observant *Observant,* when used with a preposition, takes *of* <always *observant of* social amenities>.

observation See OBSERVANCE, OBSERVATION.

obsessed When *obsessed* is used with a preposition, the choice is usually *with* <was *obsessed with* the idea>, though *by* is also common <*obsessed by* her own suspicions>.

obtuse *Obtuse* is well established in the meanings "not acute" <an *obtuse* angle> and "insensitive, stupid" <our hopelessly *obtuse* boss>. Recently, however, *obtuse* has begun to be used in the sense "difficult to comprehend, unclear" (as in "an *obtuse* explanation"), a usage probably based on confusion with *obscure* and *abstruse;* if you are chary of new uses, you may want to avoid it.

occasion **1.** *Occasion* is often followed by *for* or *of* <the *occasion for* the exercise> <the *occasion of* the discord>. It also is followed quite frequently by the infinitive, typically when *occasion* is the object of *have* <will *have occasion* to visit the site>.

2. A common error in spelling *occasion* is to use two *s*'s.

occupy When *occupy* is used with a preposition, *with* or *by* is the usual choice <was *occupied with* her extracurricular work> <seemed to be *occupied by* his thoughts>, but *in* is also used <*occupying* themselves *in* church work>.

occur See TAKE PLACE, OCCUR.

-odd When used to indicate a quantity somewhat greater than a given round number, *odd* is preceded by a hyphen <300-*odd* pages>. The redundant use of *some* with *-odd* (as in "*some* 60-*odd* people") occurs more frequently in speech than in writing.

of **1.** For use of *of* in certain compound prepositions, see INSIDE OF; OFF OF; OUTSIDE OF.

2. *Of* is occasionally mistakenly used as a spelling of the contraction *'ve* (for *have*) in sentences like "The time should *of* been listed as 8 p.m." because it sounds similar to *'ve* in such contexts *(could of, should of, would of, ought to of, might of, may of,* and *must of).*

Children and those who have not completed grammar school may have an excuse for making this mistake, but most others do not.

of a *Of a* in sentences like "He's not that good *of a* putter" is a spoken idiom that is not much used in writing except when *enough, more,* or *much* is used <is not *much of a* putter>. In writing *of* is not included <is not that good a putter>. See also KIND OF A, SORT OF A.

of a . . . nature See NATURE.

of any See ANY 3.

off *Off* in the sense of "from" (as in "we bought the tools *off* Joe," or "we recorded the show *off* the TV") has been objected to for about half a century (the use is over 400 years old), but no rational basis for the objection has ever been offered. It is found most often, however, in speech and speechlike writing. See also OFF OF.

offhand, offhanded *Offhand* has been in use as both an adjective <an *offhand* remark> and an adverb <cannot recall *offhand*> for about 300 years. The adjective *offhanded* is a more recent (19th-century) and somewhat uncommon synonym, but it is nevertheless standard and respectable <in an *offhanded* way>.

off of *Off of* is a compound preposition that is used in speech, in fictional dialogue, and in light and general writing <can't get the lid *off of* the jar> <traffic was routed *off of* the highway>. It is not found in highly formal writing.

oftener, oftenest These two inflected forms of *often* are in good use, but they occur only about half as much as *more often* and *most often.*

of this nature See NATURE.

O.K., OK, okay **1.** The spellings *O.K.*, *OK*, and *okay* are all in good use, with *okay* perhaps slightly more common than the other two.

2. *O.K.* (or *OK* or *okay*) is used as an adjective <an *OK* job>, adverb <she liked it *okay*), noun <gave it the *O.K.*>, and verb <was *okayed* by the FDA> in speech and in all except formal writing. Be advised, however, that the word is commonly condemned in college English handbooks, which seem in this instance to be out of step with contemporary usage.

on **1.** *On, upon.* Of these two prepositions, *on* is certainly the more common <places a burden *on* them>, though *upon* is far from rare <was agreed *upon* by all>. You may use whichever word you prefer.

2. See ONTO, ON TO.

on a . . . basis See BASIS 1.

on account of This phrase is commonly used as a preposition equivalent to *because of* <was denied the position *on account of* his medical condition>. Some occasionally object to it, but it has long been established as standard.

on behalf of See BEHALF.

one The use of *one* to indicate a generic individual <*one* never knows> lends formality to writing, since it suggests distance between the writer and the reader. Using *one* in place of *I* <*one* should like to be able to read more> or *me* <she gave *one* to believe that it had already been done>, though common in British English, may be thought odd or objectionably remote in American English. See also YOU 1, 2.

one another, one another's See EACH OTHER, ONE ANOTHER.

one in (out of) See AGREEMENT: SUBJECT FORMED BY *ONE IN (OUT OF)* in Glossary.

one of the . . . if not the Sentences like "It is *one of the* greatest, *if not the* greatest, mine disasters of this century" are occasionally objected to. The problem is that the part of the sentence outside the commas calls for the plural *disasters,* while the part inside the commas calls for the singular *disaster.* This construction is somewhat similar to *as good or better than* in that it contains a grammatical irregularity that normally does not bother ordinary readers but seems to trouble critics. If you feel the need to revise, you can shift the words around <*one of the* greatest mine disasters, *if not the* greatest, of this century>, but only if it feels natural to you. See also AS GOOD OR BETTER THAN.

one of those who The issue here is whether you should use a singular or a plural verb with the phrase *one of those who* <he is *one of those* people *who* rarely

takes [take] vacations>. Both have in fact been in standard use for centuries. The choice depends on whether the writer regards *one* or *those* as the word that controls the number of the verb (see NOTIONAL AGREEMENT in Glossary).

on line Do you stand *in* line or *on* line? Formerly *on line* was heard only in New York City and the Hudson Valley, but in recent decades the phrase has become known, if not actually used, nationally.

only The placement of *only* in a sentence has been a source of debate since the 18th century. After 200 years of discussion, usage remains varied. In standard spoken English, placement of *only* is not fixed; ambiguity is avoided through sentence stress <he'd *only* been there three weeks> <she *only* gave me $150> <we *only* knew enough to get by>. In casual prose that keeps close to the rhythms of speech, *only* is often placed where it would be in speech. In edited and more formal prose, *only* tends to be placed immediately before the word or words it modifies <he had been there *only* three weeks> <she gave me *only* $150> <we knew *only* enough to get by>.

on the basis of See BASIS 1.

on the part of This common idiomatic phrase <some unwillingness *on the part of* the Israelis> can often be replaced by a single preposition, such as *by* or *among*—and some critics think it always should be. Its use is easily avoided by anyone who finds it awkward or needlessly wordy, but many good writers apparently do not.

onto, on to Occasionally someone confuses the compound preposition *onto* with the adverb *on* followed by the preposition *to* (as in "traveled *onto* Seville"). This use is generally to be avoided; however, the phrase *hold onto* has become established <how long can the team *hold onto* first place?>. The preposition *onto* is, in American English, regularly closed up <opens *onto* the veranda>; in British English both *onto* and *on to* are used, though *onto* seems to be gaining ascendency.

onward, onwards *Onward* serves both as an adjective <an *onward* rush> and as an adverb <rushing *onward*>; *onwards* is an adverb only <from 1600 *onwards*>. *Onward* is the more common adverb in American English, *onwards* in British English.

opening gambit See GAMBIT.

opine This verb, used in English since the 15th century, is sometimes thought to be less than serious. It does turn up in humorous writing, but it also commonly serves to imply, seriously enough, some skepticism about the opinion being reported <she *opined* that the comet would strike the earth> or to emphasize that the opinion being reported is just that—an opinion <she *opined* that stock prices could soar>.

opportunity *Opportunity* is often used with *to* followed by an infinitive <an *opportunity to* get involved>.

Opportunity for frequently precedes a noun phrase <*opportunities for* discussions involving both parties> or a gerund <*opportunities for* investing abroad>. *Opportunity of,* once common in both American and British English, is now found chiefly in the latter.

opposite *Opposite* as an adjective or adverb is followed by either *to* or *from* <in a direction *opposite to* the one expected> <sat *opposite from* him>. As a noun, *opposite* is frequently followed by *of* <the *opposite of* what they wanted>. *To* is also sometimes used <the *opposite to* the plan announced earlier>.

opposition *Opposition,* when used with a preposition, usually takes *to* <in *opposition to* the regime>. *Opposition* is also used, in different constructions, with *between* and *of* <the natural *opposition between* imagination and reason> <the *opposition of* individual will and social norms>.

opt The verb *opt* (from French *opter,* "to choose") has a modern, clipped quality that may make it seem like a recent and perhaps illegitimate invention, but in fact it is more than a hundred years old and is established as standard <*opted* not to attend> <*opted* for short sleeves> <*opted* out of the competition>.

or See AND/OR; EITHER 3, 5; NEITHER 2; AGREEMENT: COMPOUND SUBJECTS JOINED BY *OR* (in Glossary).

oral See VERBAL, ORAL.

orchestrate Some charge that using *orchestrate* to mean "to arrange or combine for maximum effect" <*orchestrated* preparations for the banquet> is faddish or a cliché. This use, however, has been around since the late 1800s and continues to be employed by good writers.

order See IN ORDER TO.

ordinance, ordnance The more common of these two words, *ordinance* (meaning "municipal law"), is sometimes mistakenly used for the less common *ordnance* (meaning "military supplies").

Oriental See ASIAN, ORIENTAL.

originate *Originate,* when used with a preposition, is most often used with *in* <the idea *originated in* a meeting held in June>. A little less often, it is used with *from* <*originated from* outside the compound>. *Originate* is also used with *as, at, on, out of, outside of,* and *with.*

other Some critics claim that *other* can only be paired with *than* in constructions like "never looked on him in any *other* light *than* as my friend." However, use of *but* with *other* in such constructions <had no *other* choice *but* to sit and wait> is idiomatic and fully standard in American English.

ought *Ought* is a little awkward to put into the negative. In writing, *ought not* is the usual form, and it may be followed by the bare infinitive without *to* <one *ought not* complain about a tax benefit> or the infinitive with *to* <many *ought not to* be accepted as members>. Although *ought not* is used in speech, it can seem a bit stuffy for everyday use. *Oughtn't* is one spoken substitute; it is widespread but more common in the South. *Hadn't ought* is another; it too is widespread but is more common in the North. *Didn't ought* is mostly British.

ought to of The *of* here stands for *'ve* or *have.* See OF 2.

ours The possessive pronoun *ours,* like the possessive pronouns *its, theirs,* and *yours,* is properly spelled without an apostrophe.

out See OUT OF, OUT.

out loud *Out loud* was once widely decried as an error for *aloud,* and it is still sometimes described as too casual to be used in formal writing. Our evidence shows clearly that *out loud* is neither an error nor a casual spoken form, but it does appear less frequently than *aloud* in formal writing.

out of, out *Out of* and *out* are interchangeable only in a few restricted contexts. *Out* is used much more often as an adverb <turn *out* the light> than as a preposition. When used as a preposition, it seems most often to go with *door* or *window* <ran *out* the door> <looked *out* the window>. With *window, out of* is about equally common <leaned *out of* the window>. With nouns that designate places or things that can be thought of as containing or surrounding, *out of* is usual <walked *out of* the room> <step *out of* the car, please>.

outside of **1.** Some criticize using *outside of* as a synonym for *outside*. Our evidence suggests that competent writers and speakers retain the *of* when it sounds right to them for idiom and rhythm <he wasn't known *outside of* his own circle> and drop it when it does not <it falls *outside* the court's jurisdiction>. You have the same choice.

2. Some regard the use of *outside of* in the sense "except for" or "aside from" as improper. However, the usage is quite respectable in ordinary writing <*outside of* a few experts, no one was bothered by it>.

3. See INSIDE OF.

over Various reasons have been put forth as to why *over* in the sense of "more than" should be avoided, but none of these arguments holds water and they conflict with each other. *Over* has been used in this sense since the 14th century <in the business for *over* thirty years>, and there is no reason to avoid it.

overwhelmed Whether used as a passive form or as an adjective, *overwhelmed* is most often followed with *by* <the picnic area was *overwhelmed by* black flies> <a small building *overwhelmed by* its towering neighbors>, less frequently by *with* <she was suddenly *overwhelmed with* calls for interviews>.

owing to See DUE TO.

P

paid See PAY.

pair **1.** The usual plural of *pair* is *pairs,* when there is no preceding number or indicator of number (such as *several*) <*pairs* of stockings hung from various appurtenances>. When a number or indicator of number precedes *pair,* either *pair* or *pairs* may be used <five *pair* [*pairs*] of sox>.

2. *Pair* is one of those collective nouns that take a singular or plural verb according to notional agreement: If you are thinking of the individuals in the pair, you will use a plural verb <a *pair* of horses were grazing in the field>; if you are thinking of the pair as a unit, you will use the singular <a *pair* of eyes peeks out from behind the blinds>.

parallel **1.** *Parallel* is sometimes misspelled. Try thinking of the two *l*s in the middle as parallel lines cutting through the word.

2. The prepositions that occur after the adjective *parallel* are *to* and *with* <an opinion that runs *parallel to* her own> <an effort *parallel with* that of the group>. The noun *parallel* is followed by *to, with,* or *between* <looking for a *parallel to* the experience> <citing a *parallel with* Northern Ireland> <sees a *parallel between* the two methods>.

parameter This borrowing from mathematics and other technical writing has been much disparaged. Our evidence shows that it is not much used in general writing but is fairly common in technical and quasi-technical writing (such as about investment and consumer electronics).

paraphernalia Some regard *paraphernalia* (which was originally a Latin plural) as a plural noun <filled with those *paraphernalia* you see in such shops>, while others regard it as a singular <every kind of *paraphernalia* imaginable>. Both uses are proper.

part **1.** *Part with* almost always means "give up" <hated to *part with* that money>. *Part from* generally means "leave" <he *parted from* the administration in May>.

2. See ON THE PART OF.

partake As an intransitive verb, *partake* may be followed by *in* or *of*. *Partake in,* like *take part in,* implies active participation in something <*partaking in* the revelry>. *Partake of,* like *take part of,* usually means "share" or "possess" <the religion *partakes of* a certain mysticism>.

partial *Partial* is used with the preposition *to* when it means "markedly fond (of)" <*partial to* pizza>. Formerly this use was considered unacceptable by some, but nowadays it is accepted as standard.

partially, partly These two words have long been interchangeable in the sense "in some measure or degree" <her figure was *partly* enveloped in a shawl> <the hat-brim *partially* shaded his face>, though there is some tendency toward differentiation. *Partially* is used more often than *partly* to modify an adjective or past participle that names or suggests a process <the body was only *partially* concealed>. *Partly* is used more often before clauses and phrases offered by way of explanation <the work has not achieved canonical status, *partly* because of its density and length>. But there are plenty of exceptions to the general trend, and only time will tell whether the process of differentiation will continue.

participate *Participate* is most often used with *in* <always tried to *participate in* class discussions>.

partly See PARTIALLY, PARTLY.

party *Party* in the sense of "person" <didn't reach the *party* I sent it to> has been criticized from the days of Queen Victoria, apparently because it belonged to the language of the socially inferior. Criticism has continued through pure inertia, but this use is now standard.

pay *Paid* is the spelling for the past tense and past participle of *pay.* Only in the specialized nautical sense of *pay out* are they normally spelled *payed.*

peaceable, peaceful *Peaceable* means "disposed toward peace, preferring peace" <a *peaceable*

kingdom>, while *peaceful* means "characterized by peace" <a *peaceful* sleep>. However, *peaceable* and *peaceful* can also be properly used as synonyms, and they have been since the 14th century.

peak, peek, pique These soundalikes have a way of getting switched by inattentive writers. Most often, *peak* is substituted for one of the other two. Be sure to match your intended meaning to the correct spelling, using your dictionary for help as required. See also PIQUE.

pedal, peddle Once in a while the verb *peddle* is used where *pedal* is meant, as a result of carelessness.

peek See PEAK, PEEK, PIQUE.

people, persons Since the late 1800s critics have warned against using *people* to mean *persons,* especially when paired with modifiers such as *several, many,* or specific numbers like *a thousand* <several new *people* attended> <the facility can hold 22,500 *people*>. Despite the warnings, which were never based on very solid reasoning, *people* has continued to stand in for *persons* and is now recognized even by former critics as standard in such contexts. *Persons* continues to be used, often in the traditionally recommended way <eight *persons* were on board the small aircraft>, but also as an alternative where *people* has just been used <some 800 *people,* many of them older *persons*>.

per Though regarded by some as not quite an English word, *per* is completely standard when used with figures. It usually appears in the context of money <$100 *per* performance>, vehicles <65 miles *per* hour> <32 miles *per* gallon>, or sports <15 points *per* game>. It also appears regularly in business correspondence, where it means "according to" <*per* your instructions> and is standard (see also AS PER). Avoid inserting words like *a* or *each* between *per* and the word or words it modifies (as in "committed at least one typo *per* a paragraph").

percent, per cent You can use either the one-word or the two-word form, though the one-word form is more common in America. *Percent* can be followed by either a plural or singular verb; the number of the verb is usually dictated by the noun in the following *of* phrase <20 *percent* of families prefer product A> <over 75 *percent* of the population was in favor>. The percent sign (%) is generally avoided in discursive prose.

perfect The phrases *more perfect* and *most perfect* are considered by some as improper, since something is supposedly either perfect or not (see ABSOLUTE ADJECTIVE in Glossary). But *perfect* has been used in the comparative and superlative since the 14th century; and except in the minds of some critics, it has never been wrong to use the disputed phrases.

period of time This phrase, as many critics point out, can often be shortened to either *period* or *time* <during this *period* [*time*]>. However, when using the phrase improves the clarity of your sentence

<subjected to sensory deprivation for long *periods of time*>, you can safely choose the phrase.

permeate *Permeate* is used with *by* or *with* about equally. When used with *by*, the verb is almost always in the passive <was *permeated by* the stench>; when followed by *with*, the verb may appear in either the active <has *permeated* her work *with* her own sense of guilt> or the passive voice <a room *permeated with* tobacco smoke>.

permit See ALLOW 1.

permit of *Permit of*, like *admit of* and *allow of* (all of which mean "to make possible"), is almost always used with an impersonal subject <a situation that does not *permit of* a satisfying remedy>. See also ALLOW 2.

person **1.** For a discussion of choosing between *persons* and *people*, see PEOPLE, PERSONS.

2. In response to concern about sexism in language, recent decades have seen the coinage of compound terms in which the terminal element *-man* (as in *draftsman*), and sometimes *-woman* (as in *chairwoman*), is replaced by *-person*. Such terms as *chairperson, anchorperson,* and *spokesperson* are now well established. Bare designations such as *chair* and *anchor* are also common. Other terms (such as *waitperson*) have made inroads but still have a way to go before being fully accepted. Checking a recent dictionary or two should help you determine whether a given compound is established in current use.

persuade *Persuade* is most often used with *to* and an infinitive <*persuaded* us *to* drop the case>. It quite frequently introduces a clause <*persuading* them that they should go>. It is somewhat less often used with *of, by,* or *into* <to *persuade* her *of* his sincerity> <were *persuaded by* the weight of the facts> <*persuading* them *into* accepting his offer>, and occasionally with *as to, from, out of, with,* and *upon.* See also CONVINCE, PERSUADE.

pertinent *Pertinent* is usually used with *to* and a noun object <*pertinent to* the matter at hand>. Sometimes it is followed by the infinitive <it would be *pertinent* to discuss the issue at least>. It is also found with *as regards, for,* or *in.*

peruse *Peruse* has for a long time held two rather contradictory narrow meanings, namely, "to examine or consider with attention and in detail" and "to look over or through in a casual or cursory manner." In broader use it means simply "to read" and may suggest either an attentive or a quick reading. In our time it tends to have a literary flavor, whichever meaning is involved.

pervert The verb *pervert* is used with *into, to,* or *by* <*perverted* the trial *into* a media show> <*perverted* it *to* their own ends> <*perverting* the original play *by* introducing new scenes>. Somewhat less frequently, it is followed by *for, from,* or *with.*

phenomena *Phenomena* is the usual plural of *phenomenon* <scientists have yet to link these *phenomena* to a specific cause>. Use of *phenomena* as a singular (as in "St. Elmo's Fire is an eerie *phenomena*") is encountered in speech and now and then in writing, but it is nonstandard and it is safer to avoid it.

phony *Phony* is an Americanism of obscure origin first attested in print in 1900. It was originally considered slang, but over the decades it has been used in contexts that are less and less slangy <used *phony* credentials to land the job>. By now it must be regarded as standard. The spellings *phony* and *phoney* are both found, but *phony* is the predominant form by a wide margin.

pianist Our evidence shows that the pronunciation \pē-ˈan-əst\ seems to prevail among classical musicians and radio announcers, \ˈpē-ə-nəst\ being less common.

pique When the verb *pique,* in the sense "to irritate," takes a preposition, it is either *at* or *by* <was *piqued at* them for discounting her claim> <was *piqued by* this reversal of fortune>. When *pique* means "to excite or arouse," the preposition of choice is *by* <was *piqued by* the unexpected news>.

place As in the case of *anyplace, everyplace,* and *someplace,* some critics worry that *place* itself in expressions like *going places, go any place,* or *going* *no place,* is substandard. Yet these uses are solidly established in American English, and there has never been any reason to avoid them in general writing.

plan **1.** Although some critics consider phrases like *plan ahead, plan in advance,* and *plan out* redundant, preferring *plan* by itself, such combinations serve the purpose of narrowing the focus of the verb, which has more than one sense. You may safely ignore the critics' complaints.

2. *Plan on, plan to. Plan on,* followed by a gerund <is *planning on* going>, is more often found in spoken than in written use. *Plan on* is also used with a noun object <*plan on* fewer guests than the number invited>. *Plan to* (followed by an infinitive) is more usual in general written use <had *planned to* complete the project by May>.

playwright, playwrite The *-wright* in *playwright* is from an obsolete sense of *wright* that meant "maker" (as in *wheelwright, shipwright,* and *wainwright*). The spelling *playwrite* for the noun is considered an error. However, the spellings *playwrighting* and *playwriting* are both common for the verbal noun <the art of *playwriting* [*playwrighting*]>.

plead *Plead* belongs to the same class of verbs as *bleed, lead, speed, read,* and *feed,* and like them it has a past tense and a past participle with a short vowel spelled *pled* or sometimes *plead.* However, the regular form *pleaded* has always competed with the short-vowel form. Both *pled* and *pleaded* are in good use in the United States today; only *pleaded* is standard in British English.

pleased *Pleased* is often followed by *to* and an infinitive <was *pleased to* arrange the meeting>. The passive *pleased* is often followed by prepositional phrases beginning with *with, about,* or *by* <is *pleased with* the results> <was *pleased about* the news> <were *pleased by* these signs of progress>.

pled See PLEAD.

plenty **1.** Many critics advise avoiding the adverb *plenty* in writing and replacing it with *very, quite,* or a more precise word. Actually, *plenty* is often more precise than its recommended replacements <it's already *plenty* hot in the kitchen> <the complaints were piling up *plenty* fast> <has *plenty more* to say>. However, it is not used in formal writing.

2. *Plenty* was once in literary use as a predicate adjective <whisky was *plenty*> but is not much used any more; as an attributive adjective (as in "there's *plenty* work to be done"), it is primarily found in spoken English.

plethora **1.** Some critics complain that *plethora* should not mean simply "a lot," as it often seems to in ordinary usage, but rather "an excessive amount." In actual practice, *plethora* may connote an undesirable excess, an undesirably large supply but not an excess, an excess that is not necessarily undesirable, or simply an abundant supply. All of these uses are well established and standard.

2. *Plethora* often occurs in the phrase *a plethora of* followed by a plural noun. When this unit governs the verb of a sentence, notional agreement prevails. Writers who view the plethora as a lump use a singular verb <*a plethora of* chorus-line dancers is used in the production>; those who view it as a collection of discrete items use a plural verb <*a plethora of* new films were on offer>.

plunge When *plunge* is used with a preposition, it is most often *into* <*plunged into* the river>. It is also frequently used with *in* <*plunged* right *in* the water>, somewhat less frequently with *through, to, beneath, down,* and *over* <*plunging through* the morass> <*plunged to* near zero> <*plunged beneath* the surface> <sales *plunge down* sharply at this point> <*plunging over* the goal line>, and additionally with *for, on,* and *toward* (or *towards*).

plus The preposition *plus* has long been used with a meaning equivalent to *and* <two *plus* two>; it is therefore not very surprising that in time it has come to be used as a conjunction <had a sandwich and juice *plus* dessert>. This use is now established in casual prose. The related sense "in addition" that is invoked when *plus* joins clauses <the apartment was small; *plus* it was unfurnished> is used chiefly in speech and in informal writing.

point in time This phrase is often criticized as a wordy locution for either *time* or *point* by itself. And yet a great many writers use it, including the critics themselves. If you need it for rhythm or another stylistic reason, you may use it; otherwise, one of the single words will be adequate.

point of view Constructions like "from a maintenance *point of view*" or "from the *point of view* of security" are sometimes thought to be awkward or wrong because a nonhuman subject cannot have a point of view. But it is hard to see anything seriously wrong with uses like these, since the human subject is always implicitly present, being (if no one else) the speaker or writer. What needs to be avoided is not so much the construction as overreliance on it.

politics *Politics* can take either a singular or a plural verb. When it means "a person's political opinions or sympathies," it is quite likely to be plural <his *politics* have caused him trouble>. Other senses may be either singular or plural <the *politics* of space exploration is [are] again in the news> <Russian *politics* are [is] unique>.

ponder The prepositions usually used with *ponder* are *on* and *over* <*pondered on* her fate> <*pondered over* these issues>, but *about* or *upon* are also found <*pondering about* welfare reform> <would *ponder upon* it>.

pore, pour These two verbs are occasionally switched by mistake. What usually happens is that *pour* is used when the less familiar *pore,* "to read or study attentively," is called for.

portentous *Portentous,* which has as its two earliest senses "relating to or being a portent or omen" <wondrous and *portentous* signs> and "eliciting amazement or wonder, prodigious" <the *portentous* size and strength of the gorilla>, more recently began to be used in a sense close to "pretentious" <a *portentous* air of military greatness>. Though the latter use is sometimes criticized, it is fully established.

possessed When *possessed* is used as a participle or adjective meaning "influenced or controlled," it takes *by* <*possessed by* personal demons> or, less frequently, *with* <*possessed with* the idea>. The phrase *to be possessed of* means "to be the owner of" <*is possessed of* a certain talent>.

possibility When some likelihood is being considered, we usually refer to the possibility *of* its occurrence or existence <the *possibility of* life on other planets>. When *possibility* is used in the plural with a meaning close to "opportunities," it can be followed by *for* <numerous *possibilities for* trade>.

possible **1.** *Possible* is sometimes considered to be an ABSOLUTE ADJECTIVE (see Glossary).

2. Critics occasionally quibble over the use of *may* with *possible* or *possibly,* thinking it redundant <*may* *possibly* upset the balance>. However, *possibly* actually serves to reinforce *may,* underlining its seriousness. There is nothing wrong with such use.

pour See PORE, POUR.

practicable, practical *Practicable* has two basic senses, "feasible" <the most *practicable* plan of the lot> and "usable" <a *practicable* route up the west face of the mountain>. *Practical* has a much wider range of meaning, but the sense closest to those of *practicable* is "capable of being put into use, useful" <a *practical* knowledge of French>. Our evidence suggests that writers generally successfully distinguish between these two words.

practically *Practically* has a sense meaning "almost, nearly, virtually" <*practically* everyone contributed> that some critics regard as a misuse. But this sense has been in everyday use for more than two centuries and continues to come naturally from the pens of reputable writers. It is entirely standard.

practice, practise The noun *practice* is almost always spelled with the second *c* in both Britain and American. The verb is normally spelled *practise* in Britain; in America it is spelled both *practice* and *practise.*

precede, proceed These two words are occasionally mixed up or misspelled (e.g., *preceed* for *precede, procede* for *proceed*). *Precede* means "to come before," *proceed* "to advance or continue."

precedence, precedents The substitution of *precedence* ("priority") for *precedents* ("earlier examples") occurs occasionally. Be sure to match your spelling to your meaning.

precedent 1. When the adjective *precedent* is used with a preposition, the preposition is usually *to* <a condition *precedent to* any early decision>, but occasionally *of* <a condition *precedent of* advancement>.

2. When the noun *precedent* takes a preposition, the preposition is most often *for* <cited two historical *precedents for* the situation>. It is somewhat less frequently used with *of* <setting a *precedent of* abusive rule> and occasionally with *against* or *to.*

3. See PRECEDENCE, PRECEDENTS.

precipitate, precipitous Many critics insist on keeping these adjectives distinct. *Precipitate,* they say, means "headlong," "abrupt," or "rash" <the army's *precipitate* withdrawal>; *precipitous* means only "steep" <a *precipitous* slope>. Actual usage, however, is somewhat more complicated. *Precipitous* and *precipitously* are commonly used figuratively to suggest abruptness, much as *precipitate* does <*precipitous* changes> <output dropped *precipitously*>. Overlap between the two words has existed for centuries, and almost all dictionaries show that *precipitous* has as one of its senses "precipitate." The use is standard.

predominate, predominately The adjective *predominate* (and its derivative *predominately*) is today what it has been since the 17th century: a less common alternative to *predominant* (and its derivative *predominantly*). It is not an error, as some critics charge, and not even particularly rare; but it is still distinctly a minority usage.

preface **1.** The noun *preface* is usually used with *to* <served as the young man's *preface to* politics>, but also sometimes with *for* <wrote the *preface for* the book>.

2. The verb *preface* may be used with *with* <*prefaced* his speech *with* a prayer> or, less often, with *by* <the race was *prefaced by* the traditional sounding of the horn>.

prefer When *prefer* is used to compare two things, the second, especially if it is a noun or pronoun, is usually introduced by *to* <*prefers* basketball *to* baseball>. *Over* is occasionally used, especially in advertising <most *prefer* it *over* the other brand>. *Rather than* is sometimes used—especially with two infinitives, the second often without *to* <*prefers* to rent the video *rather than* see the film in the theater>.

preferable *Preferable* is sometimes considered an ABSOLUTE ADJECTIVE (see Glossary) and the combination *more preferable* has been condemned. Almost no one uses *more preferable,* but *preferable* is used with many other modifiers, such as *much, greatly, far, slightly,* and *vastly.*

preference *Preference* is often followed by *for* <expressed a *preference for* shellfish>, but also often with *in, of,* and *regarding*. The phrase *in preference to* is also common <chose unemployment *in preference to* reduced pay>.

prejudice The most frequently used preposition with *prejudice,* noun and verb, is *against* <his *prejudice against* Asians> <*prejudiced against* women>. *In favor of* is used for the opposite meaning, though much less frequently <*prejudiced in favor of* high-income earners>.

preoccupied *Preoccupied* is almost always used with *with* <became *preoccupied with* his place in history>. It may also be followed by *about* or *by* <was *preoccupied about* increases in health-care costs> <were *preoccupied by* the children>.

preparatory When used with a preposition, *preparatory* takes *to* <a sketch *preparatory to* the actual painting>. Some critics consider *preparatory to* a pretentious or wordy substitute for *before,* but *before* does not always work in its place, and writers continue to find the phrase useful. See also PREVIOUS TO; PRIOR TO.

prerequisite **1.** The noun *prerequisite* is usually followed by *for* or *to* when it takes a preposition <one *prerequisite for* admission> <a *prerequisite to* the course>, and sometimes by *of* <the first *prerequisite of* newspaper reporting>.

2. The adjective *prerequisite* is usually followed by *to* when it takes a preposition <was *prerequisite to* gaining entry to the king's court>.

present The verb *present* is most commonly found with *to* or *with,* the former marking the receiver <was *presented to* them> and the latter the thing presented <were *presented with* an award>. *Present* is also used with *as* <*presented as* a gift>, *at* <*presented at* the ceremony>, or *for* <*presented for* valor in battle>.

presently The sense of *presently* meaning "at present" has been in more or less continuous standard use since the 15th century <are *presently* accepting recommendations>, though some critics, believing it should mean only "before long," continue to warn against its use.

preside When it takes a preposition, *preside* is most commonly found with *over* <*presiding over* the festivities>. Somewhat less frequently, it is used with *at* <*presiding at* the ceremony> and occasionally with *in* <*presides in* council meetings>.

presume See ASSUME, PRESUME.

pretense, pretence The usual spelling in America is *pretense;* the usual spelling in Britain is *pretence.*

pretty *Pretty* is used to tone down a statement <*pretty* cold weather> and is in wide use across the whole spectrum of English. It is common in informal speech and writing, but is neither rare nor wrong in more serious contexts <the reasons must be *pretty* cogent>.

prevail *Prevail* is most often used with *upon* when it means "to use persuasion successfully" <*prevailed* *upon* him to change his mind>, and less frequently with *on* <*prevailed on* her to meet him for dinner> or *with* <*prevailed with* the committee to introduce the bill>. When *prevail* means "to triumph," it is often used with *over* and *against* <the tenants *prevailed over* the landlord> <the status quo *prevailed against* change>.

prevent *Prevent* is used in a number of different standard constructions. There is *prevent* + a noun or pronoun + *from* + an *-ing* form of a verb <to *prevent* that from happening>. Then there is *prevent* + possessive pronoun or noun + *-ing* <to *prevent* their leaving>. And there is *prevent* + noun or objective pronoun + *-ing* <to *prevent* the car['s] rolling>. Finally, *prevent* + an *-ing* form with no noun or pronoun is sometimes used <to *prevent* being taken to the cleaners>.

preventative, preventive Both of these words have been around for over 300 years, and both have been frequently used by reputable writers. The only real difference is that *preventive* is much more common than *preventative*.

previous to This phrase has been widely condemned by many critics on a number of different grounds, none of them adding up to a serious argument against its use, though some commentators defend it. It is true that most writers find *before* (the critics' preferred substitute) more useful most of the time, but *previous to* and other compound prepositions like it (e.g., *preparatory* *to, prior to*) are available for variety when you want them. See also PREPARATORY; PRIOR TO.

principal, principle To rehearse what you must have learned in grammar school: Only *principal* is an adjective <the *principal* source used>, but it is also a noun, usually signifying either a person <the school *principal*> or money <still owed on the *principal*>. *Principle* is only a noun, usually designating a law or rule <the *principles* of good government>.

prioritize *Prioritize* remains a jargon word used in business and other specialized fields. Unless you are working in a field where the word is commonly used, you will probably not need it.

prior to Sometimes termed pompous or affected, *prior to* is a synonym of *before* that most often appears in rather formal contexts, such as the annual reports of corporations. It may occasionally emphasize the notion of anticipation <should be verified *prior to* proceeding>. It is also sometimes used in less formal contexts. See also PREPARATORY; PREVIOUS TO.

proceed See PRECEDE, PROCEED.

proficient *Proficient,* when used with a preposition, usually takes *in* or *at* <*proficient in* translating foreign languages> <*proficient at* chess>.

prohibit *Prohibit* is often followed by *from* and a gerund <were *prohibited from* selling the property>. *Prohibit from* can also be followed by a noun <was not

prohibited from use>. Without *from,* prohibit may be followed by a noun or gerund as direct object <*prohibit* the replacement of workers> <*prohibited* his going to school>.

prophecy, prophesy Mind your spelling here: *prophecy* is a noun <the ancient *prophecy*> and *prophesy* a verb <as he had *prophesied*>.

propitious *Propitious* is usually used with *for* or *to. For* is often followed by a gerund <the environment was *propitious for* starting a new business>; *to* is often followed by an infinitive <the moment was *propitious to* declare his love>.

prostrate, prostate These two words are sometimes switched by mistake. *Prostrate* refers to lying down or to being overwhelmed by something, *prostate* to a gland at the base of the male urethra.

protect *Protect* is frequently found with *from* and slightly less frequently with *against* <to *protect* the skin *from* exposure> <to *protect* yourself *against* criminals>. It is also often used with *by* and *with* to express a different relation <is *protected by* tenure from being removed> <*protected with* multiple layers>.

protest **1.** The noun *protest* is most often used with *against* <in *protest against* the regime>, less often with *at* <a storm of public *protest at* the removal>, and occasionally with *of* or *to* <in *protest of* [*to*] the decision>.

2. The verb *protest* appears with *about, at,* or *over* <*protesting about* the treatment of women> <*protested at* the incivility of it all> <*protested over* the denial of accreditation>.

proved, proven The past participle *proven* has gradually worked its way into standard English over the past 350 years. It is now about as frequent as *proved* in all contexts <demanded that it be *proved* [*proven*]>. As an attributive adjective <*proven* [*proved*] gas reserves>, *proven* is much more common than *proved.*

provide When *provide* is used intransitively, it is most often used with *for* <*provide for* the common defense>. When it is used transitively to mean "to supply or make available," a prepositional phrase beginning with *for* or *to* often follows <*provided* new uniforms *for* the band> <*provides* job-training opportunities *to* young people>. But when *provide* is used to mean "to make something available to," the prepositional phrase usually begins with *with* <*provided* the children *with* free balloons>. When used to mean "to stipulate," it is often followed by a clause <the contract *provides* that certain deadlines will be met>.

provided, providing Although occasionally still disapproved, *providing* is as well established as a conjunction as *provided* is <no reason not to use it, *provided* [*providing*] you use it sparingly>, though *provided* is more common.

proximity The phrase *close proximity* has been called redundant, but it is not necessarily so, as some things can be nearer than others. *Close* merely emphasizes the closeness. It is used in general writing <within *close proximity* of the park> and is quite common in technical contexts as well.

publically *Publically* is an infrequent variant spelling of *publicly.* Although it is not really a misspelling—it is recognized in a number of standard dictionaries—it will look unfamiliar to many who encounter it.

punish *Punish* is found most often with *for* and an object that names the offense <*punished for* stealing>. Less often it is used with *by* or *with* and an object that names the punishment <*punished* her *by* withdrawing his love> <*punished* him *with* a whipping>.

purposefully, purposely These two adverbs can be used in similar situations, but are usually distinguished by writers. *Purposely* is the simpler word, meaning merely "on purpose, not by accident" <she *purposely* spilled the milk to get attention>, while *purposefully* is intended to suggest that the person or persons written about did what they did for a purpose, perhaps even with determination <he strode *purposefully* to the front of the stage>.

Q

question **1.** When *question* is followed by a preposition, it is usually *of* <a *question of* propriety>. *Question* is also used, but much less frequently, with *about* and *as to* <*questions about* her past> <a *question as to* whether it was warranted>.

2. Preceded by a qualifier like *no* or *little, question* is often followed by a clause introduced by *but that, but what,* or simply *that* <no *question but that* they are sincere> <little *question that* it would take place>. *Question* may also be followed by a clause introduced by *whether* or *which* <the *question whether* the practice is fair> <the *question which* came first, the chicken or the egg>.

questionnaire This word is sometimes misspelled with only one *n.*

quick, quickly The adverb *quick* (as in "Come *quick!*"), though old, is now more likely to be encountered in speech than in writing, except when the writing is deliberately informal or includes dialogue. The usual choice in more formal prose is *quickly* <she moved *quickly*>.

quote **1.** The noun *quote,* short for *quotation,* was first recorded in the late 19th century and gradually made its way into standard if somewhat casual writing <plenty of *quotes* from Shakespeare>. But there will be contexts where *quotation* sounds better.

2. The noun *quote* is also used to mean "quotation mark." Like the "quotation" sense, this "mark" sense is about a hundred years old and is by now standard in informal writing.

R

rack, wrack The prescriptions of critics who seek sharp distinctions between these two words can be stated as follows: the verb *rack,* which is related to the noun designating an instrument of torture, means "strain" or "torment" and is the correct choice in *nerve-racking, rack one's brains,* and similar expressions. The verb *wrack* and noun *wrack,* on the other hand, are etymologically related to *wreck* and should be used when wreckage or destruction is being described, as in the phrases *storm-wracked* and *wrack and ruin.* Actual usage varies somewhat, however. *Wrack* is commonly used as a verb meaning "torment" <he *wracked* his brain> <it was nerve-*wracking*>, and the noun *rack* is sometimes used interchangeably with *wrack,* especially in *rack and ruin.* Many of these phrases are, in any case, clichés and perhaps best avoided on those grounds.

racket, racquet These spelling variants are both established in reputable use. *Racket* is the more common of the two.

raise, rear The notion that we *raise* plants and animals and *rear* children is often repeated by schoolteachers and language commentators, but the facts of actual usage differ somewhat. *Raise,* used of children, is perfectly respectable American English and is very common especially in the southern United States. *Rear* is still in common use too, and some writers use it interchangeably with *raise.* You may use either word.

rarely ever This phrase is an established spoken idiom <I *rarely ever* see them>. In writing, however, *rarely* is almost always used alone.

read where See WHERE 2.

real Most critics consider the adverb *real* (as in "a *real* hard time") to be informal and more suitable to speech than writing. Our evidence shows these observations to be true in the main, but *real* is becoming increasingly common in writing of an informal, conversational style ("it was *real* fun"). It is used as an intensifier only and is not interchangeable with *really* except in that use <*really* [*real*] fine work>.

Realtor This word is sometimes pronounce \ˈrē-lə-tər\, a switched-around form of \ˈrē-əl-tər\. While the latter pronunciation is standard, the former is not very well established.

rear See RAISE, REAR.

reason is because The locution *the reason is because* has been in use—including heavy literary use—for about 350 years, usually with words intervening between *reason* and *because* <*the reason* the practice continues *is because* no one has questioned it>. Nevertheless, many critics find fault with it—on grounds that are shaky both logically and grammatically. Though the phrase must be regarded as standard, disapproval of it will doubtless continue. But if you do use it, you will be in distinguished company that includes Francis Bacon, Jonathan Swift, W. B. Yeats, and Robert Frost.

reason why *Reason why* is denounced as redundant by many critics, who prefer that *why* be omitted. But it dates back to the 13th century and is well established as standard <there is no *reason why* anyone should be upset>.

reckon **1.** When used with a preposition, *reckon* is most often followed by *with,* a combination meaning "to take into consideration" <a force to be *reckoned with*>. Occasionally *reckon* is followed by *among, as, at, by, in,* or *on* (or *upon*).

2. *Reckon* in the sense "suppose, think" <party leaders *reckon* they have the votes> is common in British English and in some American dialects ("I *reckon* I'll be going"), but is generally avoided in standard American prose.

recollect, remember A distinction that can be made between these two words is that *recollect* implies a conscious effort to recall something to the mind <he tried to *recollect* the name of the street>, while *remember* more generally implies only having something available in one's memory <he always *remembered* what she had said>. But the distinction is not a very strong one, and for many writers the real distinguishing characteristic of *recollect* seems to be that it has a folksy quality suggestive of rustic speech. Thus, the use of *recollect* without connotations of conscious effort is not an error.

reconcile Two prepositions are commonly used after *reconcile—with* and *to* <couldn't *reconcile* his ideal *with* reality> <was *reconciled to* hardship>.

recur, recurrence, reoccur, reoccurrence Of these two pairs, *recur* and *recurrence* are by far the more common. Some criticize *reoccur* and *reoccurrence* as unnecessary, but the words are useful when you want to say simply that something happened a second time <a *reoccurrence* of this astronomical event is unlikely>. *Recur* and especially *recurrence,* in contrast, often suggest a periodic or frequent repetition <a *recurring* nightmare>.

refer This verb is often used with *back* <please *refer back* to the earlier passage>, a use that is sometimes criticized as redundant. But the "backward" connotations of *refer* are usually not strong, and *back* can be useful in reinforcing them.

referendums, referenda These two plurals are about equally common in current use. You may use whichever you prefer.

refute *Refute* has two senses, both of which are in common use but one of which is widely regarded as an error. The original and uncontroversial sense is "to prove wrong, show to be false or erroneous" <*refuted* the argument point by point>. The disputed sense is "to deny the truth or accuracy of" <*refuted* the allegations>. The latter sense originated in the 20th century, and, though fairly new, is thoroughly established as standard.

regard The expressions *in regard to, with regard to, as regards,* and *regarding* are sometimes criticized as wordy and jargonistic. The critics prefer such alternatives as *about, on,* and *concerning,* and you will often find these preferable. However, the issue of wordiness is generally secondary to the issue of how your sentence sounds; when longer phrases suit the rhythm of a sentence better than short ones, the longer ones are a better choice.

relate The intransitive sense of *relate* that means "to have or establish a relationship, interact" <can't *relate* to that kind of music> established itself in general use during the 1960s. Although it has been criticized, it is established in speech and in general (but not formal) writing. It is more likely to seem acceptable when followed by a *to* phrase (as above) than when alone (as in "she just can't *relate*").

relation **1.** *Relation, relative.* These two words are synonymous in the sense "a person to whom one is related," and they are frequently plural in that sense. Various critics prefer one or the other term, but they are both standard and common.

2. *Relation* is usually used with *of* in the sense of "relative" and sometimes in other senses <a distant *relation of* mine> <the *relation of* time and space>. But *to* is more common with most senses and with most of the idiomatic expressions <in *relation to*>. *With* and *between* (and occasionally *among*) are also used <her *relation with* her employees> <*relations between* the United States and Mexico>.

relative See RELATION 1.

relatively The use of *relatively* to modify an adjective when no comparison is stated or implied <looking *relatively* calm and composed> is sometimes criticized. However, this use is common and completely standard today. *Relatively* is also standard in explicit comparisons <compared with what happened later, the start of our acquaintance was *relatively* cordial>.

remedy When used with a preposition, *remedy* is often followed by *for* <a *remedy for* inaction>. Less frequently, it is used with *against* and *to* <a *remedy against* abuse of the system> <offers no *remedy to* the problem>.

remember See RECOLLECT, REMEMBER.

reoccur, reoccurrence See RECUR, RECURRENCE, REOCCUR, REOCCURRENCE.

reprisal The most common preposition following *reprisal* is *against* <*reprisals against* the government>. *On* (or *upon*) is also used <*reprisals on* enemy targets>, as is *for* <in *reprisal for* the attack>.

repugnance When *repugnance* is used with a preposition, it is usually *to* <a *repugnance to* pretense>. Other prepositions sometimes used with *repugnance* are *for* and *toward* (or *towards*) <a *repugnance for* the military solution> <a *repugnance toward* her department chair>.

resemblance When *resemblance* is followed by a preposition, the preposition is usually *to* <bears a *resemblance to* his cousin>, often *between* <a strong *resemblance between* the two>, and sometimes *among* <the *resemblance among* works in the series>.

resentment *Resentment* takes several different prepositions, most commonly *at* <her *resentment at* being treated that way>, *of* <his *resentment of* them>, and *against* <felt no *resentment against* the legal system>. Other possibilities are *toward* (or *towards*), *over,* and *for.*

respect See IN RESPECT TO, WITH RESPECT TO.

responsibility A person is usually said to have a responsibility *for* something and *to* someone <the *responsibility for* carrying out the project> <a *responsibility to* her students>. *Responsibility* is also frequently followed by *of,* with the same meaning as *for* <the *responsibility of* organizing the affair>. Other prepositions that sometimes occur with *responsibility* include *about, in,* and *toward* (or *towards*).

reticent *Reticent* has recently developed the new sense "hesitant" or "reluctant" <lawmakers have been *reticent* to take up the issue> that is sometimes criticized. The use, however, is well established. The older senses of *reticent,* "inclined to be silent" <an extremely *reticent* man> and "restrained in expression or appearance" <his poems have a certain *reticent* charm>, are not disputed. The noun *reticence* has similarly developed an extended meaning, "reluctance," which has likewise become well established.

revel *Revel* is most often used with the preposition *in* <*reveling in* their success>, but occasionally it occurs with *at, around, on,* or *with.*

revenge The noun *revenge* is often followed by *on, against,* or *for.* The first two of these prepositions mark the object of the revenge <taking *revenge on* innocent civilians> <wants *revenge against* his tormentor>, the last its motive <*revenge for* the slaying of his brother>.

revert Although *revert back* is frequently cited as a redundancy, its occurrence in edited writing is not rare <would *revert back* to an earlier phase>. But *revert* by itself occurs far more often.

reward One is usually rewarded *for* something done, *with* (or sometimes *by*) something desirable, and *by* someone or something that provides the reward.

rich When *rich* takes a preposition, it is usually *in* <a city *rich in* traditions>, though occasionally *with* is used <life seemed *rich with* promise>.

rid *Rid* is almost always used with *of* <to *rid* the dog *of* fleas>, though once in a while an older combination with *from* is used <*ridding* fleas *from* the dog>. *Rid* is also often used in the phrases "get rid of" and "be rid of."

right **1.** Various uses of the adverb *right* have been criticized on various grounds, but the disputed uses are standard in informal writing <you could see *right* through it> <should have left *right* away> <we came *right* at the end>. When used as an intensifier <was *right* proud of the child>, *right* is sometimes associated with the speech of Southern and nearby states, but this use is in fact fairly common in the informal writing of people from various parts of the country.

2. *Right, rightly.* See WRONG, WRONGLY.

rob When *rob* takes a preposition, it usually takes *of* <*robbed* them *of* their dignity>, though occasionally it takes *from* <*robs* some intensity *from* the performance>.

round See AROUND 2.

run the gauntlet [gantlet] See GAUNTLET, GANTLET.

S

said The use of *said* as an adjective meaning "afore-mentioned" <*said* agreement is effective immediately> is today found almost exclusively in legal and business contexts.

sake In the expressions *for goodness' sake* and *for conscience' sake,* where the possessive's \s\ sound is never articulated in speech, the apostrophe alone is generally used in writing. When the word is short, the -s is likely to be pronounced and *-'s* is likely to be written: *for peace's sake, for the human race's sake.*

same The use of *same* as a pronoun, often with *the* <have enclosed *same*> <more of *the same*> is often criticized as business jargon, but the word has been in continuous use in general contexts—including literary ones—since the 14th century. Especially without *the,* it can sound wooden in awkwardly written prose, but it is often simply a mark of an informal style <will be attending *same*>.

same as **1.** Critics sometimes warn against using *the same as* in place of *as* or *just as* <he acts *the same as* he used to> (instead of ". . . just as he used to"). It is true that *as* and *just as* are more common in writing than *the same as,* but *the same as* is by no means incorrect.

2. Another old controversy has to do with whether a clause following *same* should be introduced by *as* rather than *that.* Both are in fact in reputable use <the *same* amount of compensation *as* [*that*] the others got>.

sated, satiated Both *sated* and *satiated* are followed by *with* <readers were *sated with* sensationalistic stories> <the new parents were *satiated with* others' opinions on childrearing>.

saturate When *saturate* is followed by a preposition, the usual choice is *with* <the pack's contents were *saturated with* moisture>; *by* and *in* are also occasionally used <kids are being *saturated by* television advertising> <a room *saturated in* sunlight>. When the object of *saturate* is a reflexive pronoun, the preposition that follows is *in* <*saturated* himself *in* the literature of the era>.

scared **1.** When used with a preposition, *scared* is most often followed by *of* <*scared of* snakes>. It is also used quite commonly with *about, at,* and *by* <*scared about* the change> <*scared at* the prospect> <*scared by* the news> and may be followed by *to* and the infinitive <*scared to* go out>.

2. The combination *scared of* <*scared of* snakes> has been criticized as a poor substitute for *afraid of.* But *scared of* is common—and standard—in speech and in casual and informal prose.

sceptic See SKEPTIC, SCEPTIC.

search When used with a preposition, the noun *search* is usually followed by *for* <a *search for* food>

except in the phrase *in search of* <had gone *in search of* help>.

Scotch, Scottish In Scotland, *Scottish* is the preferred adjective <*Scottish* tradition> <the *Scottish* philosopher>. *Scotch* is used chiefly in familiar compounds for well-known things like Scotch broth, Scotch whisky, the Scotch pine, and the Scotch terrier.

seasonable, seasonal Whereas *seasonable* means "suitable to the season" <*seasonable* temperatures>, *seasonal* means "of or relating to a season, occurring in a particular season" <*seasonal* migration>. They are sometimes confused.

secondly *Secondly* is used with some frequency in a series after *first* or *in the first place.* See FIRSTLY.

seeing as, seeing as how, seeing that The compounds *seeing as* and *seeing as how* (as in "*seeing as* the vote hasn't been taken" or "*seeing as how* the senator was the bill's original sponsor") are criticized by some as nonstandard, but rather they seem simply to be spoken forms. In writing, *seeing that* is the usual form <*seeing that* the climate has now changed>.

seek The verb *seek* is frequently used with *after* or *for. After* tends to occur most often with the past participle *sought* in a passive construction <the film star was much *sought after*>, but active use also occurs <we had better not *seek after* the cause>. *For* is common with all tenses and voices <*seeking for* clues>

<these results were not particularly *sought for*>. *Seek* is also commonly followed by *to* and an infinitive <*seeking to* place him at the scene>.

seem See CAN'T SEEM.

see where See WHERE 2.

seldom ever, seldom if ever These two idioms, and the related *seldom or ever* and *seldom or never,* are intensive forms of *seldom* that are sometimes criticized, rather inconsistently, as meaningless or redundant or self-contradictory. But *seldom if ever* is at least 100 years old, and the others are at least a few centuries old. There is no reason to avoid them, though only *seldom if ever* and *seldom or never* are common in 20th-century writing.

self-confessed *Self-confessed* has sometimes been regarded as a redundant substitute for *confessed.* But the meaning of *self-confessed* is typically closer to *admitted* or *avowed* than it is to *confessed* <a *self-confessed* eccentric>, and thus *confessed* will not always substitute for it comfortably.

self-destruct See DESTRUCT, SELF-DESTRUCT.

senior See JUNIOR, SENIOR.

senior citizen *Senior citizen,* though disliked by some as a vapid euphemism, is a well-established term. It is especially common in the plural.

sensitive When *sensitive* precedes a prepositional phrase, the preposition is often *to* <*sensitive to* cold>. The next most common preposition is *about* <somewhat *sensitive about* it>, followed by *of* and *on* <*sensitive of* the rights of minorities> <*sensitive on* most matters>. Very occasionally, *sensitive* has also been used with *as, to, for, in,* or *over.*

sensual, sensuous These two words are generally distinguished as follows: *sensuous* emphasizes aesthetic pleasure <the *sensuous* delights of great music> while *sensual* emphasizes gratification or indulgence of the physical appetites <a life devoted to *sensual* pleasures>. But both words have several meanings, and are close in some of them. If you are in doubt, check a good dictionary.

separate The common spelling *seperate* is considered a mistake. It may help to tell yourself that spelling this word right is *par* for the course.

service Many critics disparage the use of *service* as a verb in contexts where *serve* is also possible <we *service* the tristate area>. Nevertheless, the disapproved sense of *service* continues to be fairly common in general prose and is established as standard.

set, sit *Set* used in place of *sit* (as in "*set* next to me a spell") is primarily a spoken use, found most often in regional, uneducated, and rural speech, and is generally not used in writing except in dialogue. Some intransitive uses of *set* are standard: the sun sets, a hen sets, and so do jelly, plaster, and concrete. Intransitive *sit* <*sit* in a chair> <*sit* in Congress> is uncontroversial, and transitive *sit* is standard especially with *down* <*sit* yourself *down*> <she *sat* us *down*>.

shall, will *Shall* and *will* are generally interchangeable in present-day American English. In recent years, *shall* has been regarded as somewhat affected; *will* is much more common. However, *shall* is still common in questions expressing simple choice <*shall* we go now?>.

shame The noun *shame* can be followed by *at* or *for* or by both when you can feel shame for someone *at* something <her *shame at* the thought> <no *shame for* having done it> <*shame for* her father *at* his awkwardness>. *Over* and *about* may also follow *shame* <*shame over* her role in the affair> <no *shame about* who he is>.

share The newest sense of *share,* "tell, tell about" (as in "I'd like you to *share* what you're feeling"), is disliked by some critics. It is fairly well established in speech but is not much used in writing.

shined, shone *Shine* has had both *shined* and *shone* as its past tense and past participle since the 16th century. Today, we regularly use the transitive *shined* meaning "polished" <getting his shoes *shined*> and frequently use it for "directed the light of" <*shined* his flashlight on them>, though *shone* is also common here. The intransitive form tends to be *shone* <the sun *shone*>, though *shined* is also used in American English <the sun *shined* on the picnic>.

should of See OF 2.

showed, shown The usual past participle of *show* is *shown* <have *shown* their willingness to compromise>, though *showed* is also sometimes used <had *showed* some interest>.

show up *Show up* is sometimes considered colloquial or informal, but the phrase occurs widely in general prose, including formal prose <*showed up* my ignorance> <*showed up* late for the wedding>.

shrink *Shrank* is the usual written past tense of *shrink* <*shrank* from the challenge>, but in speech *shrunk* is also standard (as in "honey, I *shrunk* your sweater"). *Shrunk* and *shrunken* are both used as the past participle: *shrunk* is the usual choice when the participle is functioning as a verb <it seems to have *shrunk*>, *shrunken* when it is functioning as an adjective <a *shrunken* head>.

shy A person can be said to be shy *of* or *about* doing something. *Shy* can also be followed by *to* and the infinitive <*shy to* claim credit>. When *shy* means "showing a lack" or "short," it is followed by *of* <the stew is a little *shy of* seasoning> <just *shy of* six feet>.

sibling *Sibling* is to *brother* and *sister* more or less as *spouse* is to *husband* and *wife:* a formal word that is sometimes useful in contexts where either of the sexually specific words would be inappropriate. It most often occurs in scientific writing but sometimes shows up in general writing as well.

sight See CITE, SITE, SIGHT.

similar **1.** *Similar* is sometimes used as an adverb (as in "step 2 is completed *similar* to the way you completed step 1"). Such usage is regarded as an error but can easily be avoided, either by substituting *similarly* or by rearranging the parts of the sentence to make it read more smoothly: "Completing step 2 is *similar* to completing step 1."

2. One thing is said to be similar in some way *to* another, and two or more things are said to be similar *in* some respect.

simultaneous The use of *simultaneous* as an adverb in place of *simultaneously* (as in "*simultaneous* with this announcement, negotiations were taking place") is considered an error when it occurs in writing and seems to show up primarily in speech.

since Some critics warn that the conjunction *since,* when used to mean "because," can create ambiguity, particularly when both this "because" sense and the alternative "from the time when" sense are meaningful in the same context (as in "the President could have moved ahead, but *since* his opponents took the reins of Congress his efforts have been stymied"). But most writers recognize this ambiguity and try to avoid it. In most contexts there is no potential for ambiguity <*since* it was raining, she took an umbrella>. Though some critics prefer *because* as a causal conjunction in all cases, there is no need for you to adopt such a stringent policy.

sing *Sung* used as the past tense of *sing* is today not so much wrong as simply old-fashioned <*sung* out a round of praise>. *Sang* is the usual past tense, and *sung* is the past participle <they'd *sung* it every year>.

sink Both *sank* and *sunk* are used for the past tense of *sink* <*sank* [*sunk*] back into the chair>. *Sank* is used more often, but *sunk* is neither rare nor dialectal, though it occurs much more often as a past participle <had *sunk* like a stone>.

sit See SET, SIT.

site See CITE, SITE, SIGHT.

skeptic, sceptic *Skeptic* and related words (*skeptical, skepticism*) are usually spelled with a *k* in America and a *c* in Britain.

slow, slowly Some critics claim that careful writers avoid the adverb *slow,* even though it has been used for over four centuries. In actual practice, *slow* and *slowly* are not used in quite the same way. *Slow* is almost always used with verbs that denote movement or action, and it normally follows the verb it modifies <stew should be cooked long and *slow*>. *Slowly* can be used before the verb <outrage that *slowly* changed to

shame> and with participial adjectives <a *slowly* dawning awareness>; it is also used after verbs where *slow* could be used <burn *slowly* [*slow*]> as well as after verbs where *slow* would sound odd <he turned *slowly* toward the door>.

smell *Smell* is one of those verbs that are used with both adjectives and adverbs. When a writer is describing the quality of a smell, an adjective is usual <it *smells* good>. But *smell* can also be used with an adverb of manner, most often when *smell* means "stink" <began to *smell* badly>. *Smell* is also frequently followed by a prepositional phrase introduced by *of* <the place *smelled of* money and power>.

snuck From its earliest appearance in print in the late 19th century as a dialectal and probably uneducated form, the past tense and past participle *snuck* has risen to virtually equal status with *sneaked* <*snuck* down the fire escape> <had quietly *snuck* in>, and it is continuing to grow in frequency. It is most common in the United States and Canada, but has also been spotted in Australia.

so **1.** The use of the adverb *so* as an intensifier <the dialogue is *so* dull> <it is *so* unlike her to behave in that way> is widely condemned in college handbooks but is nonetheless standard in informal prose. *So* is also widely used in negative contexts <not *so* long ago> and when qualified by a dependent clause <was

so good at it that he began to consider it as a career>. These latter uses are never criticized.

2. The use of the conjunction *so* to introduce clauses of result <the acoustics are good, *so* every note is clear> and clauses of purpose <be quiet *so* he can sleep> is standard, though in clauses of purpose, *so that* is more common in formal writing than *so* alone <they want to raze the building *so that* new housing can be constructed>.

so . . . as See AS . . . AS 1.

so as to Because the *so as* of *so as to* can often be omitted <we left early [*so as*] *to* beat the traffic>, it has sometimes been called redundant. On the other hand, some critics suggest *so as to* plus an infinitive as a possible replacement for the conjunction *so* followed by a clause. Where the critics are at odds in this way, you must follow your ear. If a sentence sounds better without *so as,* omit it; if it sounds better with *so as,* keep it. And note that some contexts positively require *so as* or an equivalent like *in order* <they spoke in a whisper *so as* not *to* disturb the others>.

so-called Some critics find fault with using quotation marks to enclose a term or terms following *so-called* <you and your *so-called* "friends">. Their advice is to omit either the quotation marks <you and your *so-called* friends> or the *so-called* <you and your "friends">. In edited writing quotation marks are in fact usually omitted after *so-called,* but their use is not at all rare. Using them is not an error, but they are just as easily and sensibly omitted.

so far as See AS FAR AS, SO FAR AS.

so long as See AS LONG AS, SO LONG AS.

solution When used with a preposition, *solution* is usually followed by *of* or *to* <the *solution of* problems> <the *solution to* the puzzle>, and occasionally by *for* <a *solution for* their problems>.

some **1.** When *some* is used to modify a number, it is almost always a round number <a community of *some* 150,000 inhabitants>. But because some is slightly more emphatic than *about* or *approximately,* it is occasionally used with a more exact number <has *some* 125 tackles to his credit>.

2. When *some* is used without a number, most critics feel that *somewhat* is to be preferred. However, only when *some* modifies an adjective, usually a comparative, will *somewhat* always substitute smoothly <with *some* [*somewhat*] higher temperatures expected>. When *some* modifies a verb or adverb, and especially when it follows a verb, the substitution may prove awkward <forced me to grow up *some*> <I've been around *some* in my day>.

somebody, someone **1.** *Somebody* and *someone* are two of those curious indefinite pronouns that take a singular verb but are often referred to by the plural pronouns *they, their,* and *them* <if *someone* asks, tell *them* you're with me> <the minute *somebody* raises *their* hand>. Some critics are on record as insisting that singular pronouns be used. The governing principle in the choice of pronouns is notional agreement, and when the speaker or writer has more than one person in mind, or a very indefinite somebody, the plural pronoun tends to be used. When a singular pronoun is used to refer to *somebody* or *someone,* the speaker or writer often seems to have someone specific in mind <till *somebody* happened to note it as the second case *he* had heard of>.

2. *Somebody* used to be much more common than *someone;* today, however, *someone* is used more frequently than *somebody.* Both are equally standard; use whichever one you think sounds better in a given context.

somebody else's See ELSE.

some . . . -odd See -ODD.

someone See SOMEBODY, SOMEONE.

someplace *Someplace,* like *anyplace,* is an adverb that has become standard in American English during the 20th century <they were going *someplace* together>. A few critics continue to call it an informal word and to discourage its written use in favor of *somewhere,* but our evidence shows that *someplace* has been common even in academic writing since at least the 1940s. See also ANYPLACE; EVERYPLACE.

sometime The adverb *sometime* is written as a single word <he arrived *sometime* last night>. A phrase combining the adjective *some* and the noun *time* is written as two words <he needed *some time* to think> <we haven't seen them for *some time*>. An easy way to tell if *some* and *time* should be written as one word or two in most contexts is to insert *quite* before *some* and see if the passage still makes sense. If it does, *some* and *time* should be written separately <we haven't seen them for (quite) *some time*> <He arrived (quite) *some time* ago>. If it does not—as in "He arrived (quite) *sometime* last night"—*sometime* is the correct choice.

somewhat See SOME 2.

sooner See NO SOONER.

sort, sort of, sort of a See KIND 1; KIND OF, SORT OF; KIND OF A, SORT OF A.

so that See SO 2.

sparing *Sparing* is generally followed by *in* or *of* when it is complemented by a prepositional phrase <*sparing in* his praise> <*sparing of* their money>. Occasionally *sparing* is found with *with* <*sparing with* their money>.

spell Americans generally use *spelled* for the past tense and past participle of *spell.* British writers commonly use *spelt.*

spill In American English the usual past tense and past participle of *spill* is *spilled. Spilt* is common in British English. As an attributive adjective, *spilt* also occurs occasionally in American English <there's no use crying over *spilt* milk>.

spit The common verb *spit* has as its past tense and past participle either *spat* or *spit* <she *spat* [*spit*] out the words> <he actually *spit* [*spat*] on the ground>. The British prefer *spat.*

spoil In American English *spoiled* is usual for both the past tense and past participle of *spoil.* In British English both *spoiled* and *spoilt* are used.

spokesperson See PERSON 2.

spoonful See -FUL.

spring The past tense of the verb *spring* can be either *sprang* or *sprung. Sprang* is the more common form, but *sprung* is not at all rare. *Sprung* also serves as the past participle <the canoe had *sprung* a leak>.

staffer *Staffer* is a word that many people find handy and yet many others dislike. It has been around since the 1940s and has been a staple of journalism, though it is certainly not indispensable, even for journalists. Anyone determined to avoid it can easily replace it with such terms as *staff member, official,* or *employee.*

stanch, staunch These two spelling variants have been in reputable use for centuries, and they are standard for both the verb and the adjective, though *stanch* is much more common for the verb <used a tourniquet to *stanch* the flow> and *staunch* much more common for the adjective <a *staunch* ally>.

stationary, stationery The adjective that means "not moving" is *stationary* <a *stationary* object>; the noun that means "paper for writing letters" is *stationery* <purchased some *stationery* along with some pens and pencils>. The usual advice for remembering the distinction is to associate the *er* in *stationery* with the *er* in *letter* or *paper.*

staunch See STANCH, STAUNCH.

still and all This phrase is sometimes criticized, but it is clearly standard. Less formal than the starchy *nevertheless* and less abrupt than the simple *still,* it has a casual, conversational quality which is consistent with the informal tone of much modern prose <*still and all,* experimental economics is on the rise>.

stink Both *stank* and *stunk* are used as the past tense of *stink. Stank* is more common in edited prose, but both are standard. The past participle of *stink* is always *stunk* <the room has *stunk* of solvent ever since>.

straitened Though the adjective that means "distressed" or "deprived" <*straitened* circumstances> is actually the past participle of the verb *straiten* and has no relation to either *straight* or *straighten,* the spelling error *straightened* is still fairly easy to make in a moment of inattention.

strata, stratum The plural *strata* has occasionally been used as a singular (as in "one *strata* of society") since the 18th century and is sometimes given the plural *stratas* ("several *stratas* of bureaucracy"). However, these infrequent but persistent usages are generally considered nonstandard. See also LATIN PLURALS.

strike *Struck* is the past tense of *strike* <the clock *struck* twelve>, and usually also functions as its past participle <the tree was *struck* by lightning>. The alternative past participle *stricken* is used when *strike* has the sense "to afflict suddenly" <*stricken* with a heart attack>. It is also common for the sense "to cancel or delete" <*stricken* from the record>; and *stricken* has adjectival uses as well <*stricken* faces>.

strive *Strive* is most often followed by *to* and the infinitive <*striving to* keep a balance>. It is also frequently used with *for* <*strove for* reform>, and less frequently with *after, against, at, in, into, toward* (or *towards*), *with,* and *within.*

subject 1. *Noun.* When the noun *subject* is followed by a preposition, it is usually *of* <the *subject of* the book> and sometimes *for* <a *subject for* debate>.

2. *Adjective.* The adjective *subject* is usually used with *to* <was *subject to* asthma attacks>.

3. *Verb.* The verb *subject* is usually used with *to* <had never *subjected* himself *to* such a regimen>.

4. For a discussion of grammatical subject, see SUBJECT (in Glossary).

such Some critics disapprove of using *such* as a pronoun <*such* was the result> <tin and glass and *such*>, but dictionaries recognize it as standard.

such as See AS 2; LIKE 2.

suffer When followed by a preposition, *suffer* almost always takes *from* <*suffers from* rheumatism>. In speech, *with* is sometimes used (as in "*suffering with* this condition").

suitable The usual preposition after *suitable* is *for* <*suitable for* a wedding ceremony>. *To* is also used, but less commonly <was *suitable to* the couple>.

supersede, supercede *Supercede* has a long history as an occasional spelling variant of *supersede,* but most writers nowadays use *supersede.*

sure, surely Despite the suspicion of many writing handbooks, *sure* and *surely* are both standard adverbs. *Sure* is used much more in informal contexts than *surely,* which is the adverb of choice in a more elevated style. When they are used as intensifiers, *sure* is more emphatic and positive <he *sure* gets them to play hard>, while *surely* is less emphatic and more neutral and suggests that the writer or speaker is being hopeful or persuasive <*surely* such a book could be produced>.

sure and For constructions like *be sure and,* see TRY AND.

surprised The prepositions that occur after *surprised* are *at* and *by. By* is the choice when *surprised* means "taken unawares" <*surprised by* the force of the wind>. Both *at* and *by* are possible when *surprised* means "struck with wonder" or "taken aback" <*surprised at* [*by*] the announcement>.

swell This verb has two past participles, *swelled* and *swollen. Swollen* is the one used frequently as an attributive adjective <a *swollen* foot>; *swelled* is used in this way only in the idiom *swelled head.* Otherwise the two forms are more or less interchangeable, although *swollen* is more likely in describing a harmful or undesirable swelling <the door was *swollen* shut>, and *swelled* tends to be used in a neutral or positive way, especially in describing an increase in numbers <their ranks had *swelled* to 100,000>.

swim The standard past tense of *swim* is *swam* <Oliver and Katy *swam* by> and the standard past participle is *swum* <had *swum* the Channel>.

T

take, see BRING, TAKE.

take exception to See EXCEPTION.

take place, occur Some critics prefer to restrict *take place* to planned events and actions <the ceremony will *take place* on Friday afternoon> and *occur* to things that happen by chance <the accident *occurred* at a busy intersection>. While this tends to reflect actual usage, in much speech and writing planned events also "occur" and accidents also "take place." In short, *take place* and *occur* are synonyms, and there is no reason to adhere strictly to the critics' preference.

teaspoonful See -FUL.

tenant, tenet *Tenant,* meaning "occupant, landholder," is sometimes mistakenly used in place of *tenet,* meaning "principle, doctrine." To avoid this error, remember that *tenant* and *occupant* both end in *-ant.*

tendency A tendency may be either *to* or *toward* (or *towards*) something <a strong *tendency to* [*toward*] hyperbole>. In medical writing, *to* is preferred <a *tendency to* diabetes>.

tenet See TENANT, TENET.

terms See IN TERMS OF.

than *Than* followed by a third-person objective pronoun (as in "older *than* me," "stronger *than* him") is usually frowned upon when it occurs in edited prose. The construction is common in speech, however. In writing, *than* used as a conjunction is standard <older *than* I am> <easier said *than* done> <anywhere else *than* at home>.

than any See ANY 3.

thankfully The adverb *thankfully,* used as a sentence modifier <*thankfully,* it didn't rain>, is sometimes criticized, but the use is fairly common in general writing. See also HOPEFULLY.

thanks to *Thanks to* can be applied to negative causes <tripped over the last hurdle, *thanks to* a pulled ligament> as well as to positive or neutral ones <arrived early, *thanks to* good weather>. Both uses are standard, and in both informal and formal contexts.

that **1.** *That, which, who.* In current usage *that* refers to persons or things <the man *that* I love> <the book *that* she wrote>, *which* refers to things <a tree *which* bears apples>, and *who* refers to persons and sometimes to animals <the man *who* has everything> <buried my cat, *who* died yesterday>. The notion that *that* should not be used to refer to persons is without foundation; such use is entirely standard.

2. *That, which.* Although some critics say otherwise, *that* and *which* are both regularly used to introduce restrictive clauses—clauses essential to the description of the word they refer to <the book *that* [*which*] you ordered is in>. Only *which* is used to introduce nonrestrictive clauses—clauses that are not essential to the meaning of the preceding word <the door, *which* was painted pink, opened onto the garden>.

3. *That* is commonly used in negative statements as an intensifier <it's not *that* simple>. This use, though disliked by some, is standard. See also ALL THAT.

the both See BOTH 3.

the fact is, the fact that See FACT.

the late See LATE.

their **1.** *Their, there, they're.* It is not unusual to see these common words replace one another by mistake. Haste and inattention probably are more responsible than actual confusion about which word is which. However, for the record, *their* is a possessive pronoun <*their* house is down the street>; *there* has various uses as an adjective <that man *there*>, a noun <take it from *there*>, a pronoun <*there* shall come a time>, and, chiefly, an adverb <stop right *there*>; and *they're* is a contraction of *they are.* Remember that the spelling checker of a word processor will not identify a wrong use of one of these.

2. See THEY, THEIR, THEM.

theirs Like *its, ours,* and *yours, theirs* is spelled without an apostrophe in present-day English.

them See THEY, THEIR, THEM.

there See THEIR 1.

there is, there are When *there* is an anticipatory or "dummy" subject, the number of the verb is normally determined by the number of the true subject following: a singular verb precedes a singular noun <*there is* no more coffee>, and a plural verb precedes a plural noun <*there are* several rooms available>.

However, when a compound subject follows the verb and the first element is singular, the verb may be either singular or plural <*there is* a lake and several small streams> <*there are* a dog and a few cats in the house>, the singular construction being more common. Still, some writers insist on formal agreement and use a plural verb <*there were* an apartment house and a parking lot at the end of the block>.

When a collective noun (as subject) is followed by a prepositional phrase with a plural noun (as object) <*there is* a flock of geese overhead> <*there are* a passel of problems associated with it>, the verb is governed by notional agreement: When the speaker or writer has the collective in mind (e.g., *flock* in *flock of geese*), a singular verb is used; and when the plural noun is in mind (e.g., *problems* in *passel of problems*), a plural verb is used.

Some people prefer to say *there is* (or *there's*) in every case, even when the following subject is clearly plural (as in "a lottery where *there's* a hundred thousand losers to every winner"); such usage is generally avoided in writing.

the same as See SAME AS 1.

these kind of, these sort of See KIND 1.

they **1.** For *they* used to refer to a singular noun or pronoun, see THEY, THEIR, THEM.

2. *They* used as an indefinite subject <*they*'re tearing down the building next to my office> is sometimes objected to, primarily on the assumption that every pronoun should have an antecedent. But that assumption is without grammatical foundation; in this use *they* is an indefinite pronoun and indefinite pronouns do not require antecedents. The use is standard.

they, their, them English lacks a common-gender third-person singular pronoun that can be used to refer to indefinite pronouns such as *everyone, anyone,* or *someone*. Writers and speakers have for centuries supplied this lack by using the plural pronouns <everyone should try it once in *their* life> <anyone who knows *their* grammar knows this>. This use is well established in speech and writing, even in literary and formal contexts. You have the option of using the plural or singular pronouns according to which one you think sounds best in a given context <someone on my left kept bumping me with *his or her* [*their*] elbow>.

they're See THEIR 1.

thing *Thing* turns up frequently in speech and in writing that has something of the casual quality of speech <look at this *thing* another way> <the *thing* is to get well>. Some critics advise replacing *thing* with a more specific word or dropping it altogether (for example, "The first *thing* he told me was . . ." could be replaced by "First he told me . . ."). But should you? The answer really depends upon considerations of tone, rhythm, and idiom, and good writers are directed in such matters by their ear—their sense of what sounds right in a particular context.

this The use of *this* (and *that, which,* and *it* as well) as a pronoun to refer broadly to a preceding idea, topic, sentence, or paragraph <protest rallies were being mounted daily, but *this* only served to harden the regime's stance> used to be criticized but is now allowed to be respectable, as long as the reference is clear. See also WHICH 2.

those kind of, those sort of See KIND 1.

though See ALTHOUGH, THOUGH.

through The use of *through* to mean "finished" used to be criticized but is now considered standard. It usually describes either the completion of an activity <is *through* with the job> or a person who is washed-up <she was *through* as a box-office attraction>. See also DONE; FINISHED.

tight, tightly *Tight* is usually an adjective <security was *tight*>, but it is also commonly used as an adverb <the door was shut *tight*> <sleep *tight*>. Some of its adverbial uses overlap with those of *tightly,* but the two words are used mostly in distinct ways. *Tight* almost always follows the verb it modifies. It occurs especially in such idioms as "sit tight" and "sleep tight," as well as with such verbs as *hold, close, squeeze,* and *shut. Tightly* is a somewhat more common word that is used both before and after the verb or participle it modifies <*tightly* woven fabric> <clamped *tightly* in his hand>.

till, until The notion that *till* is a short form of *until* is erroneous; *till* is actually the older word, dating back to at least the 9th century. (*Until* is first recorded around 1200.) Today *until* is often considered somewhat more formal than *till,* and to be the better choice at the beginning of a sentence or clause. But *till,* although less common than *until,* shows up in highly serious writing and at the beginning of a sentence <*Till* his encounter with malaria, he had never known serious illness>.

times Critics sometimes complain about expressions such as "ten *times* less," "three *times* closer," and "five *times* more." Those who do not like the form with *less* insist that *times* invokes multiplication, and those who do not like the form with *more* say it creates mathematical uncertainty. These concerns are misplaced. Idiomatic expressions using *times* have been in use for over 300 years and there is no real reason to avoid them.

to, too, two These words are often inadvertently substituted for one another. Keep a sharp eye out for such errors when proofreading your writing.

to a degree See DEGREE.

to all intents and purposes This phrase has taken various forms throughout its history, including *to all intents, to all intent and purpose,* and *for all intents and purposes,* but *to all intents and purposes* has long been the most common. Critics sometimes call it wordy or hackneyed, but it is used by excellent writers and there is no compelling reason to avoid it. If you prefer a shorter alternative, the best one is usually *in effect.*

too See TO, TOO, TWO.

together with When *together with* serves to add a second noun to a singular noun that is the subject of a sentence <the singer, *together with* opening act Sir Prize, performs tonight>, the verb usually remains singular, especially when the segment introduced by *together with* is set off by commas, dashes, or parentheses. When it is not, the verb may be either singular or plural <the campaign leader *together with* selected staff members are [is] planning to review their strategy>. See also AGREEMENT (in Glossary).

total, totally The use of *total* and *totally* in such phrases as "total annihilation" and "totally destroyed" is occasionally criticized as redundant. *Total* and *totally* can usually be omitted from such phrases without a loss of meaning, but their omission will almost always result in a loss of emphasis, and the rhythm and idiom of the sentence should also be taken into account. If *total* or *totally* sounds right in its context, you may use it.

toward, towards Both *toward* and *towards* are commonly used in the United States, but *toward* is the usual choice. The British strongly favor *towards*. Otherwise, there is no difference between the two forms.

track, tract These words are sometimes confused in their outdoors senses. *Track* refers to a trail or course; *tract* refers to an area of land.

transpire Numerous critics have condemned the use of *transpire* to mean "to come to pass" or "occur" <the events that *transpired* last night> rather than "it was learned" or "it turned out" <it *transpired* that he had known all along>. However, the disputed use is firmly established in both informal and formal prose.

triple, treble Of these two forms, *triple* is the usual choice as either verb or adjective in American English, except that the verb *treble* is sometimes favored by business writers <profits have more than *trebled*>. In British usage, *treble* is the more common word.

triumphal, triumphant The distinction between these two words is basically this: *triumphal* is used with the meaning "ceremonially celebrating or commemorating a victory" <a *triumphal* procession>. and *triumphant* is used in most other cases, as with the meanings "having triumphed" <a *triumphant* army>, "rejoicing for victory" <a *triumphant* shout>, and "notably successful" <a *triumphant* performance>.

trivia *Trivia* is much like *data*—an English word that has the form of the original Latin plural but that is used as both a plural count noun <such *trivia* are his stock-in-trade> and a singular mass noun <a piece of *trivia*>. Some critics regard the singular use as unacceptable, but our evidence shows that it and the plural use are about equally common and are standard. See also LATIN PLURALS.

true When *true* means "faithful," it is often followed by *to* <*true to* her heart>. In other senses, *true* occurs commonly with *for* or *of* instead <the same is *true for* group B> <it is *true of* this particular case>.

trust The prepositions *in* and *to* both occur after the verb *trust* <*trust in* God> <*trust to* luck>. The noun *trust* is usually followed by *in* <placed her *trust in* him>.

try and The use of *try and* in sentences where *try to* would be possible <*try and* find it> <I'll *try and* write you soon> has long been criticized, but the use is an old one. It occurs mostly in speech and in casual writing, though it is not unknown in informal edited prose. A couple of other common verbs are used in similar constructions—namely, *go* <*go and* ask her> and *come* <*come and* see us>. *Be sure and* is also common <*be sure and* walk the dog today>. All these combinations are more characteristic of speech than of writing, but they are nonetheless standard. *Try and* is limited to one form; it cannot be inflected, as *try to* can <*tries to* help> <*tried to* do her best>.

two See TO, TOO, TWO.

type Objection is commonly made to the use of *type* in the sense "sort" to modify a preceding noun (as in "a sting *type* operation"). The standard way of getting around the criticism is to add *of* <a sting *type of* operation> or insert a hyphen before *type* <a sting-*type* operation> or simply drop *type* altogether <a sting operation>.

U

unaware, unawares *Unaware* is common as an adjective <seemed *unaware* of what was going on>. The usual adverb is *unawares* <was taken *unawares*>, but either is likely to occur following *catch* <caught him *unawares* [*unaware*]>.

unbeknown, unbeknownst Both *unbeknown* and *unbeknownst* are in standard use and have been for many years, but *unbeknownst* is the more common form <*unbeknownst* [*unbeknown*] to us>.

under . . . circumstances See CIRCUMSTANCES.

undoubtedly See DOUBTLESS, NO DOUBT, UNDOUBTEDLY.

undue, unduly *Undue* often means simply "not called for, not necessary or appropriate" <places *undue* hardships on the working poor>. More often, its meaning is closer to "inappropriately excessive or immoderate" <an *undue* hostility in those opposed to the accord>. And sometimes *undue* serves as a synonym of *excessive* or *great* <*undue* expansion of the state apparatus>. The same variation in meaning occurs in the adverb *unduly,* which is sometimes used to mean "excessively" or "extremely" <her *unduly* annoying voice>. Because of these variations in meaning, *undue* and *unduly* sometimes appear in contexts where they might seem to be redundant <no cause for *undue* alarm> <no reason to get *unduly* excited>. Many critics regard such usage as inelegant or simply wrong, but it is well established and perfectly standard.

uneatable See INEDIBLE, UNEATABLE.

unequal *Unequal* is often followed by *to* <was *unequal to* the task>.

unequivocally The adverb is *unequivocally* <is *unequivocally* opposed>. The nonstandard equivalent that sometimes shows up in print is *unequivocably.*

unexceptionable, unexceptional In current usage, *unexceptional* nearly always means "not out of the ordinary, not exceptional" <a standard restaurant with

an *unexceptional* menu>. *Unexceptionable,* the less common word, means "not open to objection or criticism" <a perfectly sound and *unexceptionable* argument>.

uninterested See DISINTERESTED, UNINTERESTED.

unique Critics have often claimed that *unique* is an absolute adjective and therefore cannot be modified by adverbs such as *more, most, somewhat,* and *very.* This claim is based on the mistaken assumption that *unique* can mean only "sole" or "unequaled." When *unique* is used in these senses, it is not qualified <his *unique* concern was to get everyone signed on before the project's May start date>. However, when *unique* is used with the more common meaning "unusual," words of comparison and qualification are widespread and standard <a rather *unique* program for the Senator to be sponsoring> <very *unique* diamond settings for this period>.

unlike The use of *unlike* as a conjunction <*unlike* with last year's model, there is no lack of engine power> is sometimes criticized, especially when the preposition following *unlike* is dropped ("*unlike* last year's model, . . ."), creating a false or incomplete comparison between two terms (*model* and *engine power,* rather than the engine power of last year's and this year's model). The construction with the preposition is established, whereas the one without it is not. See also LIKE, 1.

unreadable See ILLEGIBLE, UNREADABLE.

unsanitary, insanitary People sometimes express uncertainty about which of these words is the correct one. Our evidence shows that both are correct, common, and used in the same way.

unsatisfied See DISSATISFIED, UNSATISFIED.

unseasonable, unseasonal See SEASONABLE, SEASONAL.

until See TILL, UNTIL.

up, *adverb* **1.** *Up* is frequently used as a particle after a verb—for example, *burn up, end up, hurry up, climb up,* and *rise up.* Some critics have erroneously concluded that *up* is redundant or otherwise unnecessary in these combinations. But in fact these uses of *up* are a deeply rooted part of everyday conversational English and can often help a writer steer clear of awkward and stilted prose. We suggest that you let *up* fall where it naturally will and not become concerned with revising it out.

2. In two-word verbs like *hold up* or *stick up,* the particle *up* can either stay with the verb <the gunman *held up* the cashier> or follow the direct object <the gunman *held* the cashier *up*>. Some critics dislike the latter word order, but it is nevertheless established. Note that when the direct object is a pronoun, the particle almost always follows it <the gunman *held* her *up*>.

up, *verb* **1.** *Up* as a verb meaning "raise" or "increase" <*upped* the ante> is considered dubious by some. Our evidence shows that it is standard but is not used in formal writing.

2. Some critics view the phrase *up and* <expected them to *up and* walk out> with the same distaste they direct at *go and* and *try and* (see TRY AND). *Up and* is no rustic idiom, however; it is current on both sides of the Atlantic and is used in many general publications, though it is not formal.

upon See ON 1.

up until Since the meaning of *up until* is the same as that of *until* by itself, some critics recommend omitting the *up*. But *up until* is an idiomatic phrase that occurs naturally and appropriately in speech and in casual writing <*up until* the time of his enlistment>. Use your own judgment as to when the *up* sounds right and when it is not needed.

upward, upwards The adjective is *upward* <an *upward* spiral>. The adverb may be either *upward* or, less commonly, *upwards* <the kite rose *upward* [*upwards*]>. Both are standard. Both *upward* and *upwards* are used with *of* to mean "more than, in excess of"; *upwards of* is more common than *upward of* <they cost *upwards of* $25>.

us Like the other personal pronouns, *us* turns up in contexts where critics have long said it does not belong. It occurs after the verb *be* <it is *us*>. It is common in an emphatic position near the beginning of a statement <was *us* against them>. A little harder to explain is its appearance in the subject position <*us* conference attendees hadn't expected this>. These last two, particularly the latter, are more likely to be found in speech than in edited prose.

usage Critics have complained that the word *usage* should not be employed simply as a synonym of *use*. Almost any dictionary, however, defines *usage* to mean "act of use, use, employment" <a decrease in the *usage* of electricity> <their *usage* of migrant labor>. Though *use* is more common than *usage* in this sense, *usage* is not an error.

used to, use to The idiom *used to* meaning "to be accustomed or habituated" <we *used to* hike more than we do now> is extremely common in both speech and writing. Because the *d* is not pronounced, *used to* is indistinguishable in speech from *use to.* In writing, however, *use to* in place of *used to* is considered an error. When *did* is used with *used to,* we write "Did he *use to*?" rather than "Did he *used to*?" The usual negative form in American English is *didn't use to* <they *didn't use to* charge you for it>. See also SUPPOSED TO.

used to could Many writing handbooks attack *used to could* as nonstandard. It is not a complex verb form but a dialectal adverb, *used to,* tacked onto *could.* It is a speech form and is used in writing only for deliberate effect.

useful Something is said to be useful *to* somebody <should be *useful to* the beginner>. When the way in which something is useful is being described, either *in* or *for* may be used <is especially *useful in* [*for*] editing text>.

utilize Critics dislike *utilize* because they regard it as an inflated substitute for *use.* But *utilize* is actually used only when it has the meaning "to turn to practical use or account" <most homes do not *utilize* the entire array of channels available>, and it suggests, more than *use,* a deliberate decision or effort to employ something or someone for a practical purpose.

V

various *Various* is sometimes used as a pronoun, usually followed by *of* <*various of* them came up to us later>. This use was first recorded in British English in the middle of the 19th century and in American English a little later. It is fully established as standard in present-day American English and is fairly common in edited general prose <how the economy will behave if *various of* these factors change>. See also VARIOUS DIFFERENT.

various different This phrase has been criticized as redundant by those who do not recognize that its meaning is "a number of different," not "different different" <*various different* species could be seen>. Other critics have contended that it is incorrect to use *various* in this way to mean "of an indefinite number greater than one." Such use is actually well-established and is certainly standard <the *various* problems that he mentioned>. Even so, you may wish to steer clear of *various different* since it can give the appearance of redundancy. It seems not to occur often in edited prose.

vary One thing or group of things is said to vary *from* another <*vary from* the norm>. When a range of variation is being described, *vary* is followed by either *from* or *between* <the length *varies from* 20 to 25 inches> <the temperature *varies between* 38.6 and 45 degrees Fahrenheit>.

vast majority See MAJORITY.

've See OF 2.

vehicle The usual pronunciation of *vehicle* is without \h\. Pronunciation with \h\, however, is also widespread, especially in the South.

venal, venial *Venal,* which means "open to or characterized by corruption" <rooting out *venal* influences in the precinct> <a thoroughly *venal* man>, is sometimes confused with *venial,* which means "pardonable" <a *venial* fault>.

verbal, oral Some feel that *verbal* cannot be used to mean "spoken rather than written, oral" and views such use as a modern corruption. This is a popular myth; *verbal* is commonly used with such words as *agreement, commitment,* and *contract* in the disputed "oral" sense, and has been so used by major writers for centuries. There is no reason to avoid such use.

vest An abstract possession, such as a power or right, is vested *in* a person or institution <responsibilities *vested in* the federal government>, but a person or institution is vested *with* an abstract possession <*vested* the office *with* similar powers>. Both uses are common and correct.

via *Via* was taken into English directly from Latin in the late 18th century, with the meaning "by way of, by a route passing through" <traveled to Philadelphia *via* New York City>. Two centuries later it continues to be used in this sense—usually with no italics—as well as in the extended sense "through the medium or agency of" <went to Chicago *via* train> and in the sense "by way of" in contexts having nothing to do with travel <influence peddling *via* political action committees>. All of these uses are standard, though some critics dislike all but the original sense.

viable *Viable* is sometimes criticized as a fad word or cliché—especially in the phrase *viable alternative.* Although both the word and the phrase are perfectly standard, you may want to approach them with some caution.

vice, vise In American English, the "moral fault" is spelled *vice* while the "clamping tool" is spelled *vise.* In British English, *vice* is the preferred spelling for both.

vie *Vie* is typically used with the prepositions *with* and *for:* competitors vie *with* each other *for* something.

view The phrase *with a view* usually takes the preposition *to* or *toward* <*with a view to* [*toward*] establishing a consumer credit system>. When the phrase is *with the view, of* is almost invariably the preposition that follows <*with the view of* maintaining these ties>. See also POINT OF VIEW.

vigilant When *vigilant* is used with a preposition, the choice is most often *against, in,* or *to* <*vigilant against* attempts to impose such restraints> <*vigilant in* protecting these freedoms> <must be *vigilant to* prevent it>. Occasionally, *vigilant* may be followed by *about* or *for.*

vis-à-vis The literal meaning of *vis-à-vis* in French is "face to face," but in English *vis-à-vis* is used mostly in its two extended senses, "in relation to" <the role of the legislature *vis-à-vis* the judicial branch> and "in comparison with" <the new Russia *vis-à-vis* the old>. Both of these senses are standard (as they are in French), although a few critics insist on the literal sense only. *Vis-à-vis* has been in use in English since the 18th century and is usually not italicized as a foreign term.

vise See VICE, VISE.

W

wait on, wait for The use of *wait on* in contexts where some would prefer *wait for* or *await* <they no longer needed to *wait on* [*wait for, await*] Washington's approval> cannot be considered dialectal, colloquial, regional, or substandard. On the contrary, it is found in standard and widely circulated prose, even literary prose. If the use of *wait on,* or its occasional variant *wait upon,* is natural to you, there is no need to avoid it.

waitress See -ESS.

waive, wave The usual meaning of *waive* is "to relinquish" <*waived* his right> or "to refrain from enforcing" <*waiving* the rule>. When used where *wave* is expected (as in "to *waive* the whole matter aside"), it is widely regarded as an error and is undetectable by the spelling checker of a word processor.

wake *Wake* originated as two separate verbs that combined in the Middle Ages to produce our modern mixture of inflected forms (past tense: *woke* or *waked;* past participle: *woken, waked,* or occasionally *woke*). *Waked,* for the past tense, was more common formerly than it is now, but it has not disappeared from use <I *waked* just in time for breakfast>. *Woke* is at present the dominant form for the past tense <I *woke* before sunrise>. For the past participle, *woken* and *waked* are both used in American English <he had *woken*

[*waked*] the baby>, whereas British English prefers *woken. Woke* is also occasionally found as past participle <I must've *woke* him up>. To complicate matters, the separate but synonymous verb *waken* is regular (past and past participle: *wakened*).

wary *Wary* is often followed by *of* <is *wary of* phone solicitations>. Less commonly, *wary* is followed by *in,* usually when describing a cautious or hesitant approach toward *doing* something <leads us to be *wary in* believing such reports>. Occasionally *wary* is followed by *about* <*wary about* contacting them>.

wave See WAIVE, WAVE.

ways *Ways* has been used as a synonym of *way* in such expressions as "a long *ways* off" since the late 1500s, and is standard in American English. (In British English, it appears to have died out.) Its occurrence in writing is still frowned upon by some critics.

weave When *weave* is used in its literal senses, its usual past tense and past participle are *wove* and *woven* <they *wove* cloth> <a *woven* fabric>. The same forms are normally used in straightforward figurative examples of *weave* <*wove* together a number of different themes> <*woven* into the social fabric>. But when *weave* describes a winding course of movement, *weaved* usually serves as both its past tense and past participle <they *weaved* down the lane> <had already *weaved* past several obstacles>.

wed The past tense and past participle of *wed* is usually *wedded* <a poem in which he *wedded* everyday life and earthshaking events> <had long been *wedded* to the idea>, but the less common form *wed* is also used <they had been *wed* in the summer>.

well There are those who will criticize your "sing good" and your "feel badly," but you are safe no matter how you use *well. Well* has been both an adjective <I feel *well*> and an adverb <did *well* in math> for centuries, and you can use it safely either way. See also GOOD; FEEL BAD, FEEL BADLY.

well-nigh The adverb *well-nigh* has been called old-fashioned, but in fact it is a fairly common and perfectly good synonym for *nearly* <was *well-nigh* impossible>.

when, where Many critics balk at the use of *when* or *where,* preceded by *is,* in informal definitions such as "word processing *is where* you use a computer to type." These were used as standard defining patterns in reference works for many centuries, but in modern use they are mostly confined to informal defining, such as in glossaries published in newspapers, and to speech.

when and if See IF AND WHEN.

whence See FROM WHENCE.

where **1.** A number of critics worry about the use of *where* in the sense "that" after the verbs *see* and *read*

<I could see *where* he had a point> <you must have read *where* the President vetoed the bill>. This use appears to be more common in speech than in writing, but it is not rare in writing by any means. Similar uses are those in which *where* introduces a clause that modifies a noun, serving as an approximate equivalent to *in which* <an environment *where* people can thrive>, and in which it introduces a clause that is the object of a preposition <finally got him around to *where* he would listen to us>. All of these uses, though standard, are typically found in less formal writing.

2. For other senses and constructions, see WHEN, WHERE; WHERE . . . AT.

whereas See WHILE.

where . . . at The use of *at* following *where* <*where* is he *at*?> is routinely criticized, though it has been a part of American speech for well over 100 years. It was relatively rare in writing until the 1960s, when the phrases "where it's at" and "where you're [I'm, he's, etc.] at" came into widespread use. These phrases continue to be used today <that's *where* we're *at* now>, although they have some of the quality of dated slang. See also AT.

whether See IF 1.

whether or not Critics often point out that *or not* usually isn't necessary after *whether* <we don't know *whether (or not)* they'll come>. However, *or not* has gone with *whether* for more than 300 years and is good idiomatic English. In many instances the *or not* cannot be idiomatically omitted <*whether or not* you agree, this is what we're going to do>.

which **1.** For a discussion of *which* in restrictive and nonrestrictive clauses and of what it may refer to, see THAT 1, 2.

2. The use of *which* to refer to a whole sentence or clause <the language of the book is understood by only a few specialists, *which* prevents others from criticizing it> is often called a mistake by writing handbooks. The argument is that *which* should refer to a specific antecedent <this treatment, *which* has proven effective>. But the argument ignores the fact that the clause or sentence is clearly the antecedent. The handbooks also warn against the potential ambiguity of the use, but genuinely ambiguous examples are nearly impossible to find. This use is standard. See also THIS 1.

while The earliest meanings of *while* are related to time: "during the time that" <take a nap *while* I'm out> and "as long as" <*while* there's life there's hope>. But other senses, such as "whereas" <easy for an expert, *while* it is dangerous for a novice> and "although" <*while* respected, he is not liked>, have been established since Shakespeare's time. Despite misgivings among some critics, these uses do not inherently interfere with one another and are standard and common. There is no reason to avoid them, though you must be sure the context clearly indicates which meaning of *while* you intend.

who, whom **1.** *Whom* continues to flourish, though to many people it seems stilted or dated. It is used as the object of a verb <not sure *whom* he should hire> or a preceding preposition <for *whom* she has little regard>, and sometimes as the object of a preposition that follows it <the man *whom* you wrote to>. In speech and speechlike prose, *who* is commonly used in place of *whom* when the preposition or verb follows <*who* did you write to?> <*who* did you see?> <the man *who* you spoke to>. Uncertainty about whether to use *whom* or *who* has led to hypercorrect usage that is actually erroneous (as in "*whom* shall I say is calling?"). See also HYPERCORRECTION (in Glossary).

2. For a discussion of *who (whom), that,* and *which* in reference to persons or things, see THAT 1.

who else's See ELSE.

whoever, whomever These words are much less common than *who* and *whom,* but their usage problems are not substantially different. See WHO, WHOM 1.

whom See WHO, WHOM.

whomever See WHOEVER, WHOMEVER.

who's, whose See WHOSE 2.

whose **1.** *Whose, of which.* Traditional grammarians have long disapproved of the use of *whose* with inanimate things <a palace *whose* riches are magnificent>, preferring *of which* in such contexts <a palace the riches *of which* are magnificent>. The use, however, long predates any of its critics; it continues to flourish today and is appropriate in even the most formal writing.

2. *Whose, who's.* Because *whose* and *who's* are pronounced the same, people sometimes confuse them in their writing. *Whose* is a possessive pronoun <*whose* purse is this?>, while *who's* is a contraction of *who is* or *who has* <*who's* going to tell her?>.

widow, widower When a married man dies, is he survived by his widow or by his wife? A review of current practice in various newspapers shows that both *wife* and *widow* are used, but *wife* is more common. No such question is likely to arise when the person who has died is the wife rather than the husband; a woman is never said to be "survived by her widower." If the woman who has died was particularly noteworthy, her surviving husband may be identified as "widower of the late . . . ," but "husband of the late . . ." is more likely.

will See SHALL, WILL.

-wise The suffix *-wise* has been used for centuries to mean "in the manner of" (e.g., *crabwise, stepwise*) and "in the position or direction of" (e.g., *slantwise, clockwise*). Since at least the 1930s, it has also been used to mean "with regard to" <offers an advantage both price*wise* and convenience*wise*>. Critics continue to object to this use, but it is a common and handy way to create an adverb for the occasion <we are having

trouble temperature-*wise*>, and is sometimes used even in serious writing. Almost none of these coinages survive long enough to be recorded in dictionaries. Use of the hyphen before the suffix is optional.

wish *Wish* is commonly used as a transitive verb meaning "to want" or "to desire," often with an infinitive as its object <I *wished* to be gone.>. In another typical construction, the object is a proper name or personal pronoun followed by an infinitive <she *wished* John to call them>. These uses of *wish* are not controversial, although some people find them somewhat affected and prefer the use of *want* in such contexts. One point of dispute regarding *wish* is whether it should be used with a simple noun object <they *wished* a speedy resolution to the matter>. Although *wish* is certainly less common than *want* or *desire* in such constructions, it is nevertheless long-established and standard.

with a view, with the view See VIEW.

with disregard for, with disregard of See DISREGARD.

without hardly See HARDLY.

with regard to See REGARD.

with respect to See IN RESPECT TO, WITH RESPECT TO.

with the exception of See EXCEPTION.

with the hope(s) of, with the hope that See HOPE.

wont As an adjective, *wont* means "accustomed" or "inclined." It occurs only as a predicate adjective, almost always followed by an infinitive <got up early as she is *wont* to do>. As a noun meaning "habitual way of doing," *wont* occurs most often in phrases beginning with "as is" or "as was" <as was his *wont*, he slept until noon>.

won't *Won't* is one of the most irregular-looking of the negative contractions (others include *don't* and *shan't*), being a shortening of the earlier *wonnot*, which in turn was formed from *woll* (or *wol*), a variant form of *will*, and *not*. It is entirely acceptable in all varieties of writing <it *won't* be missed>.

worser See DOUBLE COMPARISON (in Glossary).

worst comes to worst This phrase has had several variants over its lifetime (it was first recorded in the late 16th century), but today the most common are *if worst comes to worst* and *if worse comes to worst*. There are those who regard the form having *worse* as incorrect, but its use is too widespread and well established for it to be regarded as anything other than standard.

would See SHALL, WILL.

would have The use of *would have* in place of *had* in the first part of a conditional sentence (as in "If they *would have* come earlier, we all could have left on time") has long been considered an error. It is characteristic of informal speech, but it is notorious in student writing. It occurs occasionally in the casual writing of others. In print it is mostly found in transcribed speech. The grammatical reasons for this use are not fully understood.

would of See OF 2.

would rather See HAD RATHER.

wrack See RACK, WRACK.

wreak, wreck Havoc is usually said to be wreaked <*wreak* havoc>, but occasionally the more familiar *wreck* is mistakenly substituted for *wreak.* Other verbs may also be used with *havoc,* including *create, play, raise,* and, occasionally, *work.* In the past tense, *work havoc* becomes either *worked havoc* or, more commonly, *wrought havoc.*

wrong, wrongly *Wrong* can be used as an adjective <took the *wrong* bus>, noun <two *wrongs* don't make a right>, or verb <a penal system that had *wronged* him>, and as an adverb. The adverbs *wrong* and *wrongly* are used differently, however. *Wrong* occurs most frequently with the verbs *do, get, have,* and especially *go* <how can you *go wrong*?>, but is also used with other verbs. It usually follows immediately after the verb, often at the end of a sentence or clause <she guessed *wrong*>. *Wrongly,* on the other hand, most often precedes the verb or participle being modified <was *wrongly* accused> <has

wrongly been criticized>, though it can also follow <applied the principle *wrongly*>. In general, the one that *sounds* correct *is* correct. If both sound right, either may be used. (This observation also holds true for the analogous adverbs *right* and *rightly*.)

X Y Z

Xmas *Xmas* has been used as a short form of *Christmas* since the 16th century. The *X* is derived from the Greek letter chi (X), which is the first letter in the Greek word for "Christ." *Xmas* is limited in current usage to advertisements, headlines, banners, and casual correspondence; in other contexts you will undoubtedly want to spell out *Christmas*.

yearn People who yearn usually yearn *for* something. Less commonly, the preposition following yearn may be *after, toward* (*or towards*), or *over.*

yet The use of *yet* with a verb in the plain past tense with *did* (as in "Did he leave *yet?*) is common and unobjectionable in ordinary speech, but in writing the present perfect is used <has he left *yet?*>.

you **1.** *You* is often used in addressing the reader directly <*you* should keep in mind the user's needs>. *One* may be used instead of *you* for a more formal, distant, and impersonal tone <*one* should be cautious in dealing with them>, but try not to mix the two. See also ONE.

2. *Indefinite you.* Related to the use of *you* to address the reader directly is the use of *you* to address no one in particular—in indefinite reference <*you* have to consider the long-term effects>. While some critics used to prefer the substitution of *one* <*one* has to consider the long-term effects>, or a passive construction <the long-term effects have to be considered>, most writers nowadays find indefinite *you* perfectly acceptable, if a bit informal.

your, you're 1. The possessive pronoun is *your* <*your* spelling is atrocious>. The contraction of *you are* is *you're* <*you're* an atrocious speller>.

2. *Your* is often used with an adjective such as *average, standard, ordinary, usual,* or *basic* <*your* average car salesman> in a sense more or less equivalent to *the.* This use is standard in casual prose.

yours Although the *-s* in *yours* marks the possessive <we'd like to have *yours* by March 28th>, and the possessive *-s* is normally preceded by an apostrophe, there is no apostrophe in *yours.*

zeal One may either have zeal *for doing* something or zeal *to do* something. Where the object is a noun rather than a gerund, *for* is the usual preposition after *zeal* <have shown tremendous *zeal for* the nationalist leader>.

Glossary

This glossary provides definitions, and sometimes discussions, of grammatical and other terms either used in the main A–Z section of the book or entered separately here to address additional problems of usage. Cross-references to entries in the main section are shown in SMALL CAPITALS; cross-references to entries within the glossary are shown in **boldface.**

abbreviation A shortened form of a written word or phrase used in place of the whole (such as *amt.* for *amount,* or *c/o* for *care of*).

Abbreviations can be used wherever they are customary, but note that what is customary in technical writing will be different from what is customary in journalism or other fields. If you are uncertain, consult a style manual. See also **acronym.**

absolute adjective An adjective that normally cannot be used comparatively <*ancillary* rights> <the *maximum* dose>.

Many absolute adjectives can be modified by adverbs such as *almost* or *near* <an *almost fatal* dose> <at *near maximum* capacity>. However, many adjectives considered to be absolute are in fact often preceded by comparative adverbs <a *more perfect* union> <a *less complete* account>. In such cases, *more* means "more nearly" and *less* "less nearly." Such use is long established in the language.

absolute comparative The comparative form of an adjective used where no comparison is implied or stated, although in some cases comparison may be inferred by the reader or hearer <*higher* education> <a *better* kind of company> <gives you a *brighter* smile> <an *older* woman>.

The absolute comparative is standard in general writing. See also **absolute adjective; comparison; double comparison; implicit comparative.**

acronym A word or abbreviation formed from the initial letter or letters of each of the major parts of a compound term, whether or not it is pronounceable as a word (such as *TQM* for *Total Quality Management,* or *UNPROFOR* for *United Nations Protection Force*); also called *initialism.*

active voice A verb form indicating that the subject of a sentence is performing the action <he *respects* the other scientists> <a bird *was singing*> <interest rates *rose*>; compare **passive voice.**

adjective A word that describes or modifies a noun <an *active* mind> <this is *serious*> <*full* and *careful* in its attention to detail>.

An adjective can follow a noun as a complement <the book made the bag *heavy*> and can sometimes modify larger units, like noun phrases <the *celebrated* "man in the street"> and noun clauses <it seemed *incomprehensible* that one senator could hold up the nomination>. See also **attributive; predicate adjective.**

adverb A word that modifies a verb, adjective, adverb, preposition, phrase, clause, or sentence.

Traditionally adverbs indicate time, place, or manner <do it *now*> <*there* they remained> <she went *willingly*>. They can connect statements <a small bomb had been found; *nevertheless,* they were continuing their search> and can tell the reader what the writer thinks about what is being said in the sentence <*luckily* I got there on time>. They can modify verbs <ran *fast*>, adjectives <an *awfully* long speech>, participles <a *well*-acted play>, adverbs <doing *fairly* well>, particles <woke *right* up>, indefinite pronouns <*almost* everyone>, cardinal numbers <*over* 200 guests>, prepositional phrases <*just* out of reach>, and more. Sometimes they modify a preceding noun <the great city *beyond*>, and some adverbs of place and time can serve as the objects of prepositions <since *when*> <before *long*>.

The notion that adverbs should not separate auxiliaries from their main verbs <you can *easily* see the river from here> <they should be *heartily* congratulated> is a false one, apparently based on fear of the split infinitive. See also **auxiliary verb; sentence adverb; split infinitive.**

adverbial genitive A form, or case, of some nouns used as adverbs of time, normally formed by adding *-s* <he worked *nights*> <the store is open *Sundays*>.

agreement A grammatical relationship that involves the correspondence in number either between the subject and verb of a sentence or between a pronoun and its antecedent; also called *concord.*

Subiect-verb agreement for compound subjects joined by and When a subject is composed or two or more singular nouns joined by *and,* the plural verb is usually used <*the sentimentality and lack of originality* which *mark* his writing> <*the bitterness and heartache* that *fill* the world>. Occasionally when the nouns form a single conceptual unit, the singular verb can be used <*the report's depth and scope demonstrates*> <*her patience and calm was* remarkable>. *See also* **notional agreement.**

Compound subjects joined by or (or nor): When singular nouns are joined by *or,* the singular verb is usually used <*the average man or woman was* not interested>; when plural nouns are so joined, the plural verb is used <*wolves or coyotes have* depleted his stock>. When the negative *neither . . . nor* is used with singular nouns, it usually takes a singular verb <*neither she nor anyone else is* fond of the idea>; when used with plural nouns, it takes a plural verb <*neither the proponents nor their adversaries are* willing to accept>. But when *neither . . . nor* is used with nouns of differing number, the noun closest to the verb usually determines its number <*neither he nor his colleagues were* present> <*neither the teachers nor the principal was* interested>. Similar rules apply to *either . . . or.* See also EITHER 3.

Compound subjects joined by words or phrases like with or along with, or by punctuation: When a singular noun is joined to another by a word or phrase like *with, rather than,* or *as well as,* a singular verb is generally used <*that story, along with nine others, was* published> <*the battleship together with the destroyer was* positioned three miles offshore>. Parenthetical insertions set off by commas, dashes, or parentheses should not affect agreement <*this book, as well as various others, has* achieved notoriety> <*their management—and the company's balance sheets—has* suffered>.

Subject formed by a collective noun phrase: The usage question is this: In constructions like "a bunch of the boys were whooping it up" or "a fraction of the deposits are insured," which make use of a collective noun phrase (*a bunch of the boys, a fraction of the deposits*), should the verb be plural or singular? The answer is that since the sense of the phrase is normally plural, the verb should be as well. See also **collective noun.**

Subject expressing money, time, etc.: When an amount of money, a period of time, or some other plural noun phrase of quantity or measure forms the subject, a singular verb is used <*ten dollars is* all I have left> <*two miles is* as far as they can walk> <*two thirds of the area is* under water>.

Subject formed by one in (out of) . . . : Phrases such as "one in five" or "two out of three" may take either a singular or a plural verb <*one in four union members was* undecided> <*one out of ten soldiers were* unable to recognize the enemy>, though grammarians tend to favor the singular.

Pronoun-antecedent agreement for nouns joined by and, or: When antecedents are singular nouns joined by *and,* a plural pronoun is used <*the computer and the printer* were moved because *they* were in the way>. But singular nouns joined by *or* can use either a singular or a plural pronoun, whichever sounds best <either *Fred or Marianne* will give *their* presentation after lunch> <*each employee or supervisor* should give what *he or she* can afford>.

Agreement for indefinite pronouns: The indefinite pronouns *anybody, anyone, each, either, everybody, everyone, neither, nobody, none, no one, somebody,* and *someone,* though some of them are conceptually plural, are used with singular verbs <*everyone* in the company *was* pleased> <*nobody is* responsible>, but are commonly referred to by *they, their, them,* or *themselves* <*nobody* could get the crowd's attention when *they* spoke> <*everybody* there admits *they* saw it>. Writing handbooks prescribe *he, she,* or *he or she,* or some other construction instead of the plural pronouns (see ANYBODY; EACH; EVERYBODY, EVERYONE), but use of the plural *they, their,* or *them* has long been established and is standard. See also THEY, THEIR, THEM.

antecedent A word, phrase, or clause to which a subsequent pronoun refers <*Judy* wrote to say *she* is coming> <they saw *Bob* and called to *him*> <I hear *that he is ill* and *it* worries me>.

appositive A word, phrase, or clause that is equivalent to an adjacent noun <a biography of *the poet*

Robert Burns> <sales of *her famous novel, Gone with the Wind,* reached one million copies in six months > <*we grammarians* are never wrong>.

Restrictive and nonrestrictive appositives play different roles in a sentence and are traditionally distinguished by their punctuation. A nonrestrictive appositive <*his wife, Helen,* attended the ceremony> is generally set off with commas, while a restrictive appositive <he sent *his daughter Cicely* to college> uses no commas and indicates that one out of a group is being identified (in this case, one daughter from among two or more). Exceptions occur where no ambiguity would result <his wife Helen>. See also **nonrestrictive clause; restrictive clause.**

article One of three words (*a, an, the*) used with a noun to indicate definiteness <*the* blue car> or indefiniteness <*a* simple task> <*an* interesting explanation>.

attributive A modifier that immediately precedes the word it modifies <*black* tie, *U.S.* government, *kitchen* sink, *lobster* salad>.

Nouns have functioned like adjectives in this position for many centuries. In more recent years, some critics have objected to the proliferation of nouns used to modify other nouns: e.g., *language deterioration, health aspects, image enhancement.* While long or otherwise unexpected strings of this sort can occasionally be disorienting to the uninitiated (e.g., *management team strategy planning session*), the practice is flourishing and usually serves to compress information that the intended audience need not always have spelled out for it. Be sure, however, that the context and audience will allow for such compression.

A fairly recent trend toward using plural attributives has been attacked by some critics. There always had been a few plural attributives—*scissors grinder, physics laboratory, Civil Liberties Union, mathematics book*—but is it proper to use the more recent *weapons system, communications technology, operations program, systems analyst, earth-resources satellite, singles bar, enemies list?* The answer is that such plural attributives are standard. The plural form is chosen to stress plurality—more than one weapon, operation, enemy, etc.—or to otherwise distinguish its meaning from whatever the singular attributive might connote.

auxiliary verb A verb that accompanies another verb and typically expresses person, number, mood, or tense (such as *be, have, can, do*) <they *can* see the movie tomorrow> <she *has* left already>. See also **verb.**

cardinal number A number of the kind used in simple counting <*one, 1, thirty-five, 35*>; compare **ordinal number.**

case In English, a form of a noun or pronoun indicating its grammatical relation to other words in a sentence. See **nominative; objective; possessive.** See also **genitive.**

clause A group of words having its own subject and predicate but forming only part of a compound or complex sentence. A *main* or *independent clause* could stand alone as a sentence <*we will leave* as soon as the taxi arrives>; a *subordinate* or *dependent clause* requires a main clause <we will leave *as soon as the taxi arrives*>. See also **sentence; subordinate clause.**

collective noun A singular noun that stands for a number of persons or things considered as a group (such as *team, government, horde*).

Subject-verb agreement: Collective nouns have been used with both singular and plural verbs since Middle English. The principle involved is one of notional agreement. When the group is considered as a unit, the singular verb is used <the *government is* prepared for a showdown> <his *family is* from New England> <the *team has won* all of its home games>. When the group is thought of as a collection of individuals, the plural verb is sometimes used <her *family are* all staunch conservatives>. Singular verbs are more common in American English and plural verbs more common in British English, though usage remains divided in each case. See also **agreement; notional agreement.**

A collective noun followed by *of* and a plural noun follows the same rule as collective nouns in general. When the notion is that of plurality, the plural verb is normally used <an *assemblage of rocks were* laid out on the table> <a *group of jazz improvisers were* heard through the window>. When the idea of oneness or wholeness is stressed, the verb is generally singular <this *cluster of stars is* the largest yet identified>.

Pronoun agreement: The usual rule is that writers should take care to match their pronouns and verbs, singular with singular <the committee *is* hopeful that *it* will succeed>, plural with plural <the faculty *are* willing to drop *their* suit>. But in fact writers sometimes use a plural pronoun after a singular verb <the audience *was* on *their* way out>. (The reverse combination—plural verb with singular pronoun—is very rare.)

Organizations as collective nouns: The names of companies and other organizations are treated as either singular <*Harvard* may consider *itself* very fortunate> or, less commonly, plural <the *D.A.R. are* going to do another pageant>. Organizations also sometimes appear with a singular verb but a plural pronoun in reference <*M-G-M hopes* to sell *their* latest releases> <*Chrysler builds their* convertible in Kentucky>. This usage is standard, though informal.

colloquial An adjective describing usage that is characteristic of familiar and informal conversation.

While not intended to carry pejorative overtones, the label *colloquial* often implies that the usage is nonstandard. See also **dialect; nonstandard; standard English.**

comma fault (comma splice, comma error) The use of a comma instead of a semicolon to link two independent clauses (as in "I won't talk about myself, it's not a healthy topic"). Modern style calls for the semicolon, but comma splices are fairly common in casual and unedited prose.

comparison Modification of an adjective or adverb to show different levels of quality, quantity, or relation. The *comparative* form shows relation between two items, usually by adding *-er* or *more* or *less* to the adjective or adverb <he's short*er* than I am> <her second book sold *more* quickly>. The *superlative* form expresses an extreme among two or more items, usually by adding *-est* or *most* or *least* to the adjective or adverb <the cheetah is the fast*est* mammal> <that's the *least* compelling reason> <the *most* vexingly intractable issue>. See also **absolute adjective; absolute comparative; double comparison; implicit comparative.**

complement An added word or expression by which a predicate is made complete <they elected him *president*> <she thought it *beautiful*> <the critics called her *the best act of her kind since Carmen Miranda*>.

compound A combination of words or word elements that work together in various ways (*farmhouse; cost-effective; ex-husband; shoeless; figure out; in view of* that; *real estate* agent; *greenish white* powder; *carefully tended* garden; *great white shark*).

Compounds are written in one of three ways: solid <*workplace*>, hyphenated <*screenwriter-director*>, or open <*health care*>. Because of the variety of standard practice, the choice among these styles for a given compound represents one of the most common and bothersome of all style issues. A current desk dictionary will list many compounds, but those whose meanings are self-explanatory from the meanings of their component words will usually not appear. Most writers try to pattern any temporary compounds after similar permanent compounds such as are entered in dictionaries.

compound sentence See **sentence.**

compound subject Two or more nouns or pronouns usually joined by *and* that function as the subject of a clause or sentence <*doctors and lawyers* reported the highest incomes for that period> <*Peter, Karen, and I* left together>. See also **agreement; collective noun.**

concord See **agreement.**

conjunction A word or phrase that joins together words, phrases, clauses, or sentences. *Coordinating conjunctions* (such as *and, or, but*) join elements of a similar kind <they came early *and* stayed late>. *Correlative conjunctions* (such as *either . . . or, neither . . . nor*) are used in pairs and link alternatives <the proposal benefits *neither* residents *nor* visitors>. *Subordinating conjunctions* (such as *unless, whether*) join subordinate clauses to main clauses <don't call *unless* you're coming>.

conjunctive adverb A transitional adverb (such as *also, however, therefore*) that expresses the relationship between two independent clauses, sentences, or paragraphs <he enjoyed the movie; *however,* he had to leave before the end>.

contact clause A dependent clause attached to its antecedent without a relative pronoun such as *that, which,* or *who* <the key [that] *you lost*> <he is not the person [who] *we thought he was*>.

The construction has been in existence for several hundred years and is appropriate even in formal writing.

The predicate noun clause not introduced by the conjunction *that* <we believe [that] *the alliance is strong*> is as long and as well established in English as the contact clause. It is probably more common in casual and general prose than in formal prose. It is also more common after some verbs (such as *believe, hope, say, think*) than others (such as *assert, calculate, hold, intend*).

contraction A shortened form of a word or words in which an apostrophe usually replaces the omitted letter or letters (such as *dep't, don't, could've, o'clock, we'll*).

Contractions involving verbs used to be avoided more than they are today. In fact, many contemporary writing handbooks recommend using contractions to help you avoid sounding stilted. See WON'T.

count noun A noun that identifies things that can be counted <two *tickets*> <a *motive*> <many *people*>; compare **mass noun.**

dangling modifier A modifying phrase that lacks a normally expected grammatical relation to the rest of the sentence (as in "*Caught in the act,* his excuses were unconvincing").

The common construction called the *participial phrase* usually begins with a participle; in "*Chancing to meet them there,* I invited them to sit with us," the subject, "I," is left implicit in the preceding phrase, which modifies it. But a writer may inadvertently let a participial phrase modify a subject or some other noun in the sentence it was not intended to modify; the result is what grammarians call a *dangling participle.* Thus in "*Hoping to find him alone,* the presence of a stranger was irksome," it is the "presence" itself that may seem to be hoping.

Dangling participles can be found in the writing of many famous writers, and they are usually hardly noticeable except to someone looking for them. The important thing to avoid is creating an unintended humorous effect (as in "*Opening up the cupboard,* a cockroach ran for the corner").

dangling participle See **dangling modifier.**

dialect A variety of language distinguished by features of vocabulary, grammar, and pronunciation that is confined to a region or group. See also **nonstandard; standard English.**

direct object A word, phrase, or clause denoting the goal or result of the action of the verb <he closed the *valve*> <they'll do *whatever it takes*> <"*Do it now,*" he said>; compare **indirect object.**

direct question A question quoted exactly as spoken, written, or imagined <the only question is, *Will it work?*>; compare **indirect question.**

direct quotation Text quoted exactly as spoken or written <I heard her say, "*I'll be there at two o'clock*">; compare **indirect quotation.**

divided usage Widespread use of two or more forms for a single entity (such as *dived* and *dove* for the past tense of *dive*).

double comparison Use of the forms *more, most, less,* or *least* with an adjective already inflected for the comparative or superlative degree (such as *more wider, most widest*).

This construction results from using *more* and *most* as intensifiers <a *most* enjoyable meal>. In modern usage, double comparison has all but vanished from standard writing. See also **comparison; intensifier.**

Double comparison can also occur by inflection. Though forms such as *firstest, mostest,* and *bestest* are most typical of the speech of young children, the form *worser* (which has a long literary background) still persists in adult speech. You will want to avoid it in writing.

double genitive A construction in which possession is marked both by the preposition *of* and a noun or pronoun in the possessive case.

In expressions like "that song of Ella Fitzgerald's" or "a good friend of ours," the possessive relationship is indicated by both *of* and the genitive inflection (Fitzgerald*'s, ours*), even though only one or the other would seem to be strictly necessary. However, this construction, also known as the *double possessive,* is an idiomatic one of long standing and is standard in all kinds of writing. See also **genitive.**

double modal The use of two modal auxiliaries in succession, resulting in such expressions as *might can, might could,* and *might should.*

Today double modals tend to be found in Southern dialect and are unfamiliar to speakers from other parts of the country.

double negative A clause or sentence containing two negatives and having a negative meaning.

In modern usage, the double negative (as in "they did*n't* have *no* children" or "it would*n't* do *no* good") is widely perceived as a rustic or uneducated form, and is generally avoided in both writing and speech, other than the most informal.

A standard form of double negative is the rhetorical device known as *litotes,* which produces a weak affirmative meaning <a *not un*reasonable request>. It is used for understatement, but should not be overused.

double passive A construction that uses two verb forms in the passive voice, one being an infinitive (as in "the work of redesigning the office space *was requested to be done* by outside contractors").

The double passive is awkward and potentially ambiguous (did outside contractors ask for the work to be done, or were they asked to do the work?) and should be avoided.

double possessive See **double genitive.**

double superlative See **double comparison.**

false titles Appositive preceding a person's name with no preceding article or following comma, which thus resembles a title, though it is rarely capitalized <organized by *consumer advocate* Ralph Nader> <works of *1960s underground cartoonist* Robert Crumb>. The use of such titles is sometimes criticized, but it is standard in journalism.

faulty parallelism See **parallelism.**

flat adverb An adverb that has the same form as its related adjective, such as *sure* <you *sure* fooled me>, *bright* <the moon is shining *bright*>, and *flat* <she turned me down *flat*>.

Although such forms were once common, later grammarians saw them as faulty because they lacked the *-ly* ending. Today flat adverbs are few in number and some are widely regarded as incorrect. See BAD, BADLY; CHEAP 2; CONSIDERABLE 2; NEAR, NEARLY; QUICK, QUICKLY; SCARCELY 1; SLOW, SLOWLY; TIGHT, TIGHTLY.

formal agreement See **notional agreement.**

gender In English, a characteristic of certain nouns and pronouns that indicates sex (masculine, feminine, neuter) <*he, him, his, she, her, it, its; actor, actress; brother, sister; emperor, empress; heir, heiress; fiancé, fiancée; testator, testatrix*>.

genitive A form, or case, of a noun or pronoun that typically shows possession or source <the girl*'s* sweater> <nobody*'s* fool> <an uncle *of mine*> <some idea *of theirs*> <the company*'s* failure> <a year*'s* salary> <the nation*'s* capital> <a stone*'s* throw>.

The form is usually produced by adding -*'s* or a phrase beginning with *of.* While the possessive is the genitive's most common function, it has certain other functions as well; these include the *subjective* <Frost*'s* poetry>, *objective* <her son*'s* graduation>, *descriptive* <women*'s* colleges>, and *appositive* <the state *of Massachusetts*> <the office *of president*> genitives. See also **double genitive; possessive.**

gerund A verb form having the characteristics of both verb and noun and ending in *-ing* (also called a *verbal noun*) <the ice made *skiing* impossible>.

A gerund can be preceded by a possessive noun or pronoun <her husband's *snoring*> <their *filling* the position>. See also **possessive; possessive with gerund.**

hypercorrection The use of a nonstandard linguistic form or construction on the basis of a false analogy to a standard form or construction (as in "*whom* should I say is calling?"; "this is between you and *I*"; "no one but *he* would notice"; "open *widely*"). See also BETWEEN YOU AND I; WHO WHOM

idiom A common expression that is peculiar to itself grammatically <*it wasn't me*> or that cannot be understood from the meanings of its separate words <I told them to *step on it*> <the newspaper *had a field day*>.

imperative The form, or mood, of a verb that expresses a command or makes a request <*come* here> <please *don't*>; compare **indicative; subjunctive.**

implicit comparative One of a small group of adjectives (primarily *major, minor, inferior, superior*) whose meaning resembles a true comparative but which cannot be used with comparative forms (such as *more, most; less, least*) <a *major* contributor> <an *inferior* wine>.

However, two other implicit comparatives *junior* and *senior* can be used with comparative forms <a *more senior* diplomat> <the *least junior* of the new partners>. See also **comparison.**

indefinite pronoun A pronoun that designates an unidentified person or thing <*somebody* ate my dessert> <she saw *no one* she knew>.

Many indefinite pronouns are involved in usage questions of one kind or another. See ANYBODY, ANYONE; EACH; EITHER; EVERYBODY, EVERYONE; NEITHER; NOBODY, NO ONE; NONE; SOMEBODY, SOMEONE; THEY,

THEIR, THEM. See also **agreement; notional agreement.**

indicative The form, or mood, of a verb that states a fact or asks a question <the train *stopped*> <they*'ll be* along> <everyone *is* ravenous> <*has* the rain *begun*?> <who *knows*?>; compare **imperative; subjunctive.**

indirect object A grammatical object representing the secondary goal of the action of its verb <she gave *the dog* a bone>; compare **direct object.**

indirect question A statement of the substance of a question without using the speaker's exact words or word order <the officer asked *what the trouble was*> <they wondered *whether it would work*>; compare **direct question.**

indirect quotation A statement of the substance of a quotation without using the speaker's exact words <I heard her say *she'd be there at two o'clock*>; compare **direct quotation.**

infinitive A verb form having the characteristics of both verb and noun and usually used with *to* <we had *to stop*> <*to err* is human> <no one saw him *leave*>. See also **split infinitive.**

infinitive phrase A phrase that includes an infinitive and its modifiers and complements <we expect them *to arrive by five o'clock*> <he shouted *to be heard above the din*> <*to have earned a Ph.D. in four years* was impressive>.

inflection The change in form that words undergo to mark case, gender, number, tense, person, mood, voice, or comparison <*he, his, him*> <*waiter, waitress*> <rat, *rats*> <blame, *blames, blamed, blaming*> <who, *whom*> <she *is* careful, if she *were* careful, *be* careful> <like, *likes, is liked*> <wild, *wilder, wildest*>. See also **case; comparison; gender; mood; number; person; tense; voice.**

initialism See **acronym.**

intensifier A linguistic element used to give emphasis or additional strength to another word or statement <a *very* hot day> <it's a *complete* lie> <what *on earth* is he doing?> <she *herself* did it>. See AWFUL, AWFULLY; DEFINITE, DEFINITELY; REAL; RIGHT 1; SO 1; SURE, SURELY; THAT 3. See also **double comparison.**

interjection An exclamatory or interrupting word or phrase <*ouch!*> <*oh,* must you?> <she's *like* clueless>.

intransitive verb A verb not having a direct object <he *ran* away> <our cat *purrs* when I stroke her>; compare **transitive verb.**

linking verb A verb that links a subject with its predicate (such as *is, feel, look, become, seem*) <she is the new manager> <the future *looked* prosperous> <he *has become* disenchanted>.

main clause See *clause.*

mass noun A noun that denotes a thing or concept without subdivisions <some *money*> <great *courage*> <the study of *politics*>; compare **count noun.**

modifier A word or phrase that qualifies, limits, or restricts the meaning of another word or phrase. See **adjective; adverb.**

mood The form of a verb that shows whether the action or state it denotes is conceived as a fact or otherwise (e.g., a command, possibility, or wish). See **indicative; imperative; subjunctive.**

nominative A form, or case, of a noun or pronoun indicating its use as the subject of a verb <three *dogs* trotted by the open door> <later *we* ate dinner>; compare **objective; possessive.**

In English, nouns in the nominative case are unmarked except for number.

nonrestrictive clause A subordinate or dependent clause, set off by commas, that is not essential to the definiteness of the word it modifies and could be omitted without changing the meaning of the main clause (also called *nonessential clause*) <the author, *who turned out to be charming,* autographed my book>; compare **restrictive clause.**

nonstandard Not conforming to the usage generally characteristic of educated native speakers of a language; compare **standard English.** See also **dialect.**

notional agreement Agreement between a subject and a verb or between a pronoun and its antecedent that is determined by meaning rather than form; also called *notional concord.*

Notional agreement contrasts with *formal* or *grammatical agreement* (or *concord*), in which overt grammatical markers determine singular or plural agreement. Formally plural nouns such as *news, means,* and *politics* have long taken singular verbs; so when a plural noun considered a single entity takes a singular verb, notional agreement is at work and no one objects <the *United States is sending* its ambassador>. When a singular noun is used as a collective noun and takes a plural verb or a plural pronoun, we also have notional agreement <the *committee are* meeting on Tuesday> <the *group wants* to publicize *their* views>. Indefinite pronouns are heavily influenced by notional agreement and tend to take singular verbs but plural pronouns <*everyone is* required to show *their* identification>. See HE, HE OR SHE; THERE IS, THERE ARE; THEY, THEIR, THEM. See also **agreement; collective noun.**

notional concord See **notional agreement.**

noun A member of a class of words that can serve as the subject of a verb, can be singular or plural, can be replaced by a pronoun, and can refer to an entity, quality, state, action, or concept <*boy, Churchill, America, river, commotion, poetry, anguish, constitutionalism*>.

noun phrase A phrase formed by a noun and its modifiers <*portly pensioners* sat sunning themselves>

<they proclaimed *all the best features of the new financial offering*>.

number A characteristic of a noun, pronoun, or verb that signifies whether it is singular or plural. See **singular; plural.**

object A noun, noun phrase or clause, or pronoun that directly or indirectly receives the action of a verb or follows a preposition <she rocked *the baby*> <he saw *where they were going*> <I gave *him the news*> <over *the rainbow*> <after *a series of depressing roadhouse gigs*>. See **direct object; indirect object.**

objective A form, or case, of a pronoun indicating its use as the object of a verb or preposition <we spoke to *them* yesterday> <he's a man *whom* everyone should know>; compare **nominative; possessive.**

ordinal number A number designating the place occupied by an item in an ordered sequence <*first, 1st, second, 2nd*>; compare **cardinal number.**

parallelism Repeated syntactical similarities introduced in sentence construction, such as adjacent phrases and clauses that are equivalent, similar, or opposed in meaning and of identical construction <ecological problems of concern *to scientists, to businesspeople,* and *to all citizens*> <he was respected not only *for his intelligence* but also *for his integrity*> <*to err is human, to forgive, divine*>.

Parallelism is mainly used for rhetorical and clarifying effects, and its absence can sometimes create problems for the reader. *Faulty parallelism* is the name given to the use of different constructions within a sentence where you would ordinarily expect to find the same or similar constructions. Very often such faulty parallelism involves the conjunctions *and* and *or* or such other coordinators as *either* and *neither.* Consider the sentence "To allow kids to roam the streets at night and failing to give them constructive alternatives have been harmful." An infinitive phrase (*To allow kids to roam* . . .) and a participial phrase (*failing to give them* . . .) are treated as parallel when they are not. The meaning would be taken in more readily if both phrases were similar; replacing the infinitive with a participle achieves this parallelism (*Allowing kids to roam* . . . and *failing to give them* . . .). When such errors are obvious, they can be puzzling. Often, however, the problem is subtle and hardly noticeable, as in the sentence "Either I must send a fax or make a phone call." Here *or* is expected to precede the same parallel term as *either;* by repositioning *either,* you solve the problem <I must *either* send a fax *or* make a phone call>. Such examples of faulty parallelism are fairly common, but your writing will be more elegant if you avoid them. See also AND WHICH, AND WHO; EITHER 3.

parenthetical element An explanatory or modifying word, phrase, or sentence inserted in a passage, set off by parentheses, commas, or dashes <a ruling by the FCC (*Federal Communications Commission*)> <all of us, *to tell the truth,* were amazed> <the examiner chose—*goodness knows why*—to ignore it>.

participial phrase A participle with its complements and modifiers, functioning as an adjective <*hearing the bell ring,* he went to the door>.

participle A verb form having the characteristics of both verb <the noise has *stopped*> and adjective <a *broken* lawn mower>. The *present participle* ends in *-ing* <*fascinating*>; the *past participle* usually ends in *-ed* <*seasoned*>; the *perfect participle* combines *having* with the past participle <*having escaped*>. See also **auxiliary verb; dangling modifier; possessive.**

particle A short word (such as *by, to, in, up*) that expresses some general aspect of meaning or some connective or limiting relation <pay *up*> <heave *to*>.

parts of speech The classes into which words are grouped according to their function in a sentence. See **adjective; adverb; conjunction; interjection; noun; preposition; pronoun; verb.**

passive voice A verb form indicating that the subject of a sentence is being acted upon.

Though often considered a weaker form of expression than the active voice, the passive nevertheless has important uses—for example, when the receiver of the action is more important than the doer <*he is respected* by other scholars>, when the doer is unknown <*the lock had been picked* expertly> or is understood <*Jones was elected* on the third ballot>, or when discretion or tact require that the doer remain anonymous <mistakes *were made*>; compare **active voice.**

person A characteristic of a verb or pronoun that indicates whether a person is speaking (*first person*) <*I am, we are*>, is spoken to (*second person*) <*you are*>, or is spoken about (*third person*) <*he, she, it is; they are*>. See also **number.**

personal pronoun A pronoun that refers to beings and objects and reflects person, number, and often gender <*you* and *I* will attend> <*she* gave *him* the book> <*they*'re just old rags>. See also **pronoun.**

phrase A group of two or more words that does not contain both a subject and a verb and that functions as a noun, adjective, adverb, preposition, conjunction, or verb <*the old sinner*> <*stretching for miles*> <*without a limp*> <*in lieu of*> <*as far as*> <*break off*>. See also **noun phrase; participial phrase.**

plural A word form used to denote more than one <the *Browns*> <the *children*> <these *kinds*> <seven *deer*> <they *are* rich> <*we* do care>.

possessive A form, or case, of a noun or pronoun typically indicating ownership <the *president's* message> <*their* opinions> <*its* meter>; compare **nominative; objective.** See also **double genitive; genitive; possessive with gerund.**

possessive with gerund Use of a possessive form before a gerund.

In "the reason for everyone['s] wanting to join," either the possessive or the common form of *everyone* can be used. Writing handbooks recommend always using the possessive form, but the possessive is mandatory only when the *-ing* word is clearly a noun <*my being* here must embarrass you>. The possessive is quite common with proper nouns <the problem of *John's forgetting* the keys> but rare with plurals <learned of the *bills* [*bills'*] *being* paid>. In most other instances, either the possessive or common form can be used.

predicate The part of a sentence or clause that expresses what is said of the subject <Hargrove *threw a spitball*> <the teachers from the surrounding towns *are invited to the dinner*> <Jennifer *picked up her books and left to catch the bus*>.

predicate adjective An adjective that follows a linking verb (such as *be, become, feel, taste, smell, seem*) and modifies the subject <she is *happy* with the outcome> <the milk tastes *sour*> <he seemed *puzzled* by the answer>.

prefix An affix attached to the beginning of a word to change its meaning <*a*historical> <*pre*sorted> <*anti*-imperialist> <*post*hypnotic> <*over*extended>; compare **suffix.**

preposition A word or phrase that combines with a noun, pronoun, adverb, or prepositional phrase for use as a modifier or a predication <a book *on* the table> <you're *in* big trouble> <*outside* himself> <*because of* that> <came *from* behind> <peeking *from* behind the fence>.

Despite a widespread belief that a sentence cannot end with a preposition, there is no such grammatical rule. In fact, many sentences require the preposition at the end <what can she be thinking *of?*> <he got the answer he was looking *for*> <there are inconveniences that we must put up *with*> <they haven't been heard *from* yet> and many others are perfectly idiomatic in placing it there <you must know which shelf everything is *on*>.

prepositional phrase A group of words consisting of a preposition and its complement <*out of debt* is where we'd like to be!> <here is the desk *with the extra file drawer*> <he drove on *in a cold fury*>.

pronoun Any of a small set of words that are used as substitutes for nouns, phrases, or clauses and refer to someone or something named or understood in the context.

Many pronouns are involved in usage questions. See BETWEEN YOU AND I; BUT; I; IT'S ME; ME; MYSELF; ONE OF THOSE WHO; THAN; THAT; THEY, THEIR, THEM; WHO, WHOM; YOU. See also **agreement; indefinite pronoun.**

proper adjective An adjective that is derived from a proper noun and is usually capitalized <*Roman* sculpture> <*Jeffersonian* democracy> <*Middle Eastern* situation> <*french* fries>.

proper noun A noun that names a particular being or thing and is usually capitalized <*Susan, Haydn, New York, December, General Motors, Mormon,*

Library of Congress, Middle Ages, Spanish Civil War, Reaganomics>.

redundancy Repetition of information in a message.

Redundancy is an implicit part of the English language; it reinforces the message. In "Two birds were sitting on a branch," the idea of plurality is expressed three times: by the modifier *two*, by the *-s* on *bird*, and by the plural verb *were*. Many words can be accompanied by small words that given them extra emphasis <*final result*> <*past history*> <*climb up*> <*refer back*>. These are often attacked as needlessly wordy, but in most instances they are harmless, and sometimes they actually promote communication. The use and employment of many more words, phrases, and expressions than are strictly needed, necessary, wanted, or required should be avoided.

reflexive pronoun A pronoun that refers to the subject of the sentence, clause, or verbal phrase in which it stands, and is formed by compounding the personal pronouns *him, her, it, my, our, them,* and *your* with *-self* or *-selves* <she dressed *herself*> <the cook told us to help *ourselves* to seconds> <I *myself* am not concerned>. See also MYSELF; YOURSELF, YOURSELVES.

relative pronoun One of the pronouns (*that, which, who, whom,* and *whose*) that introduces a subordinate clause which qualifies an antecedent <a man *whom* we can trust> <her book, *which* sold well> <the light *that* failed>. See also THAT; WHICH; WHO, WHOM; WHOSE.

restrictive clause A subordinate clause not set off by commas that is essential to the definiteness of the word it modifies and cannot be omitted without changing the meaning of the main clause (also called *essential clause*) <textbooks *that are not current* should be returned>. See also **appositive; nonrestrictive clause.**

sentence A group of words usually containing a subject and a verb, and in writing ending with a period, question mark, or exclamation point. A *simple sentence* consists of one main or independent clause <*she read the announcement in yesterday's paper*>. A *compound sentence* consists of two or more main clauses <*he left at nine o'clock, and they planned to meet at noon*>. A *complex sentence* consists of a main clause and one or more subordinate clauses <*it began to snow before they reached the summit*>. A *compound-complex sentence* consists of two or more main clauses and one or more subordinate clauses <*Susan left for Masters Hall after the presentation; there she joined the new-product workshop, which was already in progress*>.See also **clause; subordinate clause.**

A *declarative sentence* makes a statement <*the cow jumped over the moon*>. An *exclamatory sentence* expresses strong feeling <*that's ridiculous!*>. An *interrogative sentence* asks a question <*who said that?*>. An *imperative sentence* expresses a command or request <*get in here now*>.

sentence adverb An adverb that modifies an entire sentence, rather than a specific word or phrase within the sentence <*fortunately* they had already placed their order>. See also HOPEFULLY; THANKFULLY.

sentence fragment A group of words punctuated like a sentence, but without a subject or a predicate or both <*So many men, so many opinions.*> <*Yeah, when you think about it.*>. See also **sentence; clause.**

singular A word form denoting one person, thing, or instance <*man*> <*tattoo*> <*eventuality*> <*she* left> <it *is* here>.

split infinitive An infinitive preceded by *to* and an adverb or adverbial phrase <*to ultimately avoid* trouble>.

Grammarians used to disapprove of the split infinitive, but most now admit that it is not a defect. It is useful when a writer wants to emphasize the adverb <were determined *to thoroughly enjoy* themselves>. See also **infinitive.**

standard English English that is substantially uniform, well-established in the speech and writing of educated people, and widely recognized as acceptable; compare **nonstandard.** See also *dialect.*

subject A word or group of words denoting the entity about which something is said <*he* stopped> <*it's* clouding up> <*all sixty members* voted> <*orthodoxy* *on every doctrinal issue* now reigned> <*what they want* is more opportunity> <*going to work* was what she hated most> <*to sing at the Met* had long been a dream of his>.

subject-verb agreement See **agreement.**

subjunctive The form, or mood, of a verb that expresses a condition contrary to fact or follows clauses of necessity, demand, or wishing <if he *were* here, he could answer that> <it's imperative that it *be* broadcast> <they asked that the meeting *proceed*> <I wish they *would come* soon>; compare **imperative; indicative.** See also IF 3.

subordinate clause A clause that functions as a noun, adjective, or adverb and is attached to a main clause <theirs is a cause *that will prevail*>. See also **clause; sentence.**

suffix An affix attached to the end of a word to modify its meaning <editor*s*> <county*wide*> <Hollywood-*ish*> <umbrella-*like*>; compare **prefix.**

superlative See **comparison.**

tense The characteristic of a verb that expresses time present, past, or future <*see, saw, will see*>.

transitive verb A verb that acts upon a direct object <she *contributed* money> <he *runs* the store> <*express* your opinion>; compare **intransitive verb.**

verb A word or phrase that is the grammatical center of the predicate and is used to express action, occurrence, or state of being <*leap, carry out, feel, be*>. See also **auxiliary verb; linking verb; mood; voice.**

verbal One of a group of words derived from verbs. See **gerund; infinitive; participle.**

voice The property of a verb that indicates whether the subject acts or is acted upon. See **active voice; passive voice.**

Punctuation Guide

APOSTROPHE ’

1. **indicates the possessive case of nouns and indefinite pronouns** <the boy’s mother> <the boys’ mothers> <It’s anyone’s guess>.
2. **marks omissions in contracted words** <I’d> <didn’t> <o’clock>.
3. **often forms plurals of letters, figures, and words referred to as words** <You should dot your *i*’s and cross your *t*’s> <several 8’s> <She had trouble pronouncing her *the*’s>.

BRACKETS [ ]

1. **set off extraneous data such as editorial additions, especially within quoted material** <wrote that the author was “trying to dazzle his readers with phrases like *jeu de mots* [play on words]”>.
2. **function as parentheses within parentheses** <Bowman Act (22 Stat., ch. 4, § [or sec.] 4, p. 50)>.

COLON :

1. **introduces a word, clause, or phrase that explains, illustrates, amplifies, or restates what has gone before** <The sentence was poorly constructed: it lacked both unity and coherence>.
2. **introduces a series** <Three countries were represented: England, France, and Belgium>.
3. **introduces lengthy quoted material set off from the rest of a text by indentation but not by quotation marks** <I quote from the text of Chapter One:>.
4. **separates data in time-telling and data in bibliographic and biblical references** <8:30 a.m.> <New York: Random House, 1995> <John 4:10>.
5. **separates titles and subtitles (as of books)** <*The Tragic Dynasty: A History of the Romanovs*>.

6. **follows the salutation in formal correspondence** <Dear Sir or Madam:>.

COMMA ,

1. **separates main clauses joined by a coordinating conjunction (such as *and, but, or, nor,* or *for*) and very short clauses not so joined** <She knew very little about him, and he volunteered nothing> <I came, I saw, I conquered>.
2. **sets off an adverbial clause (or a long phrase) that precedes the main clause** <When she found that her friends had deserted her, she sat down and cried>.
3. **sets off from the rest of the sentence transitional words and expressions (such as *on the contrary, on the other hand*), conjunctive adverbs (such as *consequently, furthermore, however*), and expressions that introduce an illustration or example (such as *namely, for example*)** <Your second question, on the other hand, remains open> <The mystery, however, remains unsolved> <She expects to travel through two countries, namely, France and England>.
4. **separates words, phrases, or clauses in series and coordinate adjectives modifying a noun** <Men, women, and children crowded into the square> <A harsh, cold wind blew>.
5. **sets off parenthetic elements (such as nonrestrictive modifiers) from the rest of the sentence** <Our guide, who wore a blue beret, was an experienced traveler> <We visited Gettysburg, the site of a famous battle>.
6. **introduces a direct quotation, terminates a direct quotation that is neither a question nor an exclamation, and encloses split quotations** <John said, "I am leaving"> <"I am leaving," John said> <"I am leaving," John said, "even if you want me to stay">.

7. **sets off words in direct address, absolute phrases, and mild interjections** <You may go, Mary, if you wish> <I fear the encounter, his temper being what it is> <Ah, that's my idea of an excellent dinner>.
8. **separates a question from the rest of the sentence which it ends** <It's a fine day, isn't it?>.
9. **indicates the omission of a word or words, and especially a word or words used earlier in the sentence** <Common stocks are preferred by some investors; bonds, by others>.
10. **is used to avoid ambiguity** <To Mary, Jane was someone special>.
11. **sets off geographical names (such as state or country), items in dates, and addresses from the rest of a text** <Shreveport, Louisiana, is the site of a large air base> <On Sunday, June 23, 1940, he was wounded> <Number 10 Downing Street, London, is a famous address>.
12. **follows the salutation in informal correspondence and follows the closing line of a formal or informal letter** <Dear Mary,> <Affectionately,> <Very truly yours,>.

DASH —

1. **usually marks an abrupt change or break in the continuity of a sentence** <When in 1960 the stockpile was sold off—indeed, dumped as surplus—natural-rubber sales were hard hit>.
2. **introduces a summary statement after a series** <Oil, steel, and wheat—these are the sinews of industrialization>.
3. **often precedes the attribution of a quotation** <My foot is on my native heath. . . . —Sir Walter Scott>.

ELLIPSIS . . . .

1. **indicates the omission of one or more words within a quoted passage** <The head is not more native to the heart

. . . than is the throne of Denmark to thy father—Shakespeare>; **four dots indicates the omission of one or more sentences within the passage or the omission of words at the end of a sentence** <Avoiding danger is no safer in the long run than outright exposure. . . . Life is either a daring adventure or nothing —Helen Keller>.

2. **indicates halting speech or an unfinished sentence in dialogue** <"I'd like to . . . that is . . . if you don't mind . . . ." He faltered and then stopped speaking>.

EXCLAMATION POINT !

1. **terminates an emphatic phrase or sentence** <Get out of here!>.
2. **terminates an emphatic interjection** <Encore!>.

HYPHEN -

1. **marks separation or division of a word at the end of a line.**
2. **is used between some prefix and word combinations, such as prefix + proper name** <pre-Renaissance>; **prefix ending with a vowel + a word beginning with a vowel, often the same vowel** <co-opted> <re-ink>; **or stressed prefix + word, especially when this combination is similar to a different one** <re-cover a sofa> *but* <recover from an illness>.
3. **is used in some compounds, especially those containing prepositions** <president-elect> <sister-in-law>.
4. **is often used between elements of a unit modifier in attributive position in order to avoid ambiguity** <He is a small-business man> <She has gray-green eyes>.
5. **suspends the first part of a hyphenated compound when used with another hyphenated compound** <a six- or eight-cylinder engine>.

6. **is used in writing out compound numbers between 21 and 99** <thirty-four> <one hundred twenty-eight>.
7. **is used between the numerator and the denominator in writing out fractions, especially when they are used as modifiers** <a two-thirds majority of the vote>.
8. **serves instead of the phrase "(up) to and including" between numbers and dates** <pages 40-98> <the decade 1990-99>.

PARENTHESES ( )

1. **set off supplementary, parenthetic, or explanatory material when the interruption is more marked than that usually indicated by commas** <Three old destroyers (all now out of commission) will be scrapped> <He is hoping (as we all are) that this time he will succeed>.
2. **enclose numerals which confirm a written number in a text** <Delivery will be made in thirty (30) days>.
3. **enclose numbers or letters in a series** <We must set forth (1) our long-term goals, (2) our immediate objectives, and (3) the means at our disposal>.

PERIOD .

1. **terminates sentences or sentence fragments that are neither interrogative nor exclamatory** <Obey the law.> <He obeyed the law.>.
2. **follows some abbreviations and contractions** <Dr.> <Jr.> <etc.> <cont.>.

QUESTION MARK ?

1. **terminates a direct question** <Who threw the bomb?> <"Who threw the bomb?" he asked> <To ask the question Who threw the bomb? is unnecessary>.
2. **indicates the writer's ignorance or uncertainty** <Omar Khayyám, Persian poet (1048?–1122)>.

QUOTATION MARKS, DOUBLE “ ”

1. **enclose direct quotations** <He said, “I am leaving”>.
2. **enclose words or phrases borrowed from others, words used in a special way, and often slang when it is introduced into formal writing** <He called himself “emperor,” but he was really just a dictator> <He was arrested for smuggling “smack”>.
3. **enclose titles of short poems, short stories, articles, lectures, chapters of books, songs, short musical compositions, and radio and TV programs** <Robert Frost’s “Dust of Snow”> <Pushkin’s “Queen of Spades”> <The third chapter of *Treasure Island* is entitled “The Black Spot”> <NBC’s “Today Show”> <Beethoven’s “Für Elise”>.
4. **are used with other punctuation marks in the following ways: the period and the comma fall *within* the quotation marks** <“I am leaving.”> <His camera was described as “waterproof,” but “moisture-resistant” would have been a better description>; **the semicolon falls *outside* the quotation marks** <He spoke of his “little cottage in the country”; he might better have called it a mansion>; **the dash, the question mark, and the exclamation point fall *within* the quotation marks when they refer to the quoted matter only, but *outside* when they refer to the whole sentence** <He asked, “When did you leave?”> <What is the meaning of “the open door”?> <The sergeant shouted “Halt!”> <Save us from his “mercy”!>.

QUOTATION MARKS, SINGLE ‘ ’

enclose a quotation within a quotation <The witness said, “I distinctly heard him say, ‘Don’t be late,’ and then I heard the door close”>.

SEMICOLON ;

1. **links main clauses not joined by coordinating conjunctions** <Some people have the ability to write well; others do not>.
2. **links main clauses joined by conjunctive adverbs (such as *consequently, furthermore, however*)** <Speeding is illegal; furthermore, it is very dangerous>.
3. **links clauses which themselves contain commas, even when such clauses are joined by coordinating conjunctions** <Mr. King, whom you met yesterday, will represent us on the committee; but you should follow the proceedings yourself, because they are vitally important to us>.

SLASH /

1. **separates alternatives** <designs intended for high-heat and/or high-speed applications>.
2. **separates the month, day, and year in dates** <8/14/97>.
3. **serves as a dividing line between run-in lines of poetry** <Say, sages, what's the charm on earth / Can turn death's dart aside? —Robert Burns>.
4. **often represents *per* in abbreviations** <9 ft/sec> <20 km/hr>.